A Treatise on the Provincial Dialect of Scotland

Frontispiece: Portrait of Sylvester Douglas, by M. Gauoi.

A Treatise on the Provincial Dialect of Scotland

by

SYLVESTER DOUGLAS

edited by
Charles Jones

EDINBURGH UNIVERSITY PRESS

© Charles Jones, 1991

Edinburgh University Press
22 George Square, Edinburgh

Typeset in Linotron Caslon
by Nene Phototypesetters Ltd, Northampton
and printed in Great Britain by
The University Press, Cambridge

British Library Cataloguing
  in Publication Data
Douglas, Sylvester
  A treatise on the provincial dialect of Scotland.
  I. Title   II. Jones, Charles
  427

ISBN 0 7486 0300 X

FOR ISLA

Contents

Contents

Preface

The relative neglect by many students of historical English language studies of the materials from the eighteenth and nineteenth centuries is particularly acute in the domain of Scottish English. While the work of at least the major English grammarians of the period – Johnson, Lowth, Sheridan, Walker, Kenrick – are at least well known, and while reference is on occasion made to the work of Scottish grammarians like Elphinston and Buchanan, the extremely rich tradition of grammar writing which existed in Scotland throughout the last two centuries (pertaining both to the English spoken in England as well as that attested in Scotland itself) has been by and large ignored by the mainstream scholarly tradition, and its full extent and importance awaits documentation.

This edition of the work of one of the foremost exponents of the art of compiling the Pronouncing Dictionary attempts to go a little way towards rectifying this state of affairs. It will, I hope, reveal the views of a skilled observer of phonetic and phonological events, an observer who despite his obvious familiarity with much contemporary grammatical writing, has a highly individual and directed approach to his subject, one which gives us many clear insights into the workings of the pronunciation of the English Language as it was spoken in the late eighteenth century in educated circles in both England and (particularly) Scotland. Douglas' lack of prescriptive exhortation is refreshing and his observations are, in the main, detailed and reliable. His *Treatise* stands comparison with the work of the best English grammarians of the time and a recognition of his reputation as a linguist is long overdue.

I am particularly indebted to the Society of Writers to the Signet for kind permission to allow me to study the version of the *Treatise* in their care in the Signet Library, Edinburgh. My thanks are due especially to its Librarian, Mr G. H. Ballantyne and his staff for the many kindnesses they have shown me over the past eighteen months. While working on such an interesting document as Douglas' *Treatise* was a pleasure in itself, it was one much compounded by the opportunity to do so among the architectural splendours of the Signet Library.

I should like to thank, too, Dr I. D. L. Clark, a reader for Edinburgh University Press, whose diligent proof reading and general sound

advice made this edition much less defective than it would otherwise
have been.

CHARLES JONES
Department of English Language,
University of Edinburgh

Introduction

The only surviving son of John and Margaret Douglas, Sylvester Douglas was born on May 13th 1744 in Fechil, by Ellon, some twelve miles to the north and west of the city of Aberdeen:

> I was born, as appears by an entry in the blank leaf of my copy of Field's Bible in my father's handwriting, on the 13th of May, in the year 1744 in the house and on the estate of my maternal ancestors for several generations, called Fechil, pleasantly situated near the south or right bank of the almost Arcadian River Ythan, in the parish of Ellon, and county of Aberdeen.[1]

(although the *Dictionary of National Biography*, the *Complete Peerage* and *The Georgian Era* cite his birth as occuring on May 24th, 1743).[2] We have very few details relating to any aspect of his early life, other than that he ran away from his local school at Foveran at the tender age of eight years (Bickley, 1928:vol.2;21). His higher education was initially undertaken in the field of medicine, first at the university of Aberdeen and then (not unusually for a Scottish student at that time (Innes Smith, 1932)) at the University of Leiden in the Netherlands from where he graduated in February of 1766. Although his early medical interests were known to his contemporaries – cf. Sheridan's *Political Pasquinade*:[3]

> Gl-nb-e, Gl-nb-e
> What's good for the scurvy?
> For ne'er be your old trade forgot –
> In your arms rather quarter
> A pestle and mortar
> And your crest be a spruce gallipot, Gl-nb-e,
> And your crest be a spruce gallipot.

he seems at an early period to have abandoned this area of study for that of the law, since five years after graduating from Leiden we find him recorded as a student at Lincoln's Inn and four years later, in 1776, qualifying as a barrister. Although details of his early legal career are sparse, Douglas does appear to have gained something of a reputation as a reporter of Lord Mansfield's decisions at the King's Bench. Indeed, he became a King's Councillor in 1793, and a bencher in the same year. Six years later he is recorded as treasurer of Lincoln's Inn.

But it was in the mid-1790's that his political and administrative career began to take shape. By 1794 he had become Chief Secretary of Ireland and in the same year the member of the Irish parliament for Canice or Irishtown in Kilkenny. From then until 1806 he held a succession of seats in the Westminster parliament: Fowey in Cornwall from 1795; Midhurst in Sussex from 1796 to 1800; Plympton Earls in Devonshire in 1801, finally representing Hastings in Kent from 1802 to 1806. During this period he also held two important administrative posts in government, serving on the Board of Control from 1795 to 1800, and on the Board of the Treasury from 1797 to 1800. In his later years he rose to the position of vice-president of the Board of Trade, a post he held from 1801 to 1804; he was surveyor-general of Woods and Forests in 1803 and again in 1807, ultimately rising to be the first commissioner of the united offices from 1810 to 1814. There is little doubt that his connections through marriage, and his strong support for Pitt, contributed to this administrative and political success as well as to his elevation to the peerage (albeit, apparently to his considerable disappointment, only to the Irish branch) on November 29th, 1800. Douglas was at that point created Baron Glenbervie in the county of Kincardine. In the same year he was offered the governorship of the Cape of Good Hope colony, a post which he refused on this and two subsequent occasions. Douglas was, in fact, one of a large number of commoners elevated to baronies at or around the time of the (Irish) Act of Union, and the social enmity raised by such is again evident from Sheridan's satirical verse:[4]

> Gl-nb-e, Gl-nb-e,
> The world's topsy-turvy –
> Of this truth you're the fittest attester;
> For who can deny
> That the Low become High
> When the King makes a Lord of Sylvester?
>> Gl-nb-e,
> When the King makes a Lord of Sylvester?

His elevation to the peerage appears to mark the high point in Douglas' political career, and his apparent ambitions both for a post of cabinet rank and a step up to the English peerage were denied him, causing him by all accounts to lose his previously high estimation of Pitt and at the same time embroiling him in political squabbling with Grenville and others (Bickley, 1928:vol.1;Introduction p.vi). The impression we have from his *Journals* and *Diaries*, is one of a serious and perhaps even slightly pedantic individual who, on occasion (see the *Ass* entry in the *Treatise*, for instance) was capable of some wit; perhaps Sichel's assessment (1910:1–5) is fair:

Lord Glenbervie, though certainly no genius, was in many respects a notable man, who filled high offices, gained, from ordinary beginnings, such a place in society that he married one of Lord North's daughters (a rather plain daughter, it must be confessed), and knew or was brought into contact with many of the conspicuous personages of his day. A man acquainted alike with Marie Antoinette, Philippe Egalité, and 'Colonel' Cagliostro, Pitt, Lord Minto, and the Circle of Charles James Fox, Queen Charlotte and her grand-daughter, Madame de Staël, and Lady Hamilton; the intimate of Windham (his brother-in-law) through whom he was thrown with Gibbon, must have something interesting to relate. When he is most discursive, most legal, and most dry, there are always about his prose some redeeming touches of unconscious humour that recall the pomposities of a vanished age.

The Douglases had one son, the Honourable Sylvester North Douglas, who himself entered political life and became member of parliament for Banbury between 1812 and 1819. He died at the very early age of twenty-eight on October 21st, 1819, and his death was a blow from which his father seems never to have quite recovered. In the preface to his unpublished *Occasional Verses* (1820:viii), Douglas recounts how he wished to dedicate that work together with his *Diaries* to his son:

> But Providence has otherwise decreed, and the widowed childless father now, has been left to seek some, he trusts, blameless, dissipation of his disappointed thoughts, generally during the solitude of the night, in executing a task, the principal purpose of which has indeed been frustrated by that visitation of God, which at my age of upwards of 75 years, has deprived me of the cherished object of my paternal affection, long the delight, the hope, and the pride of his dear departed Mother and myself.

After a considerable period of ill-health, Sylvester Douglas died at Cheltenham on May 2nd, 1823 at the age of eighty years; his peerage terminated with his death.

LITERARY CAREER

Although never fulfilling his potential as a writer, Douglas shows a considerable variety of interests in both his surviving written works and those which he claims an interest in undertaking. He contemplated a life of his father-in-law, Lord North, planned an essay (to be produced in both English and Italian) 'deducing from Chaucer's time the history of the cultivation of literature in Great Britain,'[5] while:

> If I ever write my proposed historical and critical account of the

life and writings of Gavin Douglas, I should wish to find a proper place for introducing something concerning the Italian families who claim to be descended from the Douglases.[6]

His 'An Account of the Tokay and Other Wines of Hungary' (*Philosophical Transactions*, 1773) and 'Experiments and Observations upon a blue substance, found in a Peat-moss in Scotland' (*Philosophical Transactions*, 1765–6) show the catholicity of his interests, the former discussing a stage in the wine fermenting process called *Masslasch*, the other a chemical analysis of a substance (1765–6:181):

> accidentally dug up in the summer of 1759, in order to mix with some other materials for the purpose of manure, to be laid on some ground, at present in my possession, in the North of Scotland, about twelve miles from Aberdeen.

Other than the *Treatise* itself and his *Journals*, Douglas' most complete literary effort is a translation of *The First Canto of Ricciardetto* by Forteguerri ('with an Introduction, concerning the principal Romantic, Burlesque, and Mock Heroic Poets with Notes, Critical and Philological') surviving in a printed, but unpublished form, by John Murray of London, dated 1822. This work is mainly of interest to the scholar of translation technique, although on pp.158–185 we find expressed many of Douglas' views on versification, corresponding largely to the materials in Book 2 of the *Treatise* (*Of the Provincial Accentuation of Particular Words*) in the Signet Library, Edinburgh:

> This last note, of such disproportionate length, is an extract from an Essay I have in part composed on the different modes of versification in several of the modern languages (p.185).

MOTIVATIONS AND ATTITUDES

The audience aimed at by Sylvester Douglas in his *Treatise* (originally intended to comprise six separate books: see p.101) consists of those 'whose language has already been in a great degree refined from the provincial dross, by frequenting English company, and studying the great masters of the English tongue in their writings' (Collins, 1862; Colville, 1899; Smith, 1908; Brown, 1845). Like many eighteenth-century writers on 'good' pronunciation (notably Kenrick, 1784 and Adams, 1799), he is not concerned to correct the habits of those who profess 'the grosser barbarisms of the vulgar Scotch jargon', but addresses himself to the removal of the *vestigia ruris* from those Scots who otherwise speak with at least some of the characteristics of a refined, standard (by which is meant polite London[7]) dialect, although we have no strong impression that Douglas is advocating the total abandonment of all Scottish vernacular features in favour of an undiluted London upper class norm[8] (Holmberg, 1964). Indeed, his

Sonnet 1820 in his *Occasional Verses* (1820) suggests a rather robust attitude to the proliferation of linguistic niceties:

> How language changes with the lapse of years!
> Time was when plain *John Bull* was not abash'd
> Plain words to use; now silenced quite, and quash'd,
> Because they shock our modern eyes and ears.
> If now, in decent company, one hears
> Such words escape from lips of lout unwash'd
> Straight way each downcast eye to ground is dash'd,
> And on each cheek a scarlet blush appears.
> It was not so in bold *Eliza*'s times,
> Nor even much later, under good Queen *Anne*;
> The *nicest* then would call a wh-re, a wh-re;[9]
> And say; though purer now our *talk and rhymes*,
> If we the truth with honest candour scan,
> Are folks more *nice in conduct* than of yore?

There is little in Douglas' *Treatise* to suggest that he held strong views of the power of his work for the maintenance of some kind of immutable standard against the encroachments of more 'vulgar' speech habits (Emsley, 1933;1940; Leonard, 1929; Lehnert, 1981; Abercrombie, 1979; Aitken, 1979; Dunlap, 1940; Matthews, 1937a/b; Sturzen-Becker, 1942); nor is there anything in his work of the tenor of Sheridan (1781:xx) who claims that he has 'endeavoured to fix two anchors to our floating language, in order to keep it steady against the gales of caprice, and current of fashion':

> the regard formerly paid to pronunciation has been gradually declining; so that now the greatest improprieties in that point are to be found among people of fashion; many pronunciations which thirty or forty years ago were confined to the vulgar, are gradually gaining ground; and if something be not done to stop this growing evil, and fix a general standard at present, then English is likely to become a mere jargon, which every one may pronounce as he pleases.[10]

Douglas makes the distinction (common to many writers in the period) between local dialect (the 'vulgar Scotch jargon', the 'provincial dross' (pp.100–01)) and non-standard national linguistic characteristics,[11] the latter being that of 'a whole country or district where the common language is spoken with a barbarous and unclassical impurity' (p.111).[12] He raises too, the current issue of the effect of political union on the status of the national Scottish (albeit non-standard) dialect: seeing no sociolinguistic diversity between the ancient Greek dialects, he (like many others at the time)[13] entertains the thought that, had the nation been left fully independent, its national speech would have attained the status of a standard, parallel to that of the 'pure' dialect of England. Yet it is an hypothesis about which he remains sceptical (p.99):

> we cannot infer . . . that, if Scotland had not been incorporated with England, its idiom would have become classical, instead of being reckoned, (as I am inclined to think it always was from the days of Gawin Douglas downwards, and as it now certainly is) a provincial and vicious dialect of English.

Douglas' tone concerning the status of Scottish vernacular English is nowhere over-apologetic or condescendingly defensive and, while he claims that 'an Englishman has no inducement to collect together, and form a catalogue of such barbarisms' (p.101), he never seems either to completely endorse 'pure' English speech habits or take every opportunity of ridiculing the vernacular Scotch; nor, indeed, does he feel the necessity of equivocation in the matter of a North Briton pontificating (however subtley) on matters of 'proper' English usage[14] (Cohen, 1977). All in distinct contrast to Kenrick (1784:i):

> The natives of a country, and particularly of the metropolis, meet with none of those difficulties, which occur to others. Custom renders every thing easy and familiar, nor do they perceive any of those irregularities and apparent improprieties, that strike the ear of such as are accustomed to different dialects. At the same time, however, that these are most sensible of the difficulties and defects, they are the least qualified to obviate them. There seems indeed a most ridiculous absurdity in the pretensions of a native of Aberdeen or Tipperary, to teach the natives of London to speak and to read.[15]

Yet Douglas is conscious of the fact that his audience may accord less than appropriate weight to his attempt to provide 'a distinct, unequivocal, and infallible criterion to guide the Scotch reader to the just pronounciation of the word in question' (p.113) as a result of his own Scottish linguistic ancestry: he is careful to reassure his reader against the charge 'that I, a Scotchman, may be very liable to mistake the true English pronounciation of many words' (p.114):

> To this I can only answer that I have taken all the pains in my power to guard against errors of this sort. I have not only listened, and with the utmost attention, to the pronounciation of every word whose proper sound I have attempted to ascertain, in the mouths of English persons of both sexes, who are acknowledged to speak with propriety: But I have also submitted what I have written as well in this as in the subsequent parts of my work to the perusal and correction of several persons of a like description.

Douglas is clearly no Anglophobe[16] and his overall aim appears to be to assist the polite speaker of Scots vernacular to feel more at home in London society by the avoidance of the more obvious linguistic blemishes: 'There are, I believe, few natives of North Britain, who have had occasion either to visit or reside in this country, that have not learned by experience the disadvantages which accompany their idiom and pronounciation' (p.99). He certainly nowhere goes to the lengths expressed in the *Formal Vindication of the Scotch Dialect* set out by Adams (1799:156–160), who argues that Scottish English (his *Scoto-Saxon*) is not a provincial corruption, but has been a separate entity with an historical pedigree dating from the earliest times.[17]

> *First*, then I assert, that the broad dialect rises above reproach, scorn, and laughter: *Secondly*, That the tempered medium, still retaining its characteristic distinction of Scotch, is entitled (not exclusively) to all the vindication, personal and local congruity can inforce, by the principles of reason, national honour, and native dignity. Under this twofold distinction I enter the lists in Tartan dress and armour, and throw down the gauntlet to the most prejudiced antagonist. How weak is prejudice! The sight of the Highland kelt [sic], the flowing plaid, the buskin'd leg, provokes my antagonist to laugh! Is this dress ridiculous in the eyes of reason and common sense? No: nor is the dialect of speech: both are characteristic and national distinctions. National character and distinction are respectable. Then is the adopted mode of oral language sanctioned by peculiar reasons, and is not the result of chance, contemptible vulgarity, mere ignorance and rustic habit.

Douglas is at pains to stress that his decision to cast his *Treatise* in the form of an alphabetically arranged dictionary, rather than in the shape of a set of general language principles, stems from his strongly held belief that linguistic diversity in no way stems from the application of some set of general forces of 'analogy', or can be encompassed within the scope of any 'general rules' (p.101). Warning us 'how dangerous I think general rules in every thing relative to English pronounciation' (p.102), Douglas derides the 'rule of analogy' under his ‹Touch› entry, parodying the ludicrous consequences of its unprincipled application under the ‹Bough› entry. He is always at pains to indicate that both his pure and provincial pronunciations are the product of 'some', 'several', 'a few', 'many' speakers, while the qualifying 'are apt to' figures prominently in his claims concerning the usage of Scottish vernacular informants.

Douglas' *Treatise on the Provincial Dialect of Scotland* was, of course, not a unique undertaking for the period when it was written. Its aims and methods clearly stem from an orthoepistic tradition dating from two centuries earlier as well as from the great interest in the writing of (more or less prescriptive in tone and intention) grammars and dictionaries in the eighteenth century itself. Indeed, that tradition, partly educational in its aims (Law, 1965),[18] was not confined in the latter part of the century to those writing from London, or even from the English regions (Hornsey, n.d., from Newcastle; Smith, 1816, from Norwich; Hodgson, 1770, from Southampton; Scott, 1771, from South Shields) but was very active in Scotland itself, notably in the works of Buchanan (1753;1757), John Drummond, *A Grammatical Introduction to the Modern Pronunciation and Spelling of the English Tongue* (Edinburgh, 1767); William Adie, *A New Spelling Book* (Paisley, 1769); Cortes Telfair, *The Town and Country Spelling Book* (Edinburgh, 1775); William Perry *The Only Sure Guide to the English Tongue* (Edinburgh, 1776); John Bell, *A Concise and Comprehensive System of English Grammar* (Glasgow, 1769); William Scott, *An Introduction to Reading and Spelling* (Edinburgh, 1776); Alexander Barrie, *A Spelling and Pronouncing Dictionary of the English Language* (Edinburgh, 1794), James Gray, *A Concise Spelling Book* (Edinburgh, 1794); William Angus, *A Pronouncing Vocabulary of the English Language* (Glasgow, 1800) and many others.

THE MANUSCRIPT

The *Treatise* exists in two versions, one in Douglas' own hand, the other most probably in that of one of his clerks at Lincoln's Inn in London. The former, which is undated, is held in the National Library of Scotland, in the Catalogue of Advocates' MSS as Miscel. 45, 23.7.18–19. This version is in two volumes, the first containing ff.1–308, the other ff.309–553, with a leaf size of 20.2 × 15.5 cm. Both volumes show *Ex libris Fac. Jurid. Edinburg* on the inside board, where also to be found are *Ex Libris Sylvester Douglas* bookplates with the Douglas coat of arms thereon. The second version, a copy of the first, transcribed in a clear clerk's script with additions and corrections by Douglas in his own hand, is in the possession of the Signet Library (the library of the Society of Writers to the Signet) in Parliament Square, Edinburgh, and is catalogued as Signals MS106:41. This version contains 268ff, sized 22.5 × 18.5 cm, and on the flyleaf has the inscription: 'S. Douglas, Lincoln's Inn, 1779', in the clerk's hand. It is this version (s) upon which this edition is based, collated with that in the Advocates' Library (A). The Signet Library also possesses a volume in Douglas' hand, on the same paper and with the same watermark as the A version of the *Treatise*, entitled *Of the Provincial Accentuation of Particular Words*, running to some 331ff. This volume contains a Sylvester Douglas *Ex Libris* bookplate, with folio size 22.5 × 18.5 cm, and is catalogued as Signals MS 104c.32.

8

THE VOWEL AND CONSONANTAL SYSTEM:
REMARKS ON THE GENERAL PHONOLOGICAL DESCRIPTION

The means whereby the representation of speech sounds in a written form could be best achieved, has been one of the central concerns of spelling reformers, educationalists and orthoepists since the sixteenth century and doubtless long before. The utilisation of specialised alphabets with their individual orthographic conventions and specialised symbols has a long pedigree from Hart (1569) and Gil (1619) and includes the numerous instances of 'naive' orthographic systems produced by Machyn (c.1550) and the *Verney Papers* (c.1650) among many others (Horn/Lehnert, 1954:71–116; Buchmann, 1940; Koeppel, 1901). At the same time, there developed a tradition of descriptive nomenclature, often reliant upon observation of the anatomical methods of speech production, but equally often of an impressionistic nature, whose use was often inconsistent and uncoordinated (Jones, 1989:200ff; Langley, 1963). Both traditions are to be found in the eighteenth century, the former among those who wish to 'paint' speech sounds by means of a novel orthography, the latter fully represented by the continued use of descriptive phonological terminology combined with an ample employment of diacritic marks to indicate, among many other features, vowel height and length, as well as consonantal continuancy and voicing. Both traditions provoked equal degrees of disapproval and distrust from practitioners of the phonetic art in both camps (Sheldon, 1946;1947; Aarsleff, 1967; Davies, 1934). The 'wrackers of orthography' (*Loves Labours Lost*, c.1597) were perhaps most elegantly represented in the eighteenth century by Elphinston (1786:349; Müller, 1914; Dorow, 1935) whose aim was:

> to' perfet dhe art ov painting speech, *to' bring written language az near az possibel to' language spoken*; so dhat dhe eye shal read precisely hwat iz commited to' dhe ear; such iz *dhe sole means* ov repprezenting faithfoolly dhe pronuciation ov dhe Cappital.

Yet this technique was the subject of constant criticism throughout the period, as we can typically see from Kenrick's (1784:iii; Arthur Boggs, 1964) comments upon Buchanan's (1757:1762) attempts at the method:

> Admitting however that he had been capable of giving every word its true sound, this method of disfiguring the orthography is very prejudicial to the learner; who, thus being taught to speak and read, will forget, or never learn, how to write: an accurate method of spelling words being attained chiefly by reading books correctly printed; in which the word is literally presented in its due proportion of number and character to the eye.[19]

At the same time, considerable scepticism was also directed towards those phonological descriptions which relied heavily upon the physical characterisation of the articulators in the production of speech sounds. Notably Nares (1784:xx–xxi; Bendix, 1921; Pollner, 1976), while praising the efforts of Wallis (1653) in this kind of endeavour, urges caution:

> The sounds of some letters may, with tolerable exactness, be ascertained by rules for the management of the organs of speech in pronouncing them. The consonants may readily admit to such description; but the nice discrimination of vowel sounds, on which the principal harmony of language depends, will generally elude the efforts of the most subtile definer ... I contend that such definitions have in them more obscurity than utility. Those who doubt this may perhaps find it more difficult than they would expect, to apply ... definitions to the letters for which they were designed, without consulting the book from which they were taken.

Douglas is conscious throughout his *Treatise* of the shortcomings of the terminological apparatus available to him (as well as of the potential low interest factor it could have for his readers: 'Minute discussions concerning pronounciation, are of a dry and forbidding nature' (p.100)) and he continually puts us on our guard against accepting his description of the sound system at its face value, stressing always the symbolic and figurative character of any endeavour to depict the nature of phonology:

> In general enquiries concerning matters of this sort, the natural obscurity or subtlety of the subject, is rendered more obscure and perplexing if the established language which we must employ in treating of it is inaccurate and metaphorical. This happens to be peculiarly the case with regard to the theory and properties of sounds of every sort and especially those various modifications and combinations of sounds the aggregate of which constitute what we call speech. (*Of the Provincial Accentuation of Particular Words*, f.77)

He utilises neither diacritics nor special symbols in his attempt to characterise phonetic properties ('Can the shades and gradations of sounds be painted?' p.100), condemning the efforts of the 'knights errant in orthography' who 'endeavour to subvert by their arguments, or example, the whole established orthography of a language, and substitute in its room, together with a set of new characters, a mode of spelling entirely different from general usage', efforts which Douglas describes as 'absurd' (p.110). Douglas is content to use a rather restricted and traditional set of (partially articulatory based) terms, such as *open*, *close*, together with *long* and *short*, as well as more impressionistic nomenclature like *hollow*, *obscure*, a *shade*. His main descriptive tool is contrast, and in chapter three (pp.143–57) he sets out in great detail the phonetic and phonological criteria for the establishment and interpretation of 'perfect rhymes' as exemplars of pronunciation characteristics. But the strengths and limitations of this device and his other descriptive techniques will be commented upon at many points in our discussion below.

THE MAJOR CLASS FEATURES: THE VOWEL/CONSONANT DICHOTOMY

Douglas' description of the general phonological characteristics of his contemporary language, like that of many writers of his day, is not one which is couched in terms of discrete units, be they vowels, consonants, stops or fricatives, but is viewed as comprising a scale or hierarchy of non-quantal components which can show blends of sets of inter-related segments. This theoretical stance is seen nowhere more clearly than in his descriptive mechanism for the major or primary categorial features in the phonology. He presents the traditional vowel/consonant dichotomy in terms of the opposing ends of a cline which is defined on the basis of what can only be described as cavity resonance characteristics. Vowels are seen in relation to their propensity to be capable of durational retention, the characteristic of a highly resonant gesture configuration: vowels 'can be uttered by themselves' (p.106).[20] On the other hand:

> Consonants, as the name imports, can only be pronounced along with Vowells. Indeed pure consonants such as *p*, for example, or *t*, are not properly sounds themselves, but certain modes of commencing or terminating sound. You may begin, or you may close, the sound of *a* or *o*, with *t*, but you cannot utter *t* unaccompanied with a vowell. (p.106)

Voiceless obstruents are thus viewed as the polar opposite of vowels (the syllable essential elements, pp.107–08), are peripheral to them and are characteristic of the syllable edge, a view reflected too in Elphinston in his *Inglish Orthography Epitomized* (1790:21):

> Orthoggraphy iz dhe just Picture ov Speech, hwich consists ov vocality and articulation, repprezented by Vowels and Consonants, or dhoze letters, hwich paint independent sounds, and dhoze dhat serv onely to articulate or modify dhe vowels, havving consequently nedher sound nor signifficance widhout dhem.

Douglas observes that there is a 'middle place' set of sounds which, although they cannot be 'uttered so clearly or audibly' as vowel sounds, nevertheless can be capable of prolongation. These 'semivowels' are exemplified as the sonorant and non-sonorant continuant segments [l], [m], [f] and [s][21] – a viewpoint not far removed from that of Bullokar's (1580) description of the sonorant continuants as 'half vowels' (Turner, 1970; Jones, 1989:249–50). Further, a palatal glide like [j] is described by Douglas as 'a sound something between a vowel and a semivowel' (p.131), a position not unlike Elphinston's who sees [j] and [w] glides 'belonging to boath classes [vowel and consonant: CJ] articulate each oddher, in wy and dubel yoo; so prooving consonants and vowels by turne' (1790:iv).[22] Douglas therefore appears to envisage the phonological inventory as a scale composed of elements which are more or less relatively 'audible' or which can be in varying degrees 'uttered by themselves':

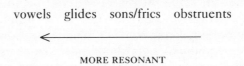

vowels   glides   sons/frics   obstruents

MORE RESONANT

a notion not at all unlike the modern 'sonority hierarchy' along which phonetic segments are arranged according to degree of relative periodicity (Hooper, 1972; Lass, 1984:282–3; Jones, 1989:56–7). Even more interestingly, we shall see that Douglas views individual vowel segments themselves not as unique entities but as relational and complex: for instance, the vowel sound in ‹all› and ‹hat›:

> gradually approaches and seems, in some measure, to confound and lose itself in that of *o*, as, on the other side, in *hat*, it approaches to the limits of and begins to mix itself with, the sound in *better*. (p.118)

Douglas claims to wish to highlight three main areas of human speech characteristics: (1) some sounds are pronounced 'in a higher, sharper or shriller tone than others', (2) all syllables show a 'difference to be observed in the length of time consumed in the respective pronounciation of the different syllables', (3) discrepancies in 'point of muscular exertion between the pronounciation of the same consonant in one syllable and another' (*Of the Provincial Accentuation*, ff.31–32). However not all of these areas achieve equal status of treatment in the *Treatise*, Douglas rarely, for instance, appealing to the sharp, shrill distinction outside the complex set of observations on stress placement (mainly in classical Greek and Latin) which constitute the bulk of *Of the Provincial Accentuation*. Yet comments on the relative duration of vowel segments (some of them of a detailed nature) abound: 'a vowel twice repeated must either form only one long syllable, or two distinct ones of the very same vocal sound' (p.107). We shall see below how Douglas differentiates long and short syllable stretches as well as durational contrasts that hold between individual vowel segments within syllables. Discrepancy in muscular exertion associated with consonantal production appears to relate to how Douglas interprets the voiced/voiceless contrast in laryngeal activity, but we shall see that he admits to some considerable scepticism as to the adequateness of this particular descriptive nomenclature.

Let us proceed to Douglas' description in the *Treatise* of his contemporary phonology and phonetics as they relate to monophthongal and diphthongal vocalic elements. We shall in turn consider pure steady state vowel sounds and the vowel transitions which constitute diphthongs, the intermediate and relatively 'vowelly' glides and (non)sonorant continuants (Douglas' 'semivowels'), and the voiced and voiceless obstruents or 'mutes'. The vowel space will be referred to throughout in terms of a three pointed, triangular configuration comprising three 'pure' high-sonority segments: [i] the pure palatal with high overall Hz characteristics; [u] the pure labial showing a resonance characteristic sympathetic to low (F2) Hz; and [ɑ] the pure sonorant showing an energy concentration relatively equally spread across the Hz range:

PALATALITY   LABIALITY
[i]   [u]

SONORITY
[ɑ]

Other vowel sounds will be considered as mixtures or composites of these three pure and primary componential vowel types, mixtures manifesting more or less of the intrinsic and primitive elements of *palatality*, *labiality* and *sonority* in their internal structure (Anderson and Ewen, 1987:§3.6.1; Lass, 1984:276–9).

We must stress, however, that the metaphorical nature of much of Douglas' descriptive terminology and the often vacuous nature of his contrastive illustrations (typically under the ‹kept› item: 'The *e* as in *step*, *stept*' (p.204)) make precise phonetic identification on many occasions an impossibility, and our attempts to provide detail in this area should be regarded as tentative. Nevertheless, we shall endeavour to set out as much of the phonological inventory of the English of late eighteenth-century England and Scotland as is recoverable from Douglas' *Treatise* and to highlight, wherever appropriate, the contrasts he brings out not only between the 'pure' and 'Scotch' regional dialects but also those he notes concerning other regional and sociophonetic types.

A. VOCALIC SEGMENTS

1 Labial Vowels

The descriptions the *Treatise* provides for the various manifestations of [u]-type, labial monophthongs in the phonology of both the pure and Scotch dialects of the late eighteenth century are detailed and revealing, yet at the same time tantalisingly complex and imprecise (Horn, 1901). While there is an extensive discussion of the nature of this vowel sound, its spelling shapes and idiosyncracies of the details of its pronunciation in regional and social contexts in chapter two (*Observations on the Alphabet*, pp.138–40), there is also to be found explicit and sometimes contradictory information under individual lexical items in the *Table of Words*, notably under ⟨above⟩, ⟨burial⟩, ⟨fill⟩, ⟨full⟩, ⟨mourn⟩, ⟨forth⟩ and ⟨pull⟩. The discussion presented in the *Observations on the Alphabet* suggests that in the pure dialect three distinctive varieties of labial-type monophthong could be distinguished at this period, Douglas listing sets of lexical items characterised by each type. The first of these Douglas describes as a *simple vocal* variety, a sound characterised by whatever is intended by the orthographic marks ⟨u⟩ and ⟨ou⟩ in Italian and French respectively (p.138). Items specifically associated with this sound (possibly the pure labial [u]) in the pure dialect are cited as: ⟨prove⟩, ⟨tomb⟩, ⟨two⟩, ⟨pulpit⟩, ⟨pull⟩, ⟨full⟩, ⟨stool⟩, ⟨good⟩, ⟨brood⟩, ⟨move⟩ (Whitehall and Fein, 1941).

Under the second labial type Douglas, in fact, describes what are two separate vowel qualities used in the pure dialect: the one, a *smothered vocal*, characteristic of what seems to be a deliberately small lexical set made up of ⟨Tully⟩, ⟨scut⟩ and ⟨rut⟩. The other, in terminology typical of Douglas, is depicted as another shade of the former, and is apparently peculiar to items such as ⟨flood⟩, ⟨blood⟩, ⟨love⟩, ⟨dove⟩, ⟨glove⟩, ⟨come⟩, ⟨couplet⟩, ⟨punt⟩, ⟨hulk⟩, ⟨rump⟩, ⟨dub⟩ and ⟨mud⟩. This labial (sub) type, Douglas is at pains to emphasise, 'approaches nearer to the first' (i.e. to the *simple vocal* [u], p.139).[23]

If we are to give any significance to the numerical size of the sets of lexical items said to manifest each labial vowel type, then we might conclude that the first and third are the commonest in the pure dialect, while the second (the *smothered vocal*) is constrained to occur with an extremely restricted lexical set, although we shall want to qualify this below. At the same time, if it is indeed the case that the other two types are perceived as being close to each other in the vowel space, i.e. both are relatively 'pure' in their labiality signature, then as a first approximation we might suggest that the most common labial sounds in the standard dialect in Douglas' time were (1) [u] and (2) [ɣ] or perhaps, as we shall suggest below, [ɯ] or [ü]. The third, *smothered*, sound (the *Tully*, *scut*, and *rut* type) might well be interpreted as a more central and sonorant [ʌ] or [ə] shape, but these possibilities too we shall investigate in more detail as we proceed.

1.a pure dialect: simple vocal u

Compared with the remarks of say Elphinston and Walker, Douglas presents us with what is a rather unusual interpretation of the manifestations of the pure labial vowel in the pure dialect. Like them, he sees what is essentially a length differential in the vowel space in items like ‹full› and ‹fool›, a distinction he sets out in some detail under the entry for ‹pull› (p.217):

> The *u* as in *full*, *bull*. The *u* in *pull*, and *full* has the same sound, in quality with that of the *oo* in *pool*, and *fool*, and they are one long syllable. Yet every body perceives, that *fool* and *full*, and *pool* and *pull*, are not, to the ear, the same words. They differ in two respects. First, the vocal part in *pull*, and *full* is short; in *pool*, and *fool*, long. Secondly, *pull* and *full* are long syllables by means of a protracted stress of the voice on *ll*; which does not take place in the pronounciation of *pool*, and *fool*.

While, under the entry for ‹full›, we find that 'the *u* has its distinct vocal sound like *oo* in *foot*, *fool*', added to which in Douglas' own hand is the insertion 'but shorter' (p.198). Elphinston distinguishes just such a long/short distinction for a similar set of lexical items, those with [uu] (his *o depressive open*) including ‹fool›, ‹soup›, ‹lose›, ‹move›, ‹prove›, ‹whom› and ‹two›; those in [u] (his *o depressive shut*) embracing ‹book›, ‹put›, ‹cushion›, ‹full›, ‹put›, ‹book›, ‹good›, ‹wood›, ‹could›, ‹should› (Rohlfing, 1984:372). Walker (1791:22–3) too sees a distinction like this, although for him there appears to be a qualitative difference as well. Long [uu] items are, he claims, rare in the lexical inventory, restricted to ‹prove›, ‹pool›, ‹move›, ‹lose›, ‹do›, ‹who›, ‹whom›, ‹wood›, ‹tomb›. In contrast, items like ‹bull›, ‹full›, ‹pull› are on the one hand like the [u] in words like ‹tube› and ‹cube›, minus their glide initial [j] component, but not so long as the ‹oo› in ‹pool›. At first sight this would suggest some kind of [u] segment, but Walker goes on to state that the vowel in the ‹bull›, ‹full› items is an 'obscure' sound, a 'middle sound' between the [uu] of ‹pool› and what we shall for the moment see as the [ʌ] in ‹dull›.

Such a segment might be interpreted as [ɷ] or [ɣ]. But Walker[24] cautions us about the difficulties of interpreting the vowel space in the ‹bull›, ‹full› items which is:

> sufficient to puzzle Englishmen who reside at any distance from the capital, and to make the inhabitants of Scotland and Ireland, (who, it is highly probable, received a much more regular pronunciation from our ancestors) not infrequently the jest of fools. (Walker, 1791:173)

Bearing in mind such strictures, as well as Douglas' own warnings concerning the metaphorical use of such terms as 'even *long* and *short*' (*Of the Provincial Accentuation*, f.27), it would seem that for the author of the *Treatise*, the pure dialect showed long/short vowel space contrasts in ‹fool›/‹full› types. Yet he paints a more complex picture, seeing some relationship between the lack of durational extension of the vowel in ‹full›, ‹pull› as in some way connected to 'syllable length', manifested by 'protracted stress of the voice on the *ll*'. While ‹pull› and ‹full› show short vowel and long syllable characteristics, the same, Douglas claims, cannot be said for ‹pully› and ‹fully›:

> But this word [*pully*] does not rhyme exactly to *fully*. In *fully* the same stress is laid upon the *ll*, as in *full*, and accordingly the first syllable is long; in *pully* there is no such stress laid on the double liquid. The voice hurries over the *ll* and the first syllable is short. (p.217)

while again in *Of the Provincial Accentuation* (ff.41–2), he claims:

> Let any one compare the three following words *foolish*, *fully* and *pully*. In each the accent is upon the first syllable and that syllable in each (as it seems to me and to others whom I have consulted) to be always, and necessarily uttered in a somewhat sharper tone than the other. But in *foolish* and *fully* the accented syllable is long, in *pully* short. Again in *foolish* the length of the accented syllable arises from our protracting the vocal part, in *fully* we hasten over the *u* and rest upon and protract the *ll* which being a liquid is capable of being lengthened, but in *pully*, no such stress is laid on the *ll* nor is there any difference between the manner of sounding this consonantal termination of the syllable single *l* in *foolish* . . .

Douglas appears to argue that while there is a long/short difference in the pure dialect in items like [puul] ‹pool› versus [pul] ‹pull›, that contrast is not simply one of stressed vowel duration: items such as ‹full› and ‹pully›, while they have short vocalic segments nevertheless manifest, he argues, long syllable characteristics, realised through the temporal extension of the highly sonorant labial coda (although there is some evidence that this characteristic is, in fact, a Scotticism[25]). Thus the phonetic contrast between ‹full› and ‹fool› is one of [full]~[fuul]. Indeed, Douglas claims to observe a rather complex

16

situation where, with morphological accretion, we can find variants such as:

LONG ACCENTED SYLLABLE		SHORT ACCENTED SYLLABLE	
‹full›	[full]	‹bull›	[bull]
‹fully›	[fullɪ]	‹bully›	[bulɪ]
‹fool›	[fuul]	‹pully›	[pulɪ]
‹foolish›	[fuulɪʃ]		
‹pull›	[pull]		
‹fool›	[fuul]		
MORPHOLOGICALLY COMPLEX		MORPHOLOGICALLY SIMPLE	

These data raise a number of interesting points. As Kohler (1966:39) observes, the long versus short accented syllable dichotomy in disyllabic items is a function of the productive versus the non-productive morphological status of the unstressed syllable; the ‹fully› and ‹foolish› cases with their meaningful accretions correlate with long accented syllables, while items like ‹pully› and ‹bully› – showing no productive morphological relationship with ‹pull› and ‹bull› – are associated with the short accented syllable. Such a relationship is apparently observed too by Elphinston (Rohlfing, 1984:144):

> Dhe shut vowel keeps distinct from dhe open, by shortnes and shutting: *fool* (filled) *foolling*, from *fool* (unwize) *fooling*; *foollish* from *foolish*, and dhe like. (*Inglish Orthography Epittomized*, 1790:49)

> Dhis *oo* shut and short, must questionles, hware possibel, appear so. Sense wil secure dhe short *pool* and *fool* from dhe long; *poolling* and *foolling*, like *pootting* and *footting*, wil secure dhem-selves. (*Propriety Ascertained in her Picture*, 1786:236)

But what is perhaps more interesting is Douglas' observation that there are, as it were, two stratagems where long accented syllable status can be achieved, especially in those items terminated by 'liquid' consonants like [l] ('*oo* is always long before a liquid', Elphinston, *The Principles of the English Language*, 1765:70). Both 'stratagems' involve an increase in vocalic weight (periodicity) in the peak or post peak area of the syllable. In the one case, the peak or central syllabic element shows its vowel with durational increase, thus [puul] ‹pool›, [fuul] ‹fool›. In the other, the vocalic increase is arrived at (perhaps in a 'weaker' fashion) by the highlighting of the sonorant coda with its durational increase – [full]. Both stratagems result in a more periodic rhyme component in the syllable.

Yet we might speculate that Douglas' observations concerning

17

syllable length may bear some relation to what he sees as vocalic length proper. We might just suggest that contrasts such as [puul]/ [fuul] versus [full]/[fullɪ] versus [bul]/[bulɪ] have something to tell us about relative stressed vowel length, such that (metaphorically),

[puul]   represents full vowel length
[pull]   represents relatively full vowel length
[bul]   represents relatively short vowel length

The ‹pool›/‹pull› length contrast is based, of course, on the etymo-logical history of the items themselves, stemming as they do from [oo] and [u] sources (Luick, 1921:§281); but if it is the case that some items showing historically short vowel origins were coming to be merged with those with a long vowel ancestry, and where that merger was incomplete, then a form such as [full] ‹full› as an 'approximation' to [fuul] might result. Certainly, it would appear from Douglas' evidence, that lexical diffusion was prevalent in the pure dialect in this area of the phonology: some historically short vowel items like ‹full› being merged (perhaps only partially) with ‹fool› types, others like ‹bull› retaining their short vowel characteristic. The Scottish dialectal manifestations of this [u]/[uu] vowel space will be discussed below in section 1.d.

1.b pure dialect: smothered vocal u

Bearing in mind the fact that Douglas' use of descriptive terminology is rarely completely consistent, the number of items described as showing a 'smothered' or even 'obscure' u in the pronouncing dic-tionary proper is extremely small; indeed (as we have already indi-cated) the specific lexical items proposed in the *Observations on the Alphabet* section as showing this vowel shape are confined to ‹Tully›, ‹scut› and ‹rut›. It is most difficult to ascribe any precise phonetic value to this 'smothered vocal' labial, mainly as a result of the problems which arise from the difficulties involved in the interpreta-tion of what Douglas means by the term 'smothered' and 'obscure' with which he sometimes appears to equate it. The Scotch pronuncia-tion of the second syllable in ‹Sunday› is described as showing an 'obscure a' (p.226); unaccented syllables 'are always pronounced in an obscure, indistinct manner, so as to be scarcely distinguishable' (p.140); there is a version of an e sound 'which has a sort of obscure and smothered sound not unlike that of the French e in *le, ce, que*' (p.123); the obscure j or y in pure dialect pronunciation of ‹calf› ([kjæ(l)f]:cJ) is said to be a 'smothered sort of y' (p.180). While we shall have cause to discuss the matter further below, the ‹fill› entry (p.193) invites us to contrast the 'obscure u' in the pure dialect in

items like ‹luck›, ‹skull›, ‹bur›, ‹but›, ‹buss›, ‹sup›, ‹scum› and ‹bun›
with the 'hollowness' characteristic of the *u* sound in ‹tug›, ‹bud›,
‹tub›, ‹buzz›. Scottish speakers are said to substitute this obscure *u* for
the palatal [ɪ] in items like ‹fill› and ‹will› and Southern English
speakers, conscious of the salientness of this Scottish characteristic,
mimic it by producing the obscure *u* or obscure *a* in expressions like
'*What's your wull*' for '*What's your will*' (p.194).

While none of this points to any unambiguous or obvious value for
Douglas' 'smothered vocal' *u* sound, his tendency to equate it with
some kind of highly sonorant [ɑ], the suggestion that it has a 'more
hollow' version and (less obviously, perhaps) its likeness to the
French unstressed vowel in ‹le›, ‹ce›, perhaps indicates a vowel with a
low F_2 feature, one which is rather sonorant and perhaps even central:
obvious candidates would be [ʌ] or [ə] with the more 'hollow' version
in the not quite fully open, central unrounded [ɐ] vowel.[26]

1.c another 'shade' of the smothered vowel

From the number of lexical items Douglas associates with this labial,
it would appear to be the most common type in this area of the vowel
space in the pure dialect. The only clue we have to the phonetics of
this segment is Douglas' statement in his *Observations on the Alphabet*
to the effect that it 'approaches nearer to the first [sound of *u*] in such
words as *punt, hulk, rump, dub, mud*' (p.139). If our observation is
correct that the first vocal *u* represents a relatively pure labial [u]
sound, while the 'smothered' *u* is a relatively sonorant [ʌ] or [ə], then
a *u* type vowel 'approaching nearer' the pure labial than the latter,
perhaps suggests a segment mixed for both sonority and labiality with
the latter predominating; perhaps some kind of [ɣ] (a back upper mid
unrounded vowel) or [ɯ] (high back unrounded) vowel space. The
difficulty with Douglas' methodology is that he rarely (if ever) distinguishes in the *Table* these two 'shades' of the second sound of *u*, so
that it is extremely difficult to decide whether he is referring to [ʌ] or
[ɣ] type vowels. We shall tend to interpret all references to the second
sound of *u* (unless they are accompanied by terms like 'obscure',
'smothered' or 'hollow') as if they are the latter, a stance also prompted
by the small lexical set accorded the smothered type in Douglas'
Observations on the Alphabet section.

The problem is typically seen under the ‹above› entry (p.159)
where the *o* 'has the second or short sound of *u*' (Douglas introducing
a new 'short' descriptive term for the first time with this item) characteristic of words like ‹love›, ‹dove›, ‹glove› and contrasted against
a long version in ‹groove›. Some of these are realised by Scottish
speakers with [u], others with [oo], again just perhaps suggesting a
pure dialect [ɣ]/[ɯ] rather than a more sonorant [ʌ],[ə] or [ɐ].

This description of a labial vowel with three phonetic manifestations ([u]/[ʌ]/[ɣ]) as observed by Douglas perhaps adds some support for Luick's ·(1921:529–30) view that the original Middle English [u] vowel developed between the late sixteenth and early eighteenth centuries into a slightly unrounded [o] sound, before becoming completely unrounded to [ʌ], a view it seems accepted by Wells (1982:197):

> The split of the old short /u/ into two distinct qualities seems to
> have been established by the middle of the seventeenth century.
> It may well have originated as an allophonic alternation, with
> unrounded [ɣ], the forerunner of the modern /ʌ/, in most
> environments, but a rounded quality (modern /ʊ/), retained after
> labials.

If Douglas' observation of a triple development for Middle English [u] is a correct and accurate one, the existence of some 'intermediate' [ɣ] stage is attested by him at a date later than most other observers.

1.d Scotch and other regional and social variants

Douglas makes detailed observations on the characteristics of labial [u] sounds in the polite Scottish English of his day. Indeed, at the beginning of his *Treatise* in the *Observations on the Alphabet* (p.139) he observes that while the pure dialect manifests (as we have just seen) a threefold [u]~[ʌ]~[ɣ] alternation:

> In the northern counties of England *oo* is always pronounced in
> this latter manner [i.e. as the shade of the second *u*: [ɣ]:ᴄɪ] as
> much as in *stood* and *good*, as in *flood* and *blood*. And so is the *u* in
> words like *scull*, *Tully*, *rut* when it has the first shade of the
> second sound [[ʌ]:ᴄɪ] in the pure dialect.

This suggests a merger of [u], [ʌ] and [ɣ] in whatever Douglas means by 'the Northern counties of England'. But although, as we shall see, Douglas' remarks on the peculiarities of Scottish realisations of the labial vowel vis-à-vis the pure dialect are detailed and observant, it is almost by chance and in passing that he comments upon what he sees as its standard shape in the southern Scottish vernacular.[27] Under his discussion of ‹Burial, Bury›, he observes that 'The true provincial sound of the *u* in the southern counties, both in these and a great many others, is like the French *u*' by which he perhaps intends a [ʉ] or [ɯ], a high central rounded or high back unrounded vowel shape. Elphinston too makes a similar observation: 'Against the English *oo* ... dhe Soddhern Scots hav garded dheir dialect widh *u* ... French; hwich dhe nodhern [Scots] found as forrain, az did the Inglish' [*Propriety Ascertained in Her Picture*, 1786:4]. Douglas tells us that speakers in the north of Scotland realise the vowel by what Douglas represents as ‹beerial‹, ‹beery›, perhaps a pure palatal [i]/[ii] sound or

a high central unrounded [ɨ] vowel.[28] But the vowels in such items, he
admits, 'are great stumbling blocks to many a Scotchman' (p.179).
Both pronunciations are recorded by Elphinston who tells us that in
Edinburgh ‹shoe› is '*chu* "Frenchly"' and ‹rude› *rude* 'French'; on the
other hand for Aberdeen speakers he cites *shee* for ‹shoe› and *rid* or
reed for ‹rude› (*Propriety Ascertained in Her Picture*, 1786:4).

However, it is perhaps the entry for the item *above* (p.159) which
gives us the greatest insight into Douglas' vision of polite Scotch
usage for labial-type vowel space. Under this entry Douglas says that
Scottish speakers generally 'confound' vowel sounds like [ɣ], [uu] and
[oo] and he takes pains to provide detailed exemplification of pure
and Scotch vernacular practice. The pure dialect, he claims, contains
both [ɣ] (the second and – now – the short sound of *u*) and [uu] (the
long vocal) lexically distributed as follows:

PURE DIALECT

[ɣ]	[uu]
‹love›	‹move›
‹above›	‹amove›
‹dove›	‹approve›
‹shove›	‹behove›
‹glove›	‹disapprove›
	‹prove›
	‹remove›
	‹reprove›
[uu]	[ɣ]

SCOTCH

All those in the second column, Douglas claims, the Scottish speaker
'often' realises with an [ɣ] as in the 'target' word ‹love›, and from the
body of the *Table* we can deduce that [ɣ] stressed vowels are a feature
of Scottish English in items like ‹duck›, ‹word›, ‹budge›, ‹trudge›,
‹gulph›, ‹pulp›, ‹but›, ‹dub›, ‹shut›, ‹hut›, and ‹cut›. From those in
the first column he claims that Scottish speakers produce a long vocal
[uu] in only the items ‹above› [əbuuv] (to rhyme to ‹groove›), ‹dove›
[duuv] and ‹shove› [šuuv]. This long vocal [uu] sound Scottish
speakers can also use where the pure dialect generally has the long
close [oo] sound in what might be the single item ‹door› (as do 'some
few English persons aiming at peculiar propriety', p.188).

Yet Douglas also hints at the possibility in Scottish English of a
[uu]~[u] alternation in his discussion under ‹mourn›, ‹mourning›
items in the pure dialect again showing, he claims, [oo] but in the

Scots vernacular 'the short close *u* as in *return*' (p.210). It is difficult to know precisely what Douglas intends by 'short, close', but while the second 'shade' of *u* – [ɣ] – is described by him on occasion as 'short' (see under ‹above›, p.159), the attribute 'close' is never otherwise given to it. Perhaps we might speculate that, on the analogy of Douglas' use of the close epithet with *o* to mean [oo] (p.133), its force here is to infer a degree of lip rounding not normally associated with [ɣ], and therefore to represent [ü]. In the same fashion Douglas records long close [oo] stressed vowels for items like ‹clover› and ‹sword› ('according to the proper pronounciation, *sword* and *soar'd* are, to the ear, a perfect rhyme', p.226) as having [ɣ] (or perhaps [ʌ]) equivalents in vernacular Scottish English, thus [klɣvər] (rhyming to ‹lover›) and [swɣrd].

Most certainly, one of the most salient features of vernacular Scottish English recorded by Douglas is the failure in that dialect then, as now (Wells, 1982:401–402), to realise length differentials in ‹full›~‹fool› type contrasts.[29] As we have noted above, Douglas records the following items with stresses [uu]~[u] contrasts in the pure dialect:

[uu]	[u]
‹fool›	‹full›
‹foot›	‹bull›
‹pool›	‹pull›
‹boot›	‹put›
	‹pulpit›

all such items he characterises as showing a short, 'unsustained' [ɣ] or [ʌ] in the Scottish vernacular.

2 Palatal Vowels

2.a pure dialect: first sound of the e

In his *Observations of the Alphabet* Douglas makes for the pure dialect what appears to be a binary split between two main types of palatal stressed vowel; one is described unhelpfully as the 'first sound of *e*', the other, only marginally more clearly, as its short close version (p.123). The first of these sounds (which Douglas asserts 'is not found in many English words', meaning, presumably, as represented by an ‹i› graph) is realised by the highlighted symbols in items such as ‹Eloisa›, ‹Clementine›, ‹Virginia›, ‹Racine›, ‹marine›, ‹magazine› and ‹caprice›. Under the E discussion he also includes as showing this sound the items ‹scene›, ‹he›, ‹the›, ‹she› and ‹people›. The *Table* is replete with items manifesting this pure palatal stressed vowel, the 'target' item often being ‹appear› (whose homophones are set out under the ‹bear› entry, pp.172–3: ‹arrear›, ‹blear›, ‹dear›, ‹clear›, ‹drear›, ‹ear›, ‹fear›, ‹gear›, ‹hear›, ‹near›, ‹rear›, ‹sear›, ‹shear›, ‹smear›, ‹spear›, ‹tear› *lacrima* and ‹year›). Under the ‹breast› entry (p.178) with a Scottish vernacular pronunciation targeting to the pure dialect realisation of ‹priest›, we also find listed ‹east›, ‹beast›, ‹feast›, ‹least›, ‹yeast› and under ‹eat› there is ‹beat›, ‹cheat›, ‹defeat›, ‹entreat›, ‹feat›, ‹heat›, ‹ascheat›, ‹meat›, ‹peat›, ‹retreat›, ‹repeat›, ‹seat›, ‹treat›, ‹wheat›.

There is some evidence to suggest too that in the pure dialect all items like the above (with the first sound of *e* or *i*) were durationally extended (Douglas' 'protracted') and that, on occasion at least, this increased length value was phonetically predicted (controlled by) the voicing characteristic of fricative consonants terminating the syllable:

> In *thief* the *ie* has the first sound of the *i* shortened. Add the *e* at the end and as in *thieve* (where indeed the consonant is also altered) and the *ie* retains the same sound but protracted. (p.124)

Likewise, under the ‹precede/preceding/precedent› head (p.216) Douglas states that while the *e* in ‹precede› has its 'long sound as in *these*, or like the *ea* in *appear*, and *ee* in *freeze* . . . In *Precedent* (subst.) the *e* is short and as in *preside*.' But it is under the ‹ease› entry (p.190) that the largest set of long/short sensitive pure palatal items is provided. Syllables terminating in voiced fricative [z] shapes show long stressed [ii] vowels, as in ‹ease›, ‹easy›, ‹appease›, ‹disease›, ‹please›, ‹lease› 'verb sinonymous to *glean*' while 'In the following words the *ea* has the same sound but shortened and the *s* hard [devoiced:CJ]': ‹cease›, ‹decease›, ‹surcease›, ‹crease›, ‹decrease›, ‹increase›, ‹grease›. But for some unaccountable reason (was the length difference in the pure dialect not as observable as he had imagined?) Douglas has scored through the entire ‹ease› entry in his revision of the Signet Library version of the manuscript.

2.b pure dialect: short close i

Douglas' description of this type of palatal sound is everywhere in the *Treatise* difficult to interpret. For the pure dialect he makes, in his *Observations on the Alphabet*, a binary distinction in this sound which he claims to be easily observable by the 'attentive ear' and which is peculiar to the English language (p.129): items he cites showing the vowel in stressed position are ‹picture›, ‹fixture› and ‹sin›. This 'short close' sound is divisible into two 'shades', the one in pre-[r], the other in all other contexts (although we shall see below that the non-rhotic environment itself may produce contextually sensitive phonetic contrasts in this palatal vowel sound).

23

The pre-[r] palatal type *i* sound in items such as ‹first› and ‹thirst› approaches, for Douglas' ear, 'nearly to but seems not exactly the same with, the short *u*' (p.129): not a very helpful description in view of our discussion above, where 'short' [u] could apparently range from [u] through [ɣ]. His statement that a ‹burst›/‹first› contrast will illustrate the difference between the two shades is not particularly enlightening either, since in his descriptions of [u] sounds, Douglas does not distinguish pre-[r] developments, except to list ‹bur› under 'obscure *u*' in contrast to the more 'hollow' *u* under his ‹fill›. entry. This might point to a pre-[r] value of [ʌ] rather than [ɣ]. So the vowel in ‹first› is 'nearly, but not exactly the same with' [ʌ]. Such a conclusion is reinforced by Douglas' ‹fir› entry, where he says that the '*i* is sounded nearly like the short obscure *u* in *burst*.' Such a vowel, we might tentatively suggest, could be the half close, upper mid, central vowel [ə]. But we shall have more to add to this discussion when we come to consider the ‹clergy› item below (Valk, 1980; Gabrielson, 1913). There would appear to be considerable evidence of lexical diffusion, from the observations of most grammarians in the period, affecting relatively central vowel shapes in the pre-[r] context; the Scotsman Gray (1814:9–14) for instance listing the items ‹sir› and ‹her› as sharing the pronunciation of ‹tun›, ‹done›, ‹touch›, ‹work›, ‹love›, with ‹first› and ‹gird› represented as ‹furst› and ‹gerd›.[30]

2.c first sound of e shortened

'Most sensibly perceived before a semivowel' this sound is evidenced in the stressed vowel spot in items like ‹fin›, ‹sin›, ‹will›, ‹ill›, ‹his›, ‹women›, ‹Lizard› (p.129). But before we speculate upon a phonetic value for this segment, it is important to realise that Douglas makes a further sub-division of it. Under the important ‹fill› entry (p.193) he observes that there is a contrast between *i* pronunciations which is a function of the shape of the segments terminating their syllable. When the syllable coda is of the 'class' voiced fricative or voiced obstruent, an 'obscure' *i* is realised, contrasting with what is described as a more 'hollow' version, where the syllable is terminated by 'the softer semivowels and mutes (viz. this soft *s*, the *v*, the soft *th* the *b* the *d* and the *g*)' and where the vowel is perhaps a low central [ʌ] or even [ɣ] (see above, pp.18–20). Such a contrast is lexically exemplified as follows:

obscure short *i*	more 'hollow'
‹fit›	‹big›
‹wit.›	‹bid›
‹fin›	‹crib›

obscure short *i*	more 'hollow'
‹is›	‹smithy›
‹skim›	‹live›
‹Liffy›	
‹Lizard›	
‹women›	
‹kick›	
‹kill›	
‹kit›	
‹ship›	
‹pith›	

Items under the first column show syllables terminated by the (rather odd) set voiceless obstruent ([t], [k], [p]), non-[r] sonorants ([l], [m], [n]), voiceless continuants ([f], [θ]) and the voiced fricative continuant ([z]). Although 'most sensibly perceived before a semivowel' (the sonorants and voiced/voiceless continuants) this set manifests, Douglas claims, stressed vowels showing a 'shade' of *i* sound which 'approaches . . . to the first sound of *e* shortened'. We might therefore speculate that in the pure dialect we are dealing in the column one items with a vowel space which, while palatal, is not so palatal as [i], and might therefore be treated as [ɨ].[31] The items under column two manifest stressed syllable codas which are either voiced fricatives or voiced obstruents. In such contexts (as we have already seen for the labial vowel segment – see p.19), the syllable space is perceived as more 'hollow', where the codas 'reflect back as it were, a sort of hollowness on a preceding obscure and short vowel' (p.193), a 'hollowness' illustrated by Douglas as typical of the stressed vowel space in items like ‹drum›, ‹sullen›, ‹dub› and ‹tub›. The column two stressed vowel might therefore be interpreted as a more sonorant (more central and lower) segment than [ɨ], perhaps [ɪ], the retracted front unrounded vowel.

Yet Douglas points out that palatal vowels in voiced fricative ([z]) contexts seem to be exceptional (although the phenomenon may be severely lexically restricted). In an item like ‹is› (and ‹his› which should 'rhyme to *is*', p.202), 'the sound seems to be somewhat different from what it is in the English pronunciation of *Fit, wit, fin,* – something nearer the *i* in *caprice*' (p.193): this might suggest an obscure short *i* in [ɨ]. But it is also possible that his observation is inaccurate here, and his attributing an [i]-like pronunciation to this item and ‹his› is a reflection of the Scottish tendency (to be described immediately below) of realising [i]/[ii] in what are otherwise [ɪ]/[ɨ] contexts:

At Edinburgh, and in the adjoining counties, this pronoun [his]

25

instead of being made to rhyme to *is*; is pronounced as if written *hees*' (p.202)

a comment suggesting that ‹is› also could have a less palatal [ɪ] realisation. Yet Elphinston too (*English Orthoggraphy Epittomized*, 1790:11) seems to see the palatal sounds in items like ‹indivizibility› as closer to the pure palatal [i] than the modern [ɪ] shape:

> Hwile the shutting dhus shortens evvery vocal sound, it guivs to *a*, *e*, and *u* new sounds, az different in quality az in quantity; but to *i*, dhat of *e* short.

His description is of a much less explicit type than that characteristic of Douglas, and he merely states that while the shortened versions of [u] and [ɑ] are different in quality from their long congeners, [ii] (his *e open*) when shortened is [i].

2.d Scotch forms of i: the short obscure i

We have observed that in the pure dialect Douglas appears to distinguish three palatal sounds, one in [r] contexts we suggested might represent an upper mid central [ə]-type segment; the second 'approaches to the first sound of *e* shortened', a segment we speculated which might be represented by [ɨ]; the third a more 'hollow' version of the last, whose value we might place somewhere near [ɪ]. Douglas claims that one of the most salient features of the Scotch dialect lies in the way it is 'apt to substitute' an [ə]-like segment in those items like ‹fin›, ‹will›, ‹ill›, ‹is›, ‹his› in which the pure dialect realises an [ɨ] vowel.[32] Indeed, he claims (p.130) 'before *n*, *l* and *t* [Scottish speakers] scarcely ever hit this exactly. Hence the English in caricaturing their pronounciation will say *wull*, *full*, *spull*, for *will*, &c'. Again, under the ‹fill› item, he asserts that:

> As there is only a slight shade, or gradation, between the Scotch method of sounding the *i*, in *fill*, *fit*, *wit* &c and the English, the difference generally escapes the attention of Scotchmen who are endeavouring to mend their pronounciation. It is however so sensible to the English, that when they mean to ridicule the Scotch dialect they frequently lay hold of this circumstance, at the same time with the provincial sound of the *ou* in *bought* and *sought*, and of the *e* in *clemency*, *memory*, *echo* &c. Indeed as caricature adds to ridicule in all sorts of mimicry the English in their imitation exaggerate the Scotch pronounciation of the short *i*, and turn it into the obscure *u* or *a*. '*What's your wull?*' '*You have a great deal of wat*'. (p.193)

But Douglas gives us no more precise information as to what this 'Scotch i' might have been like phonetically other than that it is somewhat more sonorant than [ɨ]. Indeed his terminological descriptions of the sound (assuming they all refer to it) are quite varied: *short obscure ı, short ı, obscure i, short smothered i, short close i.* The Scottish examples and their English counterparts for these descriptions are as follows:

Douglas' description	English example
short obscure	
‹Venice›	‹fin›, ‹winning›
short	
‹weather›	‹wither›
‹whether›	‹whither›
‹tremble›	‹thimble›
‹bedizen›	‹phiz›, ‹mizzen›
‹behind›	‹rescind›
obscure	
‹remember›	‹timber›, ‹window›
short smothered	
‹remainder›	‹wind›, ‹sin›, ‹fin›
short close	
‹piracy›	‹pirate›

while the Scots *i* vowels in the items ‹pencil› and ‹clever› are given no descriptive name, but are merely said to be pronounced 'as if written *Pincil*' (p.214) or made to 'rhyme to *liver*' (p.184; cf. Adams' ‹pincil› '*pencil*' ‹wist› '*west*' and ‹till› '*tell*', 1799:152–3). Perhaps we are looking here at a sound not so palatal as [ɨ] and yet not so sonorant as [ə], some more central [ɨ] or perhaps even [ə], a mid central unrounded vowel.

2.e Scotch forms of i: the first sound of e, long and short [ii]/[i]

As is the case with many modern Scots regional and social varieties, long and short pure palatal [ii]/[i] stressed vowels could be realised, in the late eighteenth century, where the pure dialect produced mid and less palatal versions. Table 2.e sets out some of the possibilities recorded by Douglas in his *Table* (the examples in column two are the items in the pure dialect with which the Scotch versions of those in column one are said to form a perfect rhyme). While we shall discuss in some detail below (see pp.31–7) the motivation for and distribution of the pure dialect [ee], [ɛɛ] and [ɛ] stressed vowel shapes in the items cited in the first column, it would seem clear that the English realisations suggest discrepancies in that dialect from the

TABLE 2.E

Pure Dialect	Scotch Rhyme Exemplars
[ɛɛ]	[ii]/[i]
‹bear›	BEER
‹chair›	CHEER
‹e'er›	EAR, APPEAR
‹mare›	MERE, HERE
‹ne'er›	NEAR
‹pear›	APPEAR
[ɛ]	
‹bread›	BREED
‹breast›	PRIEST
‹friend›	FEEND
‹head›	HEED
‹his›	HEES ('as if written')
[ee]	
‹either›	'like *ee* in *steel*'
[i]	
‹whim›	SEEM
‹build›	STEEL'D
‹liberty›	LEER, LEAVE

'standard' *modus operandi* of the set of changes known as the *Great* or *English Vowel Shift*. In one sub-set of this process, from as early as the late fourteenth century, we find evidence for a 'palatality increase' or raising of mixed palatal/sonorant vowels such that, for example, [ee] → [ii] and [ɛɛ] → [ee] and even → [ii], so that [see] → [sii] ('*see*'); [sɛɛ] → [see] ('*say*') and [mɛɛt] → [meet] → [miit] ('*meat*').[33] Yet it was commonly the case that long mixed palatal/sonorant vowels 'failed' this raising process when in pre-[r] contexts in some southern regions of the country (Jones, 1989:241–8). Thus, rather than find an alternation for the item ‹chair› such that: [čɛɛr] → [čeer] → *[čiir], we find in fact that the stressed vowel tends to 'stick' and remain 'unshifted': i.e. it retains elements of its sonority in a pre-[r] environment, an environment itself, we might claim, prominent in a sonority acoustic characteristic (see below under our ‹clergy› discussion, pp.40–1). Douglas' evidence suggests that this [r] context had no such effect in some Scottish regional types of his day – raising to pure palatal [i]/[ii] forms being readily observable. However, he also comments on the fact that while ‹chair› has a (probably long) [ii] stressed vowel 'in many parts of Scotland', 'some vulgar persons in England' produce the word with this pronunciation as well.

However, the data from the *Treatise*, like those from many present day Scottish regional types (as well as those in Australia and South Africa; Wells, 1982:598–9;612–3) suggest that this 'vowel shift' phenomenon could affect stressed vowels whose duration was not extended, as well as those with lengthened qualities so favoured as the affecting context in the standard literature (Lass, 1984:126ff; Johnston, 1980; Kohler, 1966,1967; Vianna, 1972). Items in the first column of Table 2.e like ‹bread›, ‹breast›, ‹friend› and ‹head› can be shown to have etymologically long vowels as late as the sixteenth century in many southern British dialects (Dobson, 1968:§123; Ekwall, 1975:§§15–17) and might therefore be assumed to undergo the normal palatalisation associated with the *English Vowel Shift*, vowel shortening occuring at a later date and in particular contexts – notably adjacent to [l], [m], [n] and [d] (Robinson, 1985:xxv). Yet it is very difficult to be sure whether Douglas' contemporaries heard long vowel versions in column one items in their contemporary phonology. He specifically tells us, for instance, that in the pure dialect the vowel in ‹bread› is like the '*ea* in *bear*, but short' (p.177). Were it the case that speakers heard only short vowel outputs for the stressed vowels in the column one items, then some scholars might still argue that speakers were somehow able to 'recover' the original, historical length and thus be able to input the words into the *English Vowel Shift* process, later shortening them. But (circuitous) arguments like this based upon a speaker's ability to reconstruct abstract, historically remote phonological inventories are subject to the severest criticisms (Hooper, 1976:4–11; Kiparsky, 1973). This 'short vowel shift' phenomenon appears to have been one of the most saliant characteristics of Scottish English phonology to eighteenth-century observers of the dialect.[34] Walker's (1791:xi) comments on the phenomenon, under his *Rules to be Observed by the Natives of Scotland for attaining a just Pronunciation of English*, are worth quoting at length:

> With respect to quantity, it may be observed, that the Scotch pronounce almost all their accented vowels long. Thus, if I am not mistaken, they would pronounce *habit, hay-bit; tepid, tee-pid; sinner, see-ner; conscious, cone-shus;* and *subject, soobject:* it is not pretended, however, that every accented vowel is so pronounced, but that such a pronunciation is very general, and particularly of the *i*. This vowel is short in English pronunciation where the other vowels are long; thus *evasion, adhesion, emotion, confusion,* have the *a, e, o,* and *u,* long; and in these instances the

29

Scotch would pronounce them like the English; but in *vision*, *decision*, &c. where the English pronounce the *i* short, the Scotch lengthen this letter by pronouncing it like *ee*, as if the words were written *vee-sion*, *decee-sion*, &c. and this peculiarity is universal.

Walker is clearly not (with the possible exception of the ‹subject› instance) merely observing a length dichotomy between the Scotch and English versions, but one where a vowel height discrepancy of the type [æ]/[e]; [ɛ]/[e], [i]/[i] and [ɔ]/[o] also exists, although we might wish to treat with reservation his observation that the Scotch vowel forms are durationally extended.

As well as making vowels like [ɛ], [e] and [æ] more palatal by raising them to [e], [i] and [ɛ]/[e] respectively, the *English Vowel Shift* is also a process which typically diphthongises long vowels, notably [ii] → [ei], [ɛi], [æi], [ɑi]; thus fifteenth-century [miin] '*mine*', seventeenth-century [mɛin], [mæin] (Dobson, 1968:659ff) and in its more recent stage [ee] → [ei]; [see] → [seɪ] '*say*' (Zettersten, 1974:58–60). The [ɑi] and [æi] diphthong in the first syllable of the pure ‹idea› item has arisen (as the spelling suggests) from some kind of historical [ii] source, a 'stage' which could apparently be retained in an undiphthongised form in the Scottish pronunciation of Douglas' day. Douglas claims, for instance, that the first syllable of ‹idea› is realised in the Scottish vernacular by a first syllable vowel in [ii] – a long vocal *i*, like the vowel spelt ‹i› in ‹caprice› and ‹magazine› (p.203). Perhaps like this too are his recorded Scottish pronunciations of ‹twilight› as [twiilæit] (p.230), [bihind] for [bihæind] (p.174), [bidəzən] ‹bedizen› for [bidæizən] (p.173), [klɨm] ‹climb› for [klæim] and [riið] ‹writhe› (to rhyme to WREATH) for the pure dialect [ræið] (p.233).[35] But a further discussion of diphthongal sounds, both for the pure dialect and Scottish vernacular will appear below; see pp.157–62. An excellent instance of the differential effects of the vowel shift as they relate to regional and social factors in the late eighteenth century can be seen from the information provided under Douglas' ‹weigh› entry (pp.231–2). There he distinguishes three different pronunciations for the item corresponding to three groups of speakers: the vernacular Scotch, Scotch aiming to speak with 'more propriety' and the pure dialect speaker, thus:

SCOTCH		PURE
vernacular	polite	
[wæi]	[wii]	[wee]
EYE, TRY[36]	SEE, PEA	PAY, PRAISE

where the capitalised items represent rhyming congeners in the pure dialect. The pure dialect version is in fact rather conservative, reflecting a pronunciation current in polite southern English speech since the seventeenth century at least. The polite Scottish vernacular shows the 'expected' palatalisation associated with the *English Vowel Shift* to a level not reached by southern British English (which, in fact, diphthongised to [ei] in the early nineteenth century). It is thus the vernacular Scottish version which shows the most 'advanced' stage of the vowel shift process for this item – the diphthongisation of the pure [ii] palatal to a transitional vowel space in something like [æi]. This tendency for the relatively non-prestigious dialects to realise more 'advanced' stages of phonological processes than are achieved in 'standard' versions of the language, is well attested (Dobson, 1968:§96; Milroy, 1980:181ff; Jones, 1989:212–13).

3 Mixed Palatal/Sonorant Vowels: [e]/[ε]

3.a pure dialect manifestations

In some respects Douglas' descriptions of the 'mid' [e]/[ε] front vowel are the most extensive and detailed in his *Treatise* (Flasdieck, 1900), but in others, especially when exemplification is being provided in the body of the *Table*, frustratingly and tantalisingly vague as, for instance, in the entry under ‹remember›: 'The second *e* is to be pronounced nearly as in *member*, though perhaps not quite so distinctly, and fully' (p.219) where there is no separate entry for *member* and where one would like to know precisely what Douglas means by 'nearly', 'not quite', 'distinctly' and 'fully'. The most detailed account of the nature of this type of segment as it surfaces in the pure dialect appears in his *Observations on the Alphabet*, especially in his discussion there as to the phonetic significance of the ‹a› and ‹e› symbols in contemporary orthographic practice (pp.117–19; 123–6); interesting comments are to be found too under the ‹bear› and ‹eat› entries in the *Table* proper. Although his terminology is far from consistent, Douglas seems to be suggesting that for the pure dialect he could recognise a long and short version of both the high and low mid [e] and [ε] vowels (Kohler, 1966:46). Both vowels he characterises as close and slender *a* and both, he claims, are 'more commonly long' (p.117), and he describes their contrast in terms of the 'strong slender' versus the 'short, thin or feeble slender'. According to his statements in the *Observations on the Alphabet* under the *A* and *E* headings, we can represent the kinds of mixed palatal/sonorant (mid front) vowels in the pure dialect schematically as follows:

CLOSE/SLENDER *a*

STRONG		THIN-FEEBLE	
LONG	SHORT	LONG	SHORT
(most commonly)			(most commonly)
‹stare›	‹pen›	‹phrase›	‹race›
‹share›	‹stem›	‹waste›	‹pace›
‹pare›	‹rest›	‹glare›	‹grace›
‹bare›	‹better›	‹great›	‹tale›
‹hare›	‹cellar›		‹daisy›
‹tail›	‹there›		‹baize›
‹hair›	‹fell›		‹reign›
‹bear›	‹debt›		‹weigh›
‹wear›			‹state›
‹pear›			‹pay›
[εε]	[ε]	[ee]	[e]

While we cannot completely justify the phonetic values assigned above to the four types of mid front vowel which Douglas distinguishes, the [ε] values for the stressed vowels in ‹pen›/‹debt› types would appear non-controversial for this period, while Douglas' association of the long strong type with the stressed vowels in contemporary French ‹bête›, ‹pere› and ‹ferme› suggests [εε], (a value he asserts is the shape of the Scotch pronunciation of the Greek η symbol). So too, the linking of the thin feeble slender with the final syllable vowel in French ‹porter› and both vowels in the French ‹extrait› suggests for it a more palatal [e] value (the Scotch pronunciation, he claims, for the Greek ε). Likewise, the low mid [εε] value in the predominantly pre-[r] environment for the strong slender long types agrees well with what we know about the general historical tendency for rhotic syllable terminations to 'block' the vowel shifting of mixed palatal/sonorant segments to those which are more palatal (Jones, 1989:§4.3;2). Nevertheless matters are not always so clear cut as Douglas appears to suggest as, for instance, when describing the existence in the pure dialect of an [εε]~[e] distinction he observes (p.117):

> The distinction will be still more evident if we compare the usual manner of pronouncing *tail*, and *tale*; where *ai* in the first word represents the strong, and *a* in the second the thin, slender sound. It is necessary to remark that some good English speakers, either from affectation or habit, pronounce such words as *tail* and such as *tale* in the same manner, viz with the strong slender *a*.

See too Dobson (1968:§104). In much the same fashion, Douglas' comments on relative front mid vowel duration often appear to be at variance with each other. His assigning of the item ‹glaze› to the 'protracted' vowel space agrees well with his observations that voiceless [s] codas select short stressed vowels (as in ‹erase›, ‹base›, ‹grease›) while voiced [z] is associated with long vowel variants as in the items ‹wise›, ‹praise›, ‹raise›. Yet he seems to claim too that items like ‹daisy› and ‹baize› are treated as showing *short* feeble *e* stressed vowel space.[37]

It is of interest too, with reference to the evidence provided by erasures in his revision of the Signet Library version of the MS, that Douglas clearly spotted errors in his original assignment of items to the [ε]/[e] categories. His remarks under the ‹eat› item (p.190) are illuminating:

> Eat
>
> The ea as in appear ... Pronounce in the same manner beat, bleat, cheat, defeat, entreat, feat, heat, ascheat, meat, neat, peat, retreat, repeat, seat, treat, wheat. Pronounce *it* as *in* breast *in the following words great*, threat (n & v), sweat (noun and verb.), teat. **In great (which is properly pronounced in Scotland) the ea has a thinner and somewhat longer sound like the thin slender a in pate, state.**

(where the italicised words represent erased and the bold Douglas' inserted materials in the corrected MS version). Historical phonologies almost universally point to the 'exceptional' nature of ‹great›, ‹break›, ‹steak› items vis-à-vis ‹meat›, ‹cheat› in Modern English in terms of their disparate reaction to the vowel shift process (Dobson, 1968:§109; Ekwall, 1975:§54, Luick, 1968:§312; Horn-Lehnert, 1954:§251ff).[38] While the latter have progressed by a 'double', two stage application of palatalisation increase from a source [εε] through [ee] to [ii], the former have rested at the [ee] stage: a point forcibly presented as well by Elphinston who, after listing items like ‹break›, ‹great›, ‹steak›, ‹bear›, ‹pear›, ‹there›, ‹their›, ‹where›, says:

> Nor will won ov [them:CJ] clas annymore, even in semblance, widh here, hear, speak or neat.' (*Propriety Ascertained in Her Picture*: 225)[39]

Douglas' insert to the Signet MS suggests that the Scotch pronunciation of the expected vowel shift value in [ii] is the 'proper' one, while the pure variety of the language has a 'thinner and somewhat longer sound' of the [ee] in ‹pate›. However, in the A MS version, Douglas has clearly associated the item ‹great› with the stressed vowel in ‹breast›, suggesting perhaps that some [grεεt]/[greet] alternation also existed in the pure dialect at that time, although the fact that he has scored out this material may suggest his own uncertainty as to the original accuracy of his observation on the matter. Douglas also records pure dialect, non vowel shifted [ʧεεrfəl] ‹chearful› (p.182) and [t(ε)εt] ‹teat› (the latter rhyming, he says, to ‹threat› (p.227)) pronunciations which, in the modern standard language, have reached pure palatal [ii] values.

It is worthwhile at this point to comment upon some of the ways in which Douglas represents stressed vowel length in the pure dialect. While in his general remarks in the *Observations on the Alphabet*, he states that [ɛ] low mid, less palatal types are 'most commonly' protracted or long, while the thin, feeble [e] type is 'most commonly' short, his identification of vowel length value under the entries in the *Table* proper is patchy. Certainly there are few, if any, instances there where Douglas directly comments that a pre-[r] [ɛ] shape is long or protracted, although there are a few instances where he specifically identifies short vowels of the close, slender strong type: ‹Thames›, (HEMS, GEMS), ‹threat›, ‹tremble›, ‹member›, ‹weapon›, (PEN), ‹bread› (DREAD, HEAD, INSTEAD, LEAD, SPREAD, STEAD, THREAD, TREAD), ‹breast› (DREST), ‹dead› (FED, BED, SHED), ‹delicate› (BELVIDERE, CLEMENCY, MEMORY), ‹edge›, ‹epilogue› (STEP) where the upper cased items represent perfect rhyme analogues cited under principal dictionary entry heads.

Close thin or feeble varieties ([e]/[ee]) which are 'most commonly short' in Douglas' view are marked rather more regularly and systematically for durational value in the *Table*, even though they are statistically less frequently cited there than the [ɛ]/[ɛɛ] types. The following table lists those items from the *Table* which are specifically marked as long or short:

SHORT [e]	LONG [ee]
‹base›	‹impl*a*cable›
‹place›	‹April›
‹space›	‹ape›
‹debase›	‹apron›
‹rase›	‹Babel›
‹erase›	‹babe›
	‹face›
	‹capon›
	‹acorn›
	‹rake›
	‹bake›
	‹pi*a*zza›
	‹staple›
	‹rape›

It is worth noting that despite his observations on the predictability of stressed vowel length as a function of the voicing characteristic of the syllable coda (see p. 24 above), Douglas enters ‹face› with a long [ee] vowel space. But, in general, the vast majority of [e]/[ee] type items are left unmarked as to length value in the *Table*.

3.b mixed palatal/sonorant vowels in the Scotch dialect: the [ɛ]/[ɛɛ] type

Our discussion of this and the [e]/[ee] (more palitality prominent in the mix) vowel types in Scottish English in the late eighteenth century will centre largely upon the ways in which they are manifested in that dialect vis-à-vis their behaviour with respect to the 'classical' interpretation of the *English vowel shift* process. We have already seen, for instance, how even at this early period, there is evidence to show that (in defiance of traditional interpretations of the event) the vowel shift could apparently involve *short* vowels as input – recall our [hɛd]/[hid] '*head*' alternation discussed above. We noted in the last section too how the evidence provided by Douglas for both the Scottish and the pure dialect points to a manifestation of long vowel English vowel shifting which is at once 'retarded' and 'advanced' in relation to the 'standard' and stereotypical interpretation of this phonological process. The behaviour of the predominantly sonorant weighted front mixed vowels in Douglas' description of their Scottish variants would seem to be little different in this respect. Consider the following table where once again we contrast what Douglas considers to be the pure dialect stressed vowel form against its Scotch counterpart, with upper cased items representing perfect rhyme congeners in the pure dialect. The precise phonetic values for the segments for the moment characterised as showing [æ] or [ɑ] will be the topic of discussion in the next section:

PURE DIALECT	SCOTCH
[æ]/[ɑ]	[ɛ]/[ɛɛ]
‹apple›	KEPPEL
‹chariot›	CARE, STARE
‹rather›	FEATHER, LEATHER
‹master›	MESS
‹napkin›	NEPTUNE
‹saffron›	SHARE
‹yard›	AIRED, SPARED
‹Saturday›	SHARE
‹Harry›	PARE
‹harvest›	PARE
‹large›	CLARE, WARE, STARE

Although the data are complex, they seem in general to suggest that what for the pure dialect are (long as well as short) low vowels – i.e.

more sonorant than palatal in their mix – are realised in the Scottish dialect as relatively more palatal ('raised').[40] The Scottish forms show what we might therefore metaphorically describe as an 'advanced' state of the *English vowel shift* process for the particular lexical items in question, both in the extent to which the raising occurs and in the range of the constituency which it affects.

There is evidence too from the *Treatise* to suggest that the vowel shifting of [æ]/[ɑ] segments in the Scots dialect was more 'advanced' still, since it seems to be the case that Douglas records even more palatal [e]/[ee] values for such low vowel inputs. For instance, although ‹saffron› is said to rhyme to SHARE and thus show [ɛɛ] (p.221), rhyming analogues like PAPER, WAFER are also proposed suggesting a [se(e)frən] pronunciation. In the same way, although ‹Saturday› and ‹Saturn› are said to rhyme to the SHARE [ɛɛ] vowel, they too are compared to STATE, pointing to realisations like [seetərn] and [setərde]. Perhaps evidence of Douglas' uncertainty over the [ɛɛ]/[ee] value of the pure [æ]/[ɑ] stressed vowels as they appear in Scots can be seen in the ‹napkin› entry where, although the rhyme model is given as NEPTUNE (possibly with [ɛ]) Douglas has scored through rhyming model entries like NAPE, CAPE, RAPE, the last unambiguously marked as [ee] (under ‹staple›: p.225) in the *Table*.

That items such as ‹apple› and ‹napkin› show 'raised' Scottish vowels might lead us to conclude that here again we have an instance of the *English Vowel Shift* affecting short stressed vowel segments, a view reinforced by Douglas' remark that although ‹Harry› as well as ‹parry› and ‹tarry› show a short open *a* ([æ]): 'The Scotch generally pronounce it in these words with the slender *a* as in *pare*, but shorter' (p.200) – some kind of [hɛrɪ] pronunciation. Nevertheless, Douglas' description of Scottish vernacular [ɛ]/[ɛɛ] stressed vowel shapes suggests that for some lexical items at least the result of the vowel shift was a 'retarded' one:

PURE	SCOTCH
[ii]	[ɛ]/[ɛɛ]
‹neat›	BEAR
‹retreat›	BEAR
‹spear›	BEAR
‹deal›	BREAST
‹idea›	PEN
[i]	[ɛ]
‹dinner›	‹denner›
	'as if written'

In the Scottish vernacular the ‹neat›, ‹retreat› etc items have not undergone the 'expected' English vowel shifting of [ɛɛ] to the more palatal [ee]/[ii]. At the same time, the vernacular Scottish situation reveals lexical diffusion and socio-phonetic alternation of some sort: Douglas emends his ‹deal› entry (p.187) from 'The Scotch often pronounce *all* or *some* of these words as *breast* is sounded in the pure dialect' to 'Many Scotch people pronounce *all* and most of these words as *breast* is sounded in the pure dialect.' Again, under ‹spear› (p.224) he comments:

> The *ea* as in *appear*. The Scotch often sound it as in *bear*. Tho' the other is their vernacular pronounciation.

suggesting a polite vernacular [spiir] pronunciation with a less acceptable, vowel shift retarded [spɛɛr] variant. While we might speculate that Douglas' recording of the fact that although ‹dinner› 'rhymes to *sinner*, in Scotland it is often pronounced as if written *denner*' (p.187) might indicate a 'retarded' state of some short vowel shift of [ɛ] → [ɪ]/[ɨ], it is perhaps more probable that what we are witnessing here is an instance of pre-nasal lowering (Ohala, 1974).[41]

Two further points about the Scottish vernacular [ɛ] are worth noting – firstly, Douglas observes (p.218) that in the southern counties of Scotland:

> the *e* of *question* is commonly pronounced very broad, like the sound of *a* in *bare*, or the Scotch sound of the η. This peculiarity has been often remarked in the House of Commons when the gentlemen of Scotland have happen'd to unite in calling for the *question*.

Although it is difficult to guess what Douglas means by 'broad' in this context, we might assume that it points to yet another instance of the highly salient [ee]/[ɛ] contrast in Scotch/pure dialect mixed palatal/sonorant vowels. Secondly, and more puzzling, is the record of the Scottish pronunciation of ‹launch› (in the pure as AUNT, and therefore perhaps [ɔ] or [ɒ] – see below, pp.51–5) as 'if written *lench*'. Perhaps we should mention here too the [e(e)] Scotch version for the stressed vowel in ‹caution› said to rhyme to that in PATIENCE and often used specifically in a technical legal context (p.181). But we shall return to these matters under our discussion below of the 'broad *a*' (see pp.51–7).

3.c mixed palatal/sonorant vowels in the Scotch dialect: the [e]/[ee] type

There is little doubt from the evidence in Douglas' *Treatise* that the Scottish vernacular use of the palatal weighted mixed palatal/sonorant vowel is one of the most marked, salient characteristics of its phonology:

> particularly, like the Scotch manner of pronouncing *bought, sought* &c, [which:cj] is among the things which are most striking to an

37

English ear, and are generally laid hold of in 'taking off the Scotch dialect' as the phrase is. (p.183)

On the one hand, Scottish speakers manifest [e(e)] stressed vowel shapes in a 'retarded' English vowel shift manner, in contexts where the pure dialect realises the chronologically earlier mid vowels as the pure palatal [ii] – consider the following:

PURE DIALECT	SCOTCH
[ii]	[e]/[ee]
‹recent›	[resənt]
‹cream›	[kreem]
‹tea›	[tee]

although the [kreem] pronunciation is said only to occur 'sometimes', while the [tee] version is specifically associated with 'the North of Scotland' (p.226), suggesting that the 'unshifted' [ee] for pure [ii] was infrequent in Scottish English at the close of the eighteenth century.[42] On the other hand, the use of [e]/[ee] stressed vowels for the pure dialect [ɛ] and [æ]/[ɑ] types appears to have been widespread in Scottish pronunciation. Compare the following data:

PURE DIALECT	SCOTCH
‹again›	agen
‹clemency›	PHRASE
‹delicate›	PHRASE
‹memory›	PHRASE
‹epilogue›	APE, TAPE
‹Thames›	LAME, SAME, BLAME
‹Thanet›	THANE
‹edge›	PAGE
[ɛ]/[ɛɛ]	[e]/[ee]

Items in the Scottish vernacular associated with the [ee] stressed vowel in ‹clemency› include, in addition to the above, ‹echo›, ‹Helen›, ‹jealousy› and ‹pedant›. But it is worth noting that the [ee] pronunciation is produced by Scottish speakers[43] when they 'mean to speak correctly' and, in the case of ‹again›:

Those Scotchmen who take pains to read and speak well generally make the last syllable of this word long, like *gain*, *stain*, *plain*. (p.161)

Again, compare the following pure dialect/vernacular Scottish [ɑ]/[æ]~[e]/[ee] contrasts:

PURE DIALECT	SCOTCH
[ɑ]/[æ]	[e]/[ee]
‹dragon›	PLAGUE
*‹Danish›	FAME
*‹famine›	FAME, GAME, TAME
*‹have›	SAVE
‹pageant›	PAGE
‹camel›	FAME
‹patent›	PATE
*‹plaid›	PLAY'D
‹rather›	RATE
‹ravish›	RAPE, RAVE
*‹statue›	STATE
‹talent›	TALE
‹drama›	SAME
‹garden›	CAVE

where items marked * represent those specifically referred to as long in the *Table*. Many of the Scottish vernacular [e]/[ee] versions, notably ‹dragon›, ‹Danish›, ‹camel›, ‹famine› and ‹drama›, Douglas also highlights as characteristic of the usage of those Scottish speakers who 'aim at propriety' (p.189), 'try to catch the right pronounciation' or are 'aiming at the improvement of their pronounciation' (p.181).[44] These 'advanced' English vowel shift manifestations of [e(e)] for [ɛ] and [æ]/[ɑ] are frequently associated with hypercorrections or accommodation characteristics, suggesting perhaps that Scottish speakers perceived the pure dialect palatal/sonorant mixed inventory as weighted towards the palatal end of the spectrum, hearing [æ] and [ɛ] as [æ⊥] and [ɛ⊥] respectively. Yet under the ‹cradle› entry, Douglas asserts that 'The Scotch (endeavouring to speak properly) are apt to pronounce the *a* short as in *bad, addle, paddle*. But it should be pronounced as in *shade, glade*. Or as *ladle*.' (p.186). But clearly variation existed in the extent to which palatalisation of the pure dialect [ɑ] type segments could occur in Scottish English, as can be seen from Douglas' description of the Scottish pronunciation of ‹rather›:

> The Scotch either sound it like the *ea* in *feather, leather*, so as to form a perfect rhyme with those words; and this is the vernacular pronounciation; or they make it like *a* in *rate*. (p.218)

There is just the suggestion here that the latter pronunciation in [e] represents some non-standard Scottish type, a suggestion perhaps borne out by Douglas' comments under ‹have›:

> The *a* has its short open sound as in *hat, hard*. The ill educated among the Londoners, and many of the Scotch, make it long and slender as in *save*. This is to be avoided. But all the other words

39

like these (even *behave*, which seems to be formed from *have*) rhyme to *save*. (p.200)

But Douglas is often uncertain as to the extent of the raising of [æ]-type vowels in the Scottish vernacular; commenting on the fact that the pure dialect realisation of the item ‹napkin› is a stressed short and open [æ], while the Scotch make it the [ɛ] of the highlighted vowel in ‹Neptune›, Douglas has nevertheless had to erase from the Signet Library version (f.234) his intuition that the 'Scotch pronounce it as in *nape*, *cape*, *rape*, but short' – some kind of [e] vowel. On the other hand, for the item ‹Patrick› he has erased a short and open [e] stressed vowel as in ‹pate›, ‹fate› for one which is long and open as in ‹father› (p.213), perhaps [ɑɑ], see § 5.a below. In general, the Scottish [ee]/[e] for the pure [æ]/[ɑ] is viewed by Douglas as either a hypercorrection or simply 'Scotch' without judgmental comment.

3.d pure dialect [ɛ] in pre-[r] contexts in specific lexical items

Douglas' descriptions of the pure dialect stressed vowel values in items like ‹clergy›, ‹fir›, ‹were› and so on are extremely difficult to decipher with anything even approaching a reasonable degree of phonetic certainty. The ‹clergy› item appears to be the model in the pronouncing dictionary for the majority of items showing pre-[r] mid palatal/sonorant mixed vowels: items like ‹eternal›, ‹earth›, ‹dearth›, ‹clever›, ‹fern›, ‹stern›, ‹herb›, ‹heron›, ‹maternal›, ‹paternal›. The value of the ‹clergy› stressed vowel is complicated by two factors. In the first place, Douglas seems to say quite unambiguously that in the pure dialect the vowel corresponds to the 'short close *e*' (p.183) typical of the items ‹mercury›, ‹berry› and ‹merry›, i.e. [ɛ]. He then states its Scotch pronunciation as [ɛɛ] rhyming to *bare*, but says that its 'proper sound' has another, more complex value. It is difficult to know whether he means by this 'proper sound', a prestigious pure or Scottish vernacular pronunciation. But a study of pre-[r] context palatal and mixed palatal/sonorant segments (already briefly referred to above, see p.134) is illuminating in that it shows Douglas attempting a degree of phonetic descriptive refinement rare in phonologists during and even before his time (Holmberg, 1956:31–2).[45] But we must bear in mind his own stated difficulties in perceiving fine phonetic detail, perhaps best represented under his comments on the ‹ever, every› entry (p.192):

The *e* short, and as in *bed*. The Scotch pronounce it like the short close *i* in *liver*, *livery*. In familiar conversation most English people make it a shade nearer this close *i*, than the *e* in *bed*; Yet not the same. But it requires great attention, and an ear *practised* in these niceties of articulate sound, to perceive the distinction.

The well attested sonorising (lowering) effect of a syllable terminating [r] on the stressed vowel space (Dobson, 1968: §65; see too above, pp.28–9) is manifested in the *Table* primarily under the ‹clerk› entry where we are told that 'The *e* [is] like the *a* in *far*. *Clerk*, and *lark*, *park*, *remark* rhyme together,' (p.184). Yet items such as ‹jerk›, ‹perk›, ‹Berks› and ‹Berkshire› are said to show the same stressed vowel shape as that in ‹fern›, itself realising the ‹clergy› vowel to be discussed in more detail below. ‹Hearth› too shows in the pure dialect a rhyme to *art*, *part*, *start* (while Douglas has erased from the Signet Library MS version the interesting remark that 'though some English people make it rhyme to *earth*' (p.249), a word with a stressed vowel also said to be like that in ‹clergy›). Thus the ‹e› symbol in pre-[r] contexts represents a segment which is possibly [æ] and whatever we can discover to be the nature of the ‹clergy› vowel.

The stressed vowel in the 'proper' pronunciation of ‹clergy›, Douglas claims, is 'a shade between' the stressed vowel in ‹fir› and the [ɛ] in ‹pen›. It is, of course, impossible to say with any certainty the degree of vowel space interval intended by a phrase like 'a shade between'. Yet we might conjecture that since the ‹i› in ‹fir› ('sounded nearly like the short obscure *u* in *burst*' p.194) – despite the ambiguity of 'nearly' and the difficulty of finding a precise value for obscure *u* itself – was the half close, upper mid central vowel [ə], then a sound 'a shade between' [ə] and the [ɛ] of ‹bed› might be interpreted as [ə], a mid central unrounded vowel. Still, Douglas repeatedly insists that this pre-[r] environment can produce [ɛɛ] vowels; thus for ‹e'er› we are told that this word is 'to the ear, the same with *air*', and rhymes to *there* which, as we saw above (p.33) was recorded with a short version of the long close/slender *a*: [ɛ].

Different again seems to be the stressed vowel in the item ‹were› which (under the entry for ‹e'er. *before*›, p.191) is described as 'short, and the *e* pronounced something between its sound in this word [‹e'er›:cJ] and in ‹clergy›.' A vowel segment 'something between' [ɛ] and the postulated [ə] of ‹clergy› might just be taken to represent some central unrounded [ɜ] type vowel. But perhaps we should resist the temptation to accept such fine phonetic detail too readily, on the basis of what are, after all, rather metaphorical and imprecise descriptive terms.

3.e [ɛ] in pre-[r] contexts: Scotch vernacular

Douglas provides considerable evidence for the sonorising effect of syllable terminating [r] on [ɛ] stressed vowel space, mutating it to what might be some kind of [ɑ] shape. Items such as ‹mercury›, ‹merge› are pronounced by the Scots as 'they do the *a* in *March*' (p.209).[46] Yet the most common Scottish vernacular pronunciation in this environment is the [εε] in items like ‹eternal›, ‹external›, ‹internal›, ‹infernal› and ‹clergy›, while the ‹e'er› item shows a Scottish 'advanced' English vowel shift realisation as the pure palatal [ii], the item pronounced in that dialect 'like *ear*' (p.191). On the other hand, in an item like ‹merry›, the Scottish stressed vowel is 'like the short obscure *i* in *mist*' (p.209): some kind of [ɨ] shape, perhaps reflecting a 'short' vowel shift phenomenon (see p.29).

3.f general observations on mid vowels in pre-[r] contexts

Douglas' observations of the pure dialectal manifestations of [e]/[ε] vowel types are in many ways typical of those of other phonologists writing in the late eighteenth century as we have seen in several places above, notably pp.31–5 (Holmberg, 1956:51ff). His assignation of a high mid [e] type vowel to items like ‹state›, ‹pay› and ‹tale›, contrasted with a 'lower' [ε] variety in pre-[r] contexts, in turn alternating with a yet lower, more central [ə] vowel in a specified set of lexical items is not untypical of the observation of other writers in the period. And he, like they, is careful to stress that the lowering effect is not an across the board affair, but is subject to considerable lexical diffusion. For instance Sheridan (1780: 1781) outlines a *Scheme of Vowels* where, among others, are listed three types of *a* and *e* sounds:

	First	Second	Third
a	hat	hate	hall
e	bet	bear	beer

perhaps at first sight suggesting some kind of [e]/[ε] alternation between the second sounds of *a* and *e* respectively, sensitive to the presence of a syllable final [r]; yet he is careful to warn us that his descriptive terminology is not unique and that 'the second sounds of *a* and *e*, as in *hate* and *bear*, are the same', although whether they both represent [e] or [ε] it is not possible to be certain since the second sound of *e* vowels are cited as being characteristic equally of items like ‹bear›, ‹pear›, ‹wear›, ‹tear›, as well as ‹steak› and ‹break› (p.23). Yet in the section *Different Sounds marked by the same Vowels* in his *Dictionary* (1780:23), Sheridan notes that the *e* vowel behaves differentially in pre-[r] environments in a fixed set of lexical items (Kaffenberger, 1927):

When this vowel precedes *r* it never has its own sound, but is always changed to that of first *e*, or first *u*. To *e* in the following words: *birth, firth, girt, girth, gird, girl, mirth, skirt, squirt, quirk, chirp, firm, irk, smirk, dirge, whirl, twirl*. To *u* in *dirt, flirt, shirt, spirt, first, third, bird*.

Walker too (1791:10) includes [r] full and [r] less coda items as showing the same stressed vowel before them:

> the first sound of the first letter in our alphabet is that which among the English is its name. This is what is called by most grammarians its slender sound; we find it in the words *lade, spade, trade* &c . . . and sometimes in the diphthong *ea*, as *bear, swear, pear* &c and *nay*.

Since he claims that 'It exactly corresponds to the sound of the French *e* in the beginning of the words *être* and *tête*', we might posit a value for the vowel in question as [ɛ(ɛ)] on the basis of Walker's assertion (1791:10) that 'As the short sound of the long slender *a* is not found under the same character, but in the short *e* (as may be perceived by comparing *mate* and *met*)'. Yet he too isolates out a specific lexical set where an etymological [ɛ] vowel:

> before [r] . . . is apt to slide into the short *u*, which is undoubtedly near the true sound, but not exactly. Thus pronouncing *earl, earth, dearth* as if written *url, urth, durth* is a slight deviation from the true sound, which is exactly that of *i* before *r*, followed by another consonant in *virtue, virgin*; and that is the true sound of short *e* in *vermin, vernal* &c.

We might note too his observation concerning the etymological [ɛ(ɛ)] that, 'the first *e* is pronounced like *a*, as if written *whare, thare*' (1791:13). In a very similar fashion, John Burn (1786:*Introduction*), listing sixteen different vowel sounds for his contemporary language, includes under his twelfth type what appears to be an [e(e)] high mid vowel in items such as ‹lay›, ‹they›, ‹there›, ‹steak›, ‹main›, ‹swear›, contrasting with possibly [ɛ] in his thirteenth vowel as in ‹net›, ‹let›, ‹men›: however, he lists a set of items (some again showing syllable final [r]) having his first *u* sound (probably [ʌ]) as in: ‹fur›, ‹her›, ‹sir›, ‹heard›, ‹but›, ‹front›, ‹blood›, ‹earn› and ‹worm›.

4 Mixed Labial/Sonorant Vowels: [o] and [ɔ] types

4.a the pure dialect situation

In his entry for ‹roast› (p.220) Douglas distinguishes four different kinds of *o* sound: (1) the 'short close' as in ‹rod›, (2) the 'short open' sound as in ‹rot›, (3) the 'long close' sound as in ‹rote› and (4) the 'long open' sound in ‹wrought›; similar divisions for the *o* segment are also suggested under the ‹of, off, oaf› entry (p.212). This fourfold division in fact represents an underlying bifurcation between two types of segment 'differing in quality from each other', and set out in some detail in the discussion of this mixed labial/sonorant class in the *Observations on the Alphabet* (p.133). In a short section there Douglas presents a picture of the values of such a class as it is manifested in the pure dialect which we might tabulate as follows:

OPEN (commonly short)		CLOSE (commonly long)	
LONG	SHORT	LONG	SHORT
‹corn›	‹hot›	‹bone›	‹sob›
‹horn›	‹lost›	‹stone›	‹pod›
‹bought›	‹cross›	‹post›	‹log›
‹thought›	‹horse›	‹hoarse›	
‹groat›		‹bowl›	
‹broad›		‹sow›	
		‹soul›	
		‹though›	
		‹road›	
		‹woe›	
		‹toe›	
		‹foe›	
		‹beau›	
		‹shew›	
[ɔɔ]	[ɔ]	[oo]	[o]

The values we have assigned to the above types should be regarded at this stage as tentative only, and we shall have to comment upon them as we procede. Notably, as regards the long open sound characteristic of the stressed vowel space in such words as ‹bought› and ‹thought›, Douglas points out that:

> This sound, if at all, is but just distinguishable from the long broad *a* in *all, malt*, or the *au* in *Paul*. Some writers on pronounciation consider them as entirely the same. They are generally made to rhyme with such words as *taught*, and *fraught*, but that is no proof that their sound is exactly the same. (p.176)

And again:

> This sound [the long sound of the open *o*] if not the same, is near the confines, or the external edge, if I may so speak, of the broad *a* in *all*. Some writers think them the same. I imagine I can perceive a difference. (p.133)

If we assume for the moment that the 'broad *a* in *all*' is some kind of

low back rounded [ʊ], then the long open *o* may well, if it is so close
to this as sometimes to be confused with it, be [ɔт] rather than [ɔ]. But
we shall return to this matter later (see pp.148–50 below).[47] Douglas'
description of the 'close *o*' is likewise a relativistic one, the segment,
he claims, one that 'verges towards the vowel represented by *oo*'
(p.133) and which may thus represent some raised (more labial)
version of the high mid rounded [oɪ]. Yet in general Douglas' four *o*
types and the lexical items with which he associates them bear a close
resemblance to the shape of the vowel space in their 'standard'
modern British English analogues, with the exception that there
many [oo] vowels have taken on (since the beginning of the
nineteenth century) a dipthongal ([ou], [oə] etc) configuration (Wells,
1982:§4.2.4). Yet while his assignation of open, short values to items
like ‹not›, ‹lost›, ‹cross›, ‹horse›, with close (and usually) long values
typical of ‹bone›, ‹stone›, ‹post›, ‹hoarse› is as we might expect, his
data in the *Table* do point to several interesting contrasts in the pure
dialect. Consider, as an example, his entry on p.212 under the items
‹of›, ‹off›, ‹oaf›:

> These three words afford examples, of three, out of the four
> sounds of *o*. In the first it is short, and close; in the second short,
> and open; and in the third, the *ou* has, as in other cases, the long
> close sound of the *o*.

Although we shall see in the next section how Scottish and pure
dialectal manifestations are distinguished by a widespread and
perhaps phonologically predictable alternation between [o(o)] and
[ɔ(ɔ)] stressed vowel space shapes, Douglas' data relating to the pure
dialect seem to show a similar discrepancy in the lexical distribution
of these high and low mid back vowels which in many cases appears to
belie their subsequent form in the modern standard language.
Consider the forms in the table below, where the modern standard
diphthongal shapes are assumed to have [oo] historical precedents.
Such forms could be treated respectively as lexical item specific
instances of retardation or advancement of the *English vowel shift*
process, although given the salience of the [o]/[ɔ] contrast between
the pure and Scottish dialects, we might have cause for concern as to
the accuracy of Douglas' observations in this area of the phonology.
Indeed, in many instances, Douglas' remarks are such that a particular vowel shape is regarded by him as specific to a particular item in
his lexicon. For instance, of the [ɔ] in the first syllable of ‹oat meal›,
he tells us (p.211):[48]

> In this (I believe single instance) the English pronounce the *oa*,
> like the short open *o*, in *not*, in so much that to make it long and
> close (although in the primitive word *oat*, the *oa* is sounded as in
> *oath*) would appear pedantic and affected.

	Modern [ou]/[oo]	Modern [ɔ]
(1) PURE [ɔ(ɔ)]	‹revolt›	
	‹oat meal›	
	‹Trojan›	
	‹groat›	
	‹ford›	
	‹form›	
(2) PURE [o(o)]		‹sob›
		‹pod›
		‹log›
		‹rod›
		‹of›
		‹knowledge›

This item specific identification of pronunciation is again clear from Douglas' observation on the items covered under ‹form› (p.196):

> This word in the ordinary acceptation (and its compounds) are pronounced with the long open *o*, as *fork, corn*. When it signifies a class in a school, or a bench, the *o* has the long close sound. To acquire a clear idea of the distinction between these two sounds of the *o*, I cannot recommend a better method, than to get an English man who speaks well, to pronounce *form*, first, as used in the one sense, and then, as in the other.[49]

Likewise, although ‹revolt› is described as showing an [ɔ] stressed vowel, items like ‹colt›, ‹dolt› and ‹jolt› are specifically excepted and show [oo]. That the [o]/[ɔ] alternation was, for the pure dialect, one of some considerable sociophonetic significance can be seen from Douglas' observations on the item ‹knowledge› whose stressed vowel is generally pronounced in both England and Scotland as [ɔ], yet 'some English people affect to give it the long close sound, as in *flow, know*' (p.204).[50]

4.b mixed labial/sonorant vowel shapes in the Scotch dialect

This is an area where there is perhaps the most salient contrast between the phonologies of the two dialects, and it is of a kind which partly hinges upon the way they appear to realise stressed vowel duration as well as the ways in which they react differentially to vowel shift processes. In the most general of terms, the pure and Scottish dialects alternate between [ɔ]/[oo] contrasts, contrasts involving both length as well as relative sonority/labiality. Indeed, so marked are some of the length idiosyncracies of the Scottish materials, that Douglas is moved to comment that while in the pure dialect there are

|oo| and |ɔɔ| durationally extended stressed vowel shapes, the situation in Scotland is markedly different; under the item ‹broad› he informs us:

> In this word and in *groat*, the *oa* has the same long open sound approaching the *a* in *all*, which we have described under the word *bought*. These two words are the only instances I believe where the *oa* has this sound. In *road*, *goad*, *float* &c, the *oa* has the long close sound as in *boat*. (p.178)

But although the discrepancy in the de-sonorising (raising) effect of the *English vowel shift* is one which we might expect, Douglas' follow-up remark concerning a particular peculiarity of Scots highlights the greater complexity involved: 'If there is any simple vocal sound in the pure English dialect, not to be found in the Scotch, it is the long open *o* or *oa*.'

That Scottish speakers were indeed conscious of some [o]/[oo]/[ɔ]/[ɔɔ] contrast in their contemporary phonology is again hinted at when he tells us that (despite the last categorical statement) while the English pronounce the stressed vowel in ‹gone› with the short open *o*, 'The Scotch are apt to make it long, when they endeavour to pronounce well' (p.199). Thus, while the [ɔɔ] may not be a product, for whatever reason, of contemporary Scottish phonology, it seems that it could be used (albeit occasionally) as a salient hypercorrected shape for, or accommodation to, [ɔ]. That the same kind of process is at work in the way Scottish speakers produce the [oo] segment is again suggested when we find under ‹bought› the observation that:

> The Scotch, after they get rid of the more barbarous pronunciation in which the *gh* is pronounced as a strong gutteral, generally fall into the mistake of using the long close sound of *o*, and making (for instance) *bought*, and *boat*, the same word to the ear. And this they do so generally that in endeavouring to mimic the Scotch pronounciation, I have observed that the English are apt to hit upon this particular way of sounding this class of words. Yet this, in truth, is not part of the vernacular pronounciation of Scotland. (p.176)[51]

The salience and sociophonetic value of the [ɔɔ]/[oo] alternation is well documented too in Douglas' remarks under the ‹coast, coat, coax› entry:

> Not long ago, a Scotch Gentleman, in a debate in the House of Commons upon the Affairs of America, began a speech, in which he proposed to examine whether it would be more advisable to adopt compulsive, or soothing measures towards the colonies. Unfortunately instead of *sooth*, *coax* was the word that had presented itself to his mind. And he pronounced it as if written *cox*. This, added to several other peculiarities of manner and

dialect, tickled the House extremely, and produced a general laugh ... (p.185)

While Douglas states quite categorically that sounds such as [ɔɔ] and [oo] are 'generally confounded in Scotland, so that the words pronounced in England in one way, are, in that country pronounced in another' (p.159), the alternation appears to have been not altogether random, and in the same passage he observes that ⟨Jove⟩, with [oo] in the pure dialect, 'is also properly pronounced by the Scotch' and for reasons we shall set out in what follows.[52]

Let us begin by considering those examples from the *Treatise* where Douglas records Scotch [ɔ] stressed vowel shapes where the pure dialect, he claims, shows durationally extended [oo] vowels.[53] Items in italic in Table 4.b(1) refer to the pure dialect analogues for the Scottish instances, those in capitals in the lower half of the table, the analogues of the pure. Items have been arranged under the consonantal shape of the segment terminating their stressed syllable. From data like these it would seem reasonable to speculate that in syllables with rhymes terminating in codas like [st], [t], [θ] and [rs]/[rk] (although frequency of occurrence in Douglas' *Table* is itself no indication of what an optimal phonetic context might be) Scottish English in the late eighteenth century 'preferred' stressed vowels whose duration was curtailed (and whose accessibility to the *English vowel shift* process could be expected to be constrained; but see pp.54–7 below).

TABLE 4.B(1)

[st]	[t]	[θ]	[rs]/[rk]	[b]	[k]	[s]
⟨coast⟩	⟨dotage⟩	⟨oath⟩	⟨force⟩	⟨job⟩	⟨poke⟩	⟨gross⟩
cox	*dot*	*moth*	*indorse*	*bob*	*lock*	
⟨boast⟩	*pottage*	⟨sloth⟩	⟨hoarse⟩	*mob*		DOSE
lost	⟨mote⟩	*broth*	*horse*		JOKE	
⟨roast⟩	*spot*		⟨pork⟩	ROBE		
⟨toast⟩	⟨notice⟩	BOAST	*fork*			
⟨ghost⟩	*not*	OATH				
lost			COARSE			
⟨most⟩	DOTE		COURSE			
lost	BOAT		FORCÉ			
⟨roast⟩	NOTE					
BOAST						
TOAST						
HOST						

That this was perhaps part of a wider process affecting stressed vowel duration in Scottish English at this period we shall see below. The two most general phonological features of the short vowel triggering context can be described as, (1) a *voiceless* rhyme termination (although the [st] shape might itself be a separate duration restricting feature; Haggard, 1973), and (2) the vast majority of the items in question are monosyllabic. Exceptions to this last distributional criterion such as ‹dotage› and ‹notice› might just be explained away by treating ‹age› and ‹ice› as (quasi) morphological accretions. But in general we should not be surprised at the association between durationally short vowels and voiceless syllable terminations, since the voicing coefficient of the syllabic coda is such a well attested stratagem for the cueing of stressed vowel durational characteristics (Raphael, 1972).

Consider in Table 4.b(2), by way of contrast, those instances which Douglas cites for the use by Scottish speakers of long [oo] stressed vowel space, where their English contemporaries would realise [ɔ] or (in the case of the forms in the first column) [ɣ], derived via the sonorising of an etymological [ɔ] segment.

TABLE 4.B(2)

[v]	[z]	[r]	[g]	[ð]	[l]	[t]
‹dove›	‹apostle›	‹abhor›	‹bogle›	‹froth›	‹extoll›	‹bought›
love	*abode*	*boar*	*brogue*	*loathe*	*coal*	*boat*
‹covet›	‹gosling›	*sore*	‹progress›		*foal*	‹motely›
cove		‹Horace›			*hole*	*mote*
rove	COST	*boreas*			‹olive›	
‹shove›		FOR			‹policy›	SPOT
‹hover›		OR			‹polish›	
rover					*pole*	
‹oven›					LOLL	
over					POLITICK	
love						
‹Ovid›						
over						
‹sloven›						
woven						
LOVE						
SHOVE						
LOVER						

Data like these in some ways confirm the predictions of the *Scottish Vowel Lengthening Rule* (Aitken, 1981; Lass, 1984:33–5:1974) which points to preferred vowel length extended space in syllables terminated by voiced continuant and fricative segments [v], [ð], [z] (possibly including [r] in the last category; Anderson and Ewen, 1989:159). In such environments Scottish vowels (both historically and synchronically) show a preference for extended duration, thus effectively delexicalising vowel length in the language's phonological structure. Yet Douglas' information suggests that the matter is not so simple and that length is, for instance, also a characteristic of pre-[l] vowel space and (albeit apparently infrequently) even of syllables terminated by voiced obstruents like [g] and voiceless obstruent [t] segments. The [l] environments might just be seen as a 'natural class' extension of the continuant fricative/sonorant group to embrace all highly vocalic sonorant types, but the [g]/[t] cases resist such an explanation and we must either treat them as 'exceptions' or look for other affecting factors.

The pre-[g] context is a particularly interesting one, since under the ‹bogle› entry in the Signet Library MS Douglas has, in fact, erased a *long close* value for the stressed vowel in the pure dialect, as well as a short value (exemplified by the vowels in BOG, DOG) for Scottish speakers. His correction reverses this situation, suggesting either uncertainty or that a genuine short close variant existed. Interestingly too, in the same entry he erases the item ‹ogle› as a parallel type to ‹bogle›: ‹ogle› under its own entry showing a long and close [oo] in the pure dialect, while the Scotch 'make it short and close' – one of the few items recorded with an [o] value in the whole *Table of Items*. Notably, the only others with this short [o] value are those whose stressed vowel space is terminated by an [l] initial cluster: ‹bolt›, ‹colt›, ‹dolt› and ‹jolt› with a vowel space which 'The Scotch generally make . . . short' (p.175) as against a pure 'long close sound' (cf. Holmberg, 1956:69, who says this short [o] value is 'most remarkable' in the commentary of James Douglas). In other words, both [g] and [l] syllable terminations are somehow associated with non durationally extended vowel space, and their inclusion in Table 4.b(2) alongside the continuant voiced fricatives need therefore not be over stressed: recall too Douglas' comment to the effect that 'the close *o* is sometimes short especially before the soft mutes *b*, *d*, and *g* as in *sob*, *pod*, *log*' (p.133).

But a characteristic which we have so far overlooked of those items showing long vowels in the Scottish dialect, and which might go some way to explain the anomalous (at least in terms of the *Scottish Vowel Lengthening Rule*) lengthening context, is the fact that the majority of them are *disyllabic* or *trisyllabic*: ‹hover›, ‹oven›, ‹Ovid›, ‹apostle›, ‹olive›, ‹policy›, ‹polish›. All the [oo] vowels are in 'open syllable' type contexts, contexts associated with stressed vowel durational increase in southern British English from the thirteenth century onwards (Jones, 1989:98ff; Bliss, 1952–3). That the handbooks (notably Mossé, 1952) tell us that this process is not a Northern dialectal phenomenon need not prevent us from postulating that in eighteenth-century Scottish English, stressed vowels had their timing extended such that:

$$\{ \mathfrak{I} \{_2 \underset{1}{l}\} \, \iota y\} \rightarrow \{ \mathfrak{I} \mathfrak{I} \{_2 \underset{1}{l}\} \, \iota y\}$$

with a vowel shift effect converting the derived [ɔɔ] to a less sonorant [oo] shape. It would therefore appear from the above data that variations in regional dialect reaction to post stressed vowel contexts such as [r], [v], [ð], [z] and the open syllable produced a differential reaction to the *English vowel shift*. In environments such as [st], [t] and [θ], where the pure dialect retained historical long vowels, vowel shifting them to some kind of [oo] shape, Scottish speakers for whom length was phonologically predictably extended in the voiced continuant fricative environment, realised them with short [o], subsequently sonorised to [ɔ]. On the contrary, historically short vowels in items such as ‹covet›, ‹oven› and those perhaps shortened through the agency of earlier phonological changes, such as ‹shove› (OE ‹scūfan›), were lengthened (or had their lexical length preserved) in Scottish dialects in such a context, and desonorised subsequently to [oo] by vowel shifting.

It is remarkable that Douglas appears to make no mention of what is now (and what was to some observers in the eighteenth century) a particularly salient characteristic of Scottish English: the [bon]/[ben], [ston]/[sten] contrast (Luick, 1921:360ff). While Adams (1799:152–3) records ‹aik› '*oak*', ‹aits› '*oats*', ‹aith› '*oath*', ‹ain› '*own*', ‹sai› '*so*', ‹bain› '*bone*', ‹stein› '*stone*', and ‹grain› '*grown*' (and even ‹flai› '*flaw*', ‹jai› '*jaw*'), Douglas perhaps sees this phonological characteristic as too 'dialectal' to be dealt with in a work whose main purpose is to refine still further the already polite (albeit non-standard) English of educated Scottish speakers (see pp.99–101).

5 (Relatively) Pure Sonorant Vowel Sounds

There is little doubt that Douglas found some difficulty in describing this area of the vowel space, yet his treatment of it in terms of 'gradations' and 'mergers' rather than as composed of discrete, individually identifiable segments, points both to his sophistication as an observer and to his foresight and inventiveness in the metaphor of phonological modelling. His main comments on [ɑ]-like sounds are to be found in the *Observations on the Alphabet* section (notably pp.117 and 133) and under the ‹aunt› and ‹wax› entries in his *Table*. Three principal *a* sounds are described for both the pure and the Scottish dialects: (1) the *long open a* as in the item ‹father›, (2) the *short open a* as in ‹hat› and (3) the *broad a* characterised by the vowel in the item ‹all›. We shall discover that it is quite difficult to assign any precise and unambiguous phonetic values to these three types, since Douglas' description of them is a relativistic one. For instance, the broad and open *a* sounds are, he claims, 'only to be considered as shades and gradations of the same sound', and Douglas' description of phonetic segments as non-discrete, analagous to the continuum of the colour spectrum, is not unlike that put forward by many modern proponents of phonological description (notably Donegan, 1978; Stampe, 1972):

> For, as in the rainbow, although the pure middle part of each of the different stripes of colours is clearly distinguishable from the others, yet, while the eye gradually passes outwards, to the edge of such stripes on either side, it seems to die away insensibly into the neighbouring tint, and is at length so like it, that it is impossible for the mind to draw the line, or fix the limit where the one ends, and the other begins; so the same thing is observable in our perception of vocal sounds. (p.118)[54]

5.a pure dialect characteristics

The *long open a* characteristic of the stressed vowel in ‹father› Douglas describes rather strangely as 'a sound placed between *o* and the strong slender *a*' (p.118).[55] It is difficult to assess what he means by *o* in this context, but we might surmise that since [oo] (the *long close* variety) is such a common feature of the pure dialect as he records it, this high mid sonorant rather than some [ɔ] type is referred to here. The strong slender *a*, we have suggested, represents [ɛɛ] (see above, p.36). A low sound 'placed between' a long back rounded and a long front unrounded segment we might see literally as referring to a long unrounded central(ised) shape like [ä]. On the other hand, if Douglas intends us to envisage a low segment with the backness characteristic of [oo] and the unrounded feature of [ɛɛ], then some low back unrounded [ɑ] segment may be what he means us to understand by this description.

Items with such an unambiguous vowel specification appear to be relatively rare in the *Table*, only ‹Patrick› showing a clear analogue to the ‹father› model, although even here Douglas has deleted the description in the A version of the vowel as *short* and open for one in the s MS where it is *long* and open, while the ‹pat›, ‹fat› and ‹patent› rhyming analogues are also deleted from A. That the pure dialect realised short versions of this long [ɑɑ] vowel seems to be inferred from a comparison between the ‹father› and its immediately preceding ‹famine› entry. The stressed vowel in ‹father› is described as 'the *a* as in the foregoing word but longer' (p.193).[56] If the *a* in ‹father› is indeed [ɑɑ], then ‹famine› would seem to show an [a] stressed vowel space, analogues to which are given as ‹ham›, ‹swam› and ‹ram›. Likewise, ‹lather› is described as 'the *a* short. In other respects as in ‹father›' (p.204). ‹Rather› too is cited as a pure dialect analogue of ‹lather› (p.218).

What Douglas intends by the much more frequently exemplified *short open a* is clearly not merely a durationally curtailed version of [ɑɑ]. The vowel sound in ‹hat› 'approaches to the limits of, and begins to mix itself with, the short and strong slender sound in *better*' (p.118).[57] Such a description might fit a phonetic entity with a palatal/sonorant mix, where the sonority component was more prominent that the palatal, a segment like [æ], rather than [a]. Items very commonly cited for this [æ] vowel are those whose stressed rhyme peaks terminate in [r] codas, a context which we might expect to produce stressed vowel length. But Douglas repeatedly refers to these as 'short open', thus ‹art›, ‹start›, ‹cart›, ‹dart›, ‹car›, ‹claret› and so on. Yet there are some suggestions that an [æ]/[æː] alternation existed in the pure dialect too. For instance, under the ‹March› entry we find (p.207):

> The *a* in Scotland, is commonly pronounced as in *have*. But it ought to be pronounced exactly as in *art, part. Starch* and *March* form a perfect rhyme. The Scotch pronounce the latter word also improperly. Sounding it as they do *March* but shorter.

This suggests perhaps that the pure dialect ‹March› stressed vowel is [æː] and thus for ‹art› and its many analogues. Perhaps pointing to a 'preferred' short vowel in ‹art›, ‹start› type items, Douglas (p.164) nevertheless (under the ‹art› entry) warns Scots speakers who, we recall, regularly use [εε] in such words, not to fall into the trap of substituting for that sound 'the long open *a* as the inhabitants of the north of England particularly do, in the word *cart*.'

The identifying feature of the (usually durationally extended) *broad open a* rests in Douglas' observation that it is 'a mixture of the long open *a* and the *o*.' Such a description – recently echoed in non linear phonologies of the *Dependency* type (Anderson and Ewen, 1989:206ff) – would perhaps point to a mixed labial/sonorant [ɔ] or [ɒ] shape; and given Douglas' insistence upon the complete lack of a long open [ɔɔ] segment in Scots, together with his record of the broad open *o* in that dialect, we might be persuaded to believe that the last was indeed some relatively highly sonorant [ɒɒ] long low back rounded configuration. And it is worth recalling Douglas' observation (p.133) concerning the [ɔɔ] (the long sound of the open *o*) in items like ‹corn›, ‹horn› when compared with the vowel (broad open long) in ‹all›:

> This sound ([ɔɔ];cj] if not the same, is near the confines, or the extended edge, if I may so speak, of the broad *a* in *all*. Some

writers think them the same. I imagine I can perceive a difference.[58]

This difference between [ɑɑ] and [ɒɒ] is once more brought to our
attention by Douglas in his detailed description of the ‹aunt› item
(pp.165–6):

In this word *aunt*, and several others, [the stressed vowel] has the
long open sound of *a* – yet less open than that in *father*.

And he points too to the fact that among the vernacular Scotch 'those
who try to catch the English method sound it [‹aunt›] long and broad,
like the *a* in *all*, or as the English pronounce it in *haunt*.' Again, while
the vowel in ‹wax› should, in the pure dialect be 'sounded something
between the *a* in *wafer*, and that in *father*', the Scotch pronounce it
'*too* open' (where Douglas underscores *too* in the Signet version)
probably as [ɑ] or [ɑɑ].[59]

Unlike for the [ɑɑ] vowel, Douglas lists many items which show
the 'broad open *a*' sound, both in his *Observations on the Alphabet* and
in the *Table* proper, e.g. ‹all›, ‹also›, ‹altar›, ‹halt›, ‹halter›, ‹hall›, etc.
He seems to suggest too that in the pure dialect a short [ɒ] version of
the sound was also to be found; for instance, under the ‹causeway›
entry (p.181) he describes the '*au* as in *cause* or *paul*, but short', while
under ‹want› we find 'The broad *a* as in *all*, but not quite so long'
(p.231). Indeed, although we should perhaps not read too much into
it, Douglas oscillates in his nomenclature for the [ɒ] type vowel space
between *long broad open* and merely *broad open*. But the data seem too
scant to warrant any predictive process for length assignment to this
segment. It is perhaps William Angus (1814), a Scottish contemporary
of Douglas who, in his *An English Spelling and Pronouncing Vocabulary
on a New Plan*, makes the most unambiguous statement as to the
presence of both [ɔɔ] and [ɒɒ] sounds in the phonology. Indeed,
Angus distinguishes no less than seven non palatal vowels in the
phonology of his contemporary language, symbolically represented as
follows:

Â	Ă	o	ö	â	ă	a
[ɒɒ]	[ɒ]	[ɔ]	[oo]	[ɑɑ]	[ɑ]	[æ]
chord	wash	college	clothe	clerk	castle	galaxy
gnaw	wad	gone	goal	gnarl	draft	carry
ball	wast	column	close	charter	ghastly	dalley
pall	wan	comedy	ghost	embalm	glass	damn
gall	want	cough	holy	guardian	rascal	habit
warm	what	doll	proclaim	hearth	pasture	imagine
war	swab	model	soldier	laughter	tranced	magpie
false	wasp	occur	post	psalm	vast	marry

Although he does not suggest any special symbol or diacritic for a long [ɔɔ] segment, it is difficult to believe that none existed in his phonology. Pre-[r] [ɒ] segments are usually perceived by Angus as durationally extended and marked with the ˆ diacritic: cf. the ‹warp› [wɒɒrp]/‹wad› [wɒd] contrast. It might not be unreasonable to conjecture that there existed a ‹cord› [kɔɔrd]/‹model› [mɔdəl] length sensitive contrast as well, and perhaps his failure overtly to record it might be a reflexion (if we are to believe Douglas' observation that the lack of [ɔɔ] was a salient Scottish characteristic) of his own speech habits.

5.b [relatively] pure sonorant sounds in the Scotch dialect

It is difficult to assess from Douglas' observations just how common the [ɒɒ], [ɑɑ] and [ææ] stressed vowel segments actually were in the Scottish English of his day. His entries containing these vowel shapes usually merit comment only as pure pronunciations, and Scottish variants are given simply because they are just that. The extent to which Scottish English speakers used such vowel shapes is difficult to calculate from the kind of information the *Treatise* provides. However, that there are genuine Scottish variants for the highly sonorant vowels of the pure dialect emerges clearly from Douglas' remarks. Consider the data in the table below. The Scottish [ɑɑ] types, few in number, represent instances where no palatalisation of [ɑɑ] → [ææ] appears to have occurred with subsequent re-palatalisation to the [ɛɛ] and ultimately [ee] of the pure dialect; a reversal of the state of affairs we observed above in our discussion of the mixed palatal/labial [ee]/[ɛɛ] types, where we found pure/Scotch [ɑ]~[æ]/[e]~[ee] contrasts in items like ‹pageant›, ‹camel›, ‹rather›, etc. (see pp.38–40 above). In the same way, the Scotch ‹half›, ‹ant› show a resistance to the palatalisation (*English vowel shift*) effect which had occurred in the pure dialect in Douglas' day: the entry under ‹aunt› (pp.165–6) is very clear on the matter:

> the short open *a*, as in *ant, scant, scar, cant, fast* &c is not only not the same in quantity, but also differs in quality, from the long open *a* in *father*. That it is, in short, a shade lying between that last mentioned sound and the slender *a*. This, I think will be manifest to any one who will carefully attend to the English and Scotch modes of pronouncing the word *ant*. The difference between them will be very perceptible, and in the latter the sound of the *a*, seems exactly the same in quality, but shorter, than in *father*.

The description of the pure short *a* as 'a shade lying between [[ɑɑ]: cɟ] and the slender *a*' recalls that in the *Observations on the Alphabet* mentioned above, where it is seen as approaching 'the limits of and

55

begins to merge itself with, the short and strong slender sound in *better* (p.118) and reinforces our interpretation of it as some kind of palatality contaminated sonorant [æ] vowel sound.

PURE DIALECT	SCOTCH VERNACULAR
[ee]	[ɑɑ]
‹ape›	‹apron›
‹fane›	‹dative›
‹fate›	‹David›
‹fame›	‹ham›
[æ]	[ɑ]
‹part›	‹half›
‹hat›	‹ant›
‹pan›	‹wax›

Douglas points to several substitutions of this [æ] sound in the Scottish dialect for a number of different pure 'equivalents', consider:

PURE DIALECT	SCOTCH VERNACULAR
[ee]	[æ]
‹bake›, ‹rake›	‹acorn› BACK
‹shade›, ‹glade›,	‹cradle› BAD, APPLE, PADDLE
‹rake›, ‹Ralph›	‹impl*a*cable› BLACK
‹race›	‹Raphael› RAP
[ɒɒ]	[æ]^{60}
‹all›, ‹hall›	‹altar›,
‹cause›, ‹pause›,	‹because›,
‹walk›	‹water›
[ɣ]	[æ]
‹wonder›	‹one› WAN
[ɛ]	[æ]
‹then›	‹then› THAN

where again items in capitals represent rhyming analogues in the pure dialect. The Scotch [æ] for pure [ee] and [ɒɒ] variants seems to indicate items where stressed vowel lengthening has not occurred and where *English vowel shift* by sonority reduction has not resulted. Yet the situation is clearly more complex, and since the [ææ] → [ee] raised stressed vowel process was anyway less 'advanced' in the pure than in the Scottish dialect regions referred to by Douglas (see pp.38–9 above and the [drægən]~[dre(e)gən] alternants there), so that when 'the Scotch (endeavouring to speak properly) are apt to pronounce the *a* short as in *bad . . .*' in an item like ‹cradle› (p.186),[61] they are bearing witness to the sociophonetic salience of the relative degree of palatalisation in the front vowel set. In the same vein, the Scotch pronunciation of ‹one› using an·[æ] type stressed vowel would appear to be a (perhaps hypercorrect) accommodation to the pure [ɣ] shape:

> Very few Scotchmen acquire the true pronounciation of *one*. The English fanaticks of the last age used to sound it like *bone*, and that method has remained with some people in Scotland when they read. Most Scotch people when they try to adopt the common pronounciation of England say *wan*. It should be sounded short, and like the first syllable of *wonder*. (p.199)

B. DIPHTHONGAL VOWEL SPACE: GENERAL OBSERVATIONS

Douglas tends to treat as diphthongs (the 'combination of two vocal sounds into one syllable', p.107)[62] both lexical and derived complex vowel space as in ‹foil› and ‹climb› as well as glide initial [ju]/[wu] sequences derived from long vowel or diphthongal sources involving some kind of syllabicity (vowel centre) shifting as in items like ‹yes› and ‹beauty›:

> In the words *sigh*, and the first syllable of the word *unity*, the vocal part is a compound sound, consisting of a combination, in the first of these words, of the two simple vowels, commonly represented by the characters *a* and *e* . . . in the second, of the same sound of *e* and that represented by the Italian, German, and Scotch *u*, or the English *u* in *put*, *pull*, and other words of that sort. (p.108)

In his *Treatise* he seems to recognise in both the pure and the Scottish dialect at least four dipthongs of the former type and two of the latter. Among the first group Douglas cites a 'front rising', sonorant to palatal type; a 'back rising', sonorant to labial type; a labial to palatal and a 'French' [eu]. The second group embraces the glide initial combinations [ju], [jə] and [wu].

1 The [æi]/[ɑi] Diphtong: the pure dialect and Scotch situation

Under his discussion of the phonetic value of the orthographic ‹i› (p.129), Douglas includes the 'diphthongal sound':

> being in truth a diphthong composed of the short open *a*, and the first sound of *e*. Although a diphthong, this sound is sometimes short, as in *dice*, often long, as in *wise*. When it is long the ear can with the greatest facility discriminate the two vocal sounds, of which it is composed. When short, this cannot be done without a considerable effort of attention.

This long/short dichotomy (at least in part conditioned by the voicing coefficient of the syllable final segment: see his p.136 remarks) appears to refer to diphthongal complexes with different starting points rather than to any inherent durational characteristics of their composite vowels.[63] The fact that the 'long' diphthong is the more audibly perceptible might just suggest that its 'degree of travel' is greater than its 'short' equivalent. That Douglas describes the first element of the 'long' version as 'short open *a*', i.e. [æ], infers that the complex is [æi], while the short version, with the lesser degree of travel, represents some kind of [ɛi] (or even [ei]) shape. In his *Table*, Douglas only occasionally describes pure dialect samples as showing the long diphthong (e.g. ‹precise›, ‹privateer›, ‹short lived›) generally characterising [æi] merely as 'dipthongal *i*' or as the 'diphthongal sound of *i*', thus ‹direct›, ‹dizen›, ‹Friday›, ‹idea›, ‹oblige›, ‹scite› and some others. In the pure dialect Douglas lists ‹ice›, ‹nice›, ‹precise›, ‹twice› and ‹entice› as 'short' [ɛi] types. There is some pure/Scotch alternation between the two dipthongal types: in general the pure [ɛi] items with syllable final [s] (‹ice›, ‹nice›, ‹twice›, ‹thrice›, ‹entice›, ‹precise›) are realised in the Scotch dialect with [æi], he claims; the Scotch ‹precise› rhyming to ‹wise›, and presumably showing a syllable final voiced segment.

At the same time, there is recorded considerable dialectal discrepancy between the advanced/retarded state of the *English vowel shift* [ii]~[æi]/[ɛi] alternation. While pure dialect speakers show [æi] dipthongs for items like ‹tw*i*light›, ‹*ei*ther› and ‹*i*dea›, their Scottish contemporaries are claimed to produce [ii] segments in the stressed vowel space of the same words. On the contrary, items like ‹privy›, ‹reprieve›, ‹shire› and ‹vicar› show diphthongal [æi] shapes compared with long [ii] (and probably [i] in ‹vicar›) in the pure dialect (cf. Walker, 1791:18–19).[64] Even further vowel shift discrepancy is shown in items such as ‹eight›, ‹wade› and ‹weigh›, where Scottish vernacular speakers are seen to 'advance' the vowel shift process beyond [ee] (possibly through [ii], to [æi]), although 'those who endeavour to speak with more propriety make ‹weigh› rhyme to *sea, pea*' (p.231). Within the pure dialect itself, Douglas observes (p.211) of ‹oblige› that:

> There are two ways of pronouncing this word, and both practised by good speakers. Viz. either to give the *i* its diphthongal sound, as in *hide*, or its long vocal sound as *Eloisa*. The latter pronunciation is, I believe, considered as the most elegant.

And while, in the pure dialect, ‹shire› has an [ii] stressed vowel, 'The Scotch and some English provincials make *shire* rhyme to *fire, hire*' (p.223).

2 The /ou/ Diphthong in the pure and Scotch dialects

Douglas' treatment of this diphthong in the pure dialect perhaps reflects, more than any other area in the *Treatise*, aspects of his specifically Scottish speech characteristics. 'The combinations of *o* and *u*, and *o* and *w* very frequently represent a proper dipthong (as in *foul, howl, now*) composed of the close *o*, and the simple vowel sound of the *u* in *full, pull*' (p.000). This apparently northern [ou] diphthong is commonly attested by Douglas as being characteristic of items in the pure dialect throughout the *Treatise*: ‹bough›, ‹how›, ‹allow›, ‹avow›, ‹enow›, ‹now›, ‹vow›, ‹owl›, ‹cowl›, ‹fowl›, ‹growl›, ‹howl›, and many others. The etymological source for this diphthong is complex, but its most developmentally usual pathway (other than Middle English [uu]) is through Old and early Middle English [o], subsequently lengthened and lowered by *Open Syllable Lengthening* to [ɔɔ] vowel shifted to [oo]; together with lexical Middle English [oo] vowel shapes, the segment is again vowel shifted to [uu] and, as we shall see, eventually to a diphthongal complex whose first element has been made less labial and more sonorant in varying degrees (Bronstein, 1949).

While it seems to be the case, according to Douglas' observations, that the majority of items showing an etymologically [uu] labial sound in the pure dialect (from whatever source) are realised in the late eighteenth century by some kind of [ou] diphthong, this is an observation not shared by many of his contemporaries, who tend to see its first element as a more heavily sonorant [ɔ] or [ɑ]. For instance, Sheridan (1781:16) whose *a3* possibly represents some kind of [ɑ] (or at least [ɔ] shape) records that: 'The diphthong *ou* or *ow* is composed of the sounds *a3* and *o3* ([u]:cɹ)', while Walker (1791:36) describes the diphthong as 'composed of the *a* in *hall*, and the *oo* in *woo*';[65] even the Scot Elphinston in his *The Principles of the English Language, Digested for the Use of Schools* (1766:4) describes the '*ou* or *ow*' combination as one where 'shuts *a* broad by the sound of *oo* or *w*', some kind of [ɑu] value (Rohlfing, 1984:166–8). Perhaps not unexpectedly, it is Buchanan (1762:17–18; Meyer, 1940) who provides a description of the diphthong, like Douglas', with some kind of [o] (or perhaps [ɔ]) first element:[66]

> How many sounds have *ou* and *ow*? *Ou* and *ow* have four; the first Sound is composed of both (*o*) and (*uw*), and if we Sound *o-oo* extremely quick, it discovers this Sound exactly; as *louse, mouse, fowl, town*, &c. which are sounded quick, *lo-oos, mo-oos, fo-ool, to-oon*.[67]

Cortes Telfair[68] sees ‹ou› diphthongs as comprising what he describes as the 'second long *A* and *W*' (1775:156–7), where the 'second long *A*' in his system is the vowel sound in items like ‹all›, ‹ball› and ‹stall› and therefore, presumably, some kind of [ɔ] shape.

Douglas lists a few pure dialect instances which, in comparison at any rate with modern British standard usage, appear anomalous. For instance, items such as ‹cucumber›, ‹pronounciation›, ‹wound› '*lesion*', ‹mow› '*of barley*' and ‹low› (as a cow), seem to appear with [ou]/[ɔu] stressed vowel space. There are also a few instances of a 'retarded' application of the vowel shifted process, manifested in [proo] '*prow*' and [droot] '*drought*', although Douglas observes that 'Formerly perhaps this word (‹drought›) was pronounced in England as in Scotland, with the diphthongal sound of the *ou*' (p.189), perhaps attesting the survival of the thirteenth to fifteenth century Middle English diphthongisation ('*Breaking*') of [o] → [ou] in pre [xt] syllable final contexts (Jones, 1989:146–7). Douglas also records the Scottish dialect as showing a diphthongal stressed vowel space in the item ‹shoulder› (an item with the long close *o* sound in the pure dialect): 'The Scotch are apt (when they aim at propriety) to give it the diphthongal sound as in *foul*' (p.223). On the other hand, Scots speakers are claimed to make the item ‹frown› rhyme to ‹shown›, i.e. with [oo] stressed vowel space, where the pure dialect 'has its diphthongal sound as in *cow, vow*' (p.198). However (with the exception of the items we are about to discuss immediately below) pure and vernacular Scottish dialectal differences, as regards contrasts between diphthongal and steady state vowel shapes, are not particularly marked in this area of the phonology and discrepancies are worthy of comment, as for the item ‹touch›:

> The Scotch in general, pronounce this word properly, so as to rhyme to *such, much*. But I know a Scotchman who from the rule of analogy had persuaded himself that it should be pronounced so as to rhyme to *crouch, pouch*: and constantly did pronounce it in that manner. The reader will judge of the ridicule this necessarily brought upon him. (p.229)

But perhaps some of the most interesting observations Douglas makes in this area of the phonology relate to items such as ‹bow›, ‹row›, ‹bowl› and ‹sow›; items which even in the seventeenth century were appearing in homophone lists and 'near alike' lists (with either [oo] or [uu]) (Dobson, 1968:161–172) despite being etymologically diversely derived. The ‹bow› item, lexically representing '*arcus*' (OE ‹bōga›) or '*to bend*' (OE ‹būgan›) shows, according to Douglas, both [bou] and [boo] manifestations in the pure dialect. However, the [bou] pronunciation is restricted, he claims, to the '*to bend*' interpretation, the [boo] to the '*arcus*':

> But Scotchmen, who have acquired a good and ready pronounciation in other respects, often find themselves puzzled and confounded between the different pronounciations of this word. (p.177)

The 'true provincial' pronunciation, he asserts, is [buu], to which if the Scotch speaker does not aspire, then [bou] is the favoured alternative, with [boo] the least preferred (and by implication the least prestigious) in the Scotch vernacular.

This tendency in the pure dialect to differentiate phonetically between lexical contrasts is also noted by Douglas for the item ‹sow›. When referring to a female pig, the pure dialect realises an [ou] vowel, the '*act of sowing*' with [oo], Scottish speakers pronouncing the latter as [suu] (to rhyme to SHOE), but they 'often pronounce it with the diphthongal sound so as to rhyme to *Now, cow*' (p.224). In the same way, ‹bowl› '*a basin*' and ‹bowl› '*ball in the game of bowling*' are distinguished as [bool] and [boul] respectively – only the Scots pronunciation of the former as [boul] is recorded by Douglas.[69] Yet both the pure and the Scottish vernacular dialect treat the two lexical specifications of ‹row› ('*a line*', '*to paddle*') as homophones, the former dialect in [roo], the latter in [rou]. But it seems in general that the Scotch vernacular treats ‹row›, ‹bow› and ‹sow› items homophonously, generally under [ou] and does not reflect the lexical/phonological matching that Douglas claims to exist in the pure dialect.

3 The [oi] Diphthong in the pure dialect

That Douglas saw the value of this diphthong as [oi] rather than [ɔi] is clear from his description in the *Observations on the Alphabet* (p.133) where, after characterising the first vowel of the *ou* diphthong as *close*, he goes on to observe that '*O* and *i* also form a proper diphthong composed of *the same sound of the o* [italics mine:CJ] and the first sound of *e*, as *boil, foil*.' Since 'there are great disputes among the English about the proper method of pronouncing the *oi* in this [‹boil›]; and many other words, *foil, oil, anoint, point, void*' (p.175)[70] we may assume this diphthong to have been a salient sociophonetic marker in the pure speech of Douglas' period (Wells, 1982:208–210). Unusually for Douglas, he comments on non-standard 'vulgar' English to tell us that the ‹foil›, ‹oil› diphthong is homophonous with the [æi] of ‹bile›, ‹file› and ‹pint›, a view also set out at length by Nares (1784:73–4).

> This diphthong (oi) has a full, rich, and masculine sound, peculiar to itself, and its substitute *oy*. It is distinctly heard in *noise, voice, rejoice*, &c. Those who are zealous for the harmony of our language, have lamented that this sound has been in danger of being lost, by a corrupt and vicious mode of pronunciation. It has been, indeed, the custom to give to this diphthong, in several words, the improper sound of the *i* long; as *boil, broil, choir, join, joint, point, poison, spoil*. The banished diphthong seems at length to be upon its return; for there are many who are

now hardy enough to pronounce *boil* exactly as they do *toil*, and
join like *coin*, &c.[71]

Douglas points, under his ‹boil› entry (p.175), to what is probably the
hypercorrect pronunciation of those 'admirers of a full and solemn
manner of speaking, [who] sound the *o* long, and very distinctly: and
hurry over the *i*', suggesting pronunciations like [noojz] *'noise'* and
[boojz] *'boys'*: 'But this method is generally thought too stiff and
formal'. That the last items terminate in a voiced fricative (a favoured
lengthening context in Douglas' descriptions, cf. p.136), might
suggest that as well as vowel length, Douglas is inferring a 'long
syllable' description in this context.

Yet there is, he claims, 'a middle way' for the realisation of this
diphthong. The first element represents an *o*-like sound 'distinguishable from *a*', perhaps [ɔ] or [ɒ] 'compressed together' with [i], thus
[bɒil], [bɔil]; although if we take 'compressed together' more literally
and see a monophthongal mixture of [ɒ] and some more palatal
sound, we might tentatively suggest an [ɞ] pronunciation, a half open,
central rounded vowel, intermediate between [œ] and [ɔ].[72]

Douglas himself, it should be noticed, is not averse – in his own
poetical writings – to rhyme the 'long *i*' with the [oi]/[ɔi] diphthong:

In the Goddess' tender smiles
Fuel of eternal fires!
Sweet oblivion drowns his toils!
Discord from his train retires.
     (Imitation of Michel Angelo Buonaroti: *Occasional Verses*, 1820:9)

And all thy mingled charms together join'd
With equal rapture fill the ravish'd mind.
     (ibid:11)

Not that I ever, ever shall recoil
And cry, 'No, No, you shall not,' all the while.
     (Madrigal; De Marot; *Occasional Verses*, 1820:40)

4 *Diphthongs with phonetically reduced first elements: [ju], [jə] and [wə]*

Douglas' general description of the [ju] diphthong is a clear one,
attempting to capture his intuitions concerning the relative prominence between the vocalic items which go to make up the complex
vowel space, as well as pointing to the fact that the highlighting of
one element brings about a concomitant reduction in vowelness in
the other:[73]

> The third sound of *u*, and that from which it takes its name in
> England, is diphthongal; consisting of the first sound of the *e*
> followed by the first of the *u*; but so that the *e* is hurried over, and

leaves the *u* to predominate. Of this we have examples in *usage* (which some old authors have written *yeusage*) *curious, unity, pure.* (p.139)

The modern British English standard [ju] complex derives from mainly two historical sources: the [iu] diphthong and the [uu] vowel. In both instances it appears that some kind of syllabicity shifting has occurred, making the 'right hand side' vowel the more prominent and, in consequence, bringing about a vowel level reduction in the 'left hand' half to [j] or, as we shall see, to [w] (Jones, 1989:180–2). Items cited by Douglas as showing [ju] in the pure dialect are not numerous, but include: ‹excuse›, ‹use›, ‹profuse›, ‹humility›, ‹Hume›, ‹humane›, ‹curious›, ‹unity›, ‹pure›, ‹pew›, ‹dew› and ‹hue›.[74] There seem to be a few others where [ju] appears which have not survived into the modern British English standard, notably ‹Bruce›, ‹spruce›, ‹truce›, ‹recluse›,[75] a fact perhaps accountable for in terms of Douglas' observation (p.192) that although ‹excuse›, the noun, with its voiceless [s], has a diphthongal *u* sound, it 'is short', a statement very much in keeping with his general rule proposing short vowels in [s]-, and long vowels in [z]-syllable terminating fricatives (p.136). Perhaps rather than suggest some kind of [juu]/[ju] alternation in these voice differentiated environments, he means something akin to the long/short syllable notion set out on p.217 under the ‹pull› entry, and in *Of the Provincial Accentuation of Particular Words*, chapter four, ff.41–2. In 'short syllable' environments, we might speculate, the less vocalically prominent [j] glide element is liable to go unperceived.

Douglas almost everywhere treats as either accommodations or as grave errors in taste, the Scottish [ju] substitute for pure [u], [y] and [i] shapes in the items ‹blue› and ‹pursue› where the '*ue* represents the first sound of *u* where the Scotch give it the diphthongal sound' (p.139) as well as ‹build› (rhyming to GILD, GILT in the pure dialect). Under ‹luxury› we are told pointedly that 'the second *u* has not the dipthongal sound which some Scotch people give it' (p.207); under ‹build› while 'many Scotch people sound the *ui* like the diphthongal *u* in *mule*' such a pronunciation is 'erroneous' (p.178). Perhaps Douglas' most strenuous injunction against [ju] pronunciations appears under the ‹burial› item, that great 'stumbling block' in Scotch vernacular speech. Scotch speakers, realising that their [ii] stressed vowel is highly stigmatised, then 'generally adopt the diphthongal *u*, and make *bury* and *fury* ... rhyme together';[76] this accommodation is 'equally wrong'. It would seem that in general Douglas regards the contemporary Scottish [ju] vernacular pronunciation for the pure [u], [y] or [i] as an unacceptable hypercorrection; cf. Sir Walter Scott's observation in *The Heart of Midlothian* (1818):

The Magistrates were closely interrogated before the House of

Peers, concerning the particulars of the Mob, and the *patois* in which these functionaries made their answers, sounded strange in the ears of the Southern nobles. The Duke of Newcastle having demanded to know with what kind of shot the guard which Porteous commanded had loaded their muskets, was answered naively: 'Ow, just sic as ane shoots *dukes* and *fools* with.' This reply was considered as a contempt of the House of Lords, and the Provost would have suffered accordingly, but that the Duke of Argyle explained, that the expression, properly rendered into English, meant *ducks and water-fowl*. (Parker, ed. 1971:207n)

Diphthongs in [wə] are also attested by Douglas, especially under his description of the ‹guardian› item where he tells us that:

Some Scotch people pronounce the *u* in the same manner as the Italians do in *guardiano*: i.e. so as to form the same diphthong with the *u*, that *w* does, in *ward*, *wander*. But the *u* is of no use in the true pronounciation. (p.200)

Yet he also observes that in the item ‹language› 'the Scotch ... suppress the *u*, sounding the *a* like the short *i*, as if it were written *langige*' (p.204).[77]

Under his discussion of the item ‹calf› (p.180) Douglas notes as a feature unique to the pure dialect, another context where some kind of epenthetic [j] is introduced into the vowel space to precede the highlighted component there. He tells us that in a set of items containing 'short open *a*' (in our interpretation, some kind of [æ] sound: cf. pp.51–6) – such as ‹cart›, ‹carriage›, ‹casuist›, ‹garden›, ‹gadso›, as well as those with the diphthongal *i* or *y* sound – as ‹kind›, ‹sky›, there appears some kind of 'smothered *y*' or 'short obscure *i*' which 'the voice hastens over ... to the *a*, or dipthongal *y*'. Indeed, he claims that this epenthetic palatal glide has the same status as that in the 'diphthongal *u*' – 'this unwritten *y* before the *a*, is exactly the same with that, which makes the first part of the diphthongal sound of *u* in *use*, *abuse*.' These [kjæ(l)f], [kjær] and [kjæind] pronunciations (also noted by Walker)[78] are difficult to explain unless we see the possibility for the pure dialect of durationally extended [ææ] in some of the contexts Douglas cites for the [jæ] occurrences. Lengthened vowels in pre syllable final [r] and [nd] contexts are hardly unusual events in the phonology of English, and we have already observed that, under his discussion of the item ‹March›, Douglas himself notes that:

The *a* in Scotland, is commonly pronounced as in *have*. But it ought to be pronounced exactly as in *art*; *past*, *starch*, and *March* form a perfect rhyme. The Scotch pronounce the latter word also improperly. Sounding it as they do *March* but shorter. (p.207)

If indeed ‹art›, ‹cart› and ‹calf› can show [æœ] vowel space, then a
'syllabicity shifting', 'vowel space prominence linear adjustment'
such that [æœ] becomes [æœ] becomes [jæ] would appear to be a
possible phonological event. But Douglas nowhere records a development like this for the Scotch vernacular, although the phenomenon
in the pure dialect is noted by other Scots, notably Elphinston
(Rohlfing, 1984:246) who records '*card, gard*; *skirt, guird, kind, sky*:
hwich must be duly *herd* (dho not seen) *kyard*, and so on', and James
Gray (1814:99) – 'late of Peebles and Dundee' – who attests the
existence of ‹kyind› '*kind*' and ‹skyi› '*sky*' pronunciations (Lloyd,
1904). For present day regional English distributions of epenthetic
[j] types, see Orton, Sanderson and Widdowson (1978: Maps 2, 9,
14, 162).

C. NON-VOWEL SEGMENTS IN THE *TREATISE*

Although it is probably true to say that Douglas is more concerned to
record both the typology and varieties of contemporary vocalic
segments (especially in syllable highlighted position), his *Treatise*
contains considerable amounts of information both as regards the way
in which he categorises non-vocalic segments in the terms of his
phonological description, but also the principles according to which
they contrast between pure and Scottish usage. Douglas' main classi-
ficatory device for non-vowel segments hinges upon a *mute* versus
semivowel distinction:

> in the utterance of the semivowels, aspiration is in some degree
> performed. The fauces are made to approach, but yet not so as to
> preclude entirely the passage of the breath. Whereas the sound
> of the hard *c* or *k*, before *h* or any other vowel or consonant,
> the breath must be suddenly and totally stopt and the act of
> expiration suspended. (p.122)

While most consonantal segment types normally include both the
voiced and voiceless occlusives, his semivowel class embraces segments containing the class of sonorant and non-sonorant continuants:
[f], [l], [m], [n], [r] and [s]. Douglas' perception of the shared
characteristic of the semivowel group is clearly related to the relatively prominent vowel-like qualities of its members which they, unlike
the obstruents, manifest. Commenting upon the fact that their
alphabetic nomenclature involves the presence of a vocalic element,
he observes:

> Thus *ef, el, em, en, ar, es*, because by that means their disting-
> uishing quality by which they are capable of being protracted to
> any length is rendered more obvious. (p.120)

Such a description points to a perception of continuants as containing
relatively highly sonorant and resonant characteristics. At the same

time it is clear from his remarks in several places in the *Treatise* that Douglas recognises the continuant/non-continuant pairing of mutes and semivowels and that, for instance, [d]/[t], [f]/[z] contrasts are non minimal but the result of a single characteristic the nature of which we shall comment upon immediately below:

> *B* and *p* are pronounced by the same position of the organs of speech, and are as much entitled to be considered as one letter, as the two sounds of the *s* and *th* are. The same is true of the hard *g* and *k*. And of *d* and *t*. Now each of these has a corresponding semivowel, which have the same sort of affinity together as the co-relative mutes. The semi-vowel of *b* is *v*; of *p*, *f*; of the hard *g*, the Dutch and German *g*; of *k*, the Scotch and German *ch*; of *d*, the soft *th*. It is to this affinity between these different sets of consonants that we are to ascribe the frequent changes from one of them to another, in words which have been transplanted out of one language into another. (p.140)

This view of the consonantal inventory in terms of 'sets' of sounds rather than as a list of discrete, unique and separately identifiable segments is a hallmark of Douglas' descriptive phonology, and colours many of the observations he makes concerning contemporary alternations.

The principal phonological and phonetic contrasts between the pure and Scotch dialects to which Douglas draws our attention are (1) voicing differentials; (2) the voiced and voiceless palatal and velar fricatives; (3) [l] vocalisation; (4) [r] segments; (5) nasal segments; (6) consonantal cluster simplifications; (7) *h* dropping and adding; (8) continuancy adjustments and (9) metathesis phenomena.

1 Voicing Contrast

Douglas has some difficulty in convincing both himself and his reader of what he considers to be the cogent characteristic differentiating such non discrete 'sets' as [d]/[t], [g]/[k] and [p]/[b]. Even the terminology he employs ('hard' for voiceless, 'soft' for voiced) seems to give him some concern:

> It may be proper to remark that Dr Johnson calls the sound of *z*, or the second sound of *s*, the hard *s*. Whereas I have applied the epithet soft to that sound, and have called the other hard. It matters little which is used. Both expressions are metaphorical. But according to my ear and to the ears of those whom I have consulted on the subject, there is more propriety in calling the *s* in *praise* soft, than that in *past*. (p.142)

But Douglas never appears to realise that [s]/[z] and [p]/[b] type contrasts have anything to do with laryngeal activity, far less vocal fold agitation; his explanation for the physics of the difference within the 'set' hinges on rather uncertain references to the 'particular exertion of the organs of speech' (p.122).[79] Voiced [g], for example, 'is a single consonant formed by the organs of speech in the very same manner with *k*; except that the last mentioned requires a stronger exertion' (p.127). Again [p] 'has but one uniform sound, being formed in the same manner with *b*, but with a more forceful exertion of the lips' (p.133) and '*t* is formed in the same manner with *d*, and only differs from it by being uttered with more energy, as *k* does from the hard *g*, and *p* from *b*' (p.138). This seems to represent a tendency to see the voiceless forms as differentiated from the voiced purely in terms of some additional degree of aspiration or ejectiveness. Elphinston sees the distinction in not unsimilar terms, voiced pairs like [t]/[d], [p]/[b] characterised by the one 'uttered by a direct and forceful emission of the breath, and the other by one indirect or depressed' (*Principles of the English Language* 1766:7).[80] Yet Douglas is clearly unhappy with criteria like these:

> The difference which takes place in point of muscular exertion between the pronounciation of the same consonant in one syllable and in another has not been in general so much attended to, but that such a difference may take place, any one may discover by trying the experiment with his own voice, and that it really occurs in the usual pronounciation of languages may be perceived by one who will attend to the phenomenon of speech. On the stage, in the pulpit, at the bar, and in the senate, we may observe some speakers who in uttering certain words, to which they mean to draw the particular attention of their hearers, use a very marked effort of the muscles in forming the beginning of consonants of those words, and the concluding consonants of certain syllables are by all speakers pronounced with a more forcible exertion of the muscles than the same consonants are in others. This is particularly observable in our language where the same consonantal character is doubled at the end of a syllable. Thus the single *t* before *e* in the first [sic] syllable of the word *appetite* and the *tt* in *petty* represent exactly the same consonantal modification, and the only difference is that in the word *petty* there is a more vigorous and forcible pressure of the tongue against the upper part of the mouth. Here again I find that I was hampered in a former part of this work by the sterility of language of which I have more than once taken notice, for I have there described the *d* as differing from *t* only in the degree of muscular exertion, but this diversity between the *tt* and the *t* in such words as *petty* and *appetite*, being of a nature very different from the difference between either and *d*, it should seem that I

ought to have described the exertions in forming the *d* and *t* as differing in kind as well as degree, and agreeing exactly only in the same position of the organs. (*Of the Provincial Accentuation*, ff.31–34)

1.a [s]/[z] alternations

While the pure dialect differentiates nominal/verbal usage in lexical items such as ‹excuse› and ‹grease› with stressed syllable final [s] and [z] respectively, we have to conclude from Douglas' general observations that Scottish English speakers make no such phonetically signalled contrast, realising [z] for both; there are, however, several lexical items where there is a direct pure/Scottish voiced determined contrast.[81] Consider data like the following:

PURE	SCOTCH	
[s]	[z]	
debase, rase	base	
erase, place		
base		
precise	precise	WISE
profuse	profuse	
design	design	
nusance	nusance	

PURE	SCOTCH	
[z]	[s]	
damsel		
resign	resign	
possess	possess	
preside	preside	PRECEDENT
president	president	
reside	reside	PRECEDE
residence		RECEDE

where again items in capitals indicate rhyming congeners cited by Douglas for items in the column immediately to their left. Douglas also records a [ʃ]/[ʒ] contrast under his discussion of the ‹Asia› item, where the pure dialect is said to realise the former, as in ‹nation› and ‹Dacia›, the Scotch [ʒ] as in ‹pleasure› or as the French ‹j› in ‹ajouter›. Elphinston too notes the use of Scottish vernacular [s] for the standard [z] in items like ‹sion› '*Zion*', ‹design›, ‹curiosity›, ‹December›, ‹precentor›, while Scottish [z] for standard [s] is the norm, he claims,

68

in the items ‹base›, ‹case›, ‹choice›, ‹else›, ‹excuse›, ‹precise›, ‹rejoice›, ‹rise›:

> Inglish verbs and dheir accions, hwen coincident in all else, ar butifooly apt to discriminate final sibbilacion. Verb assumes dhe genial depressive, noun dherfore dhe oppozite power, thus ‹abuse›, noun; ‹abuze›, verb; ‹close›, noun; ‹cloze›, verb. (1786:82)

1.b [θ]/[ð] alternations

Douglas records [θ] voiceless fricative shapes in the pure dialect – 'To our ear accustomed to it there is something peculiarly mellow in its softer sound (for it has two) as in *thou*, and *though*' (p.112) – for items such as ‹thought›, ‹breath›, ‹death›, ‹sheath› (noun) and ‹cloth›, while with [ð] he notes ‹thou›, ‹breathe› and ‹bequeath›.[82] Verbal/ nominal distinctions are also made via the [ð]/[θ] contrast in the pure dialect in pairs like ‹sheath›, ‹wreath› and ‹clothe›/‹cloth›. Pure versus Scotch voicing differences, on the other hand, are not all that numerous, but include the following:

PURE	SCOTCH	
[θ]	[ð]	
froth	froth	LOATHE
oath	oath	
both	both	
[ð]	[θ]	
thence	thence	THOUGHT
thither	thither	
heather	heather	

1.c [f]/[v] alternations

In his description of these labial fricative continuants, Douglas distinguishes three distinct sounds. The sounds represented by the symbol ‹f›:

> May be pronounced by the pressure of the lips together as in uttering *p* or *b*, but so as to leave some slight issue for the breath. In the act of blowing out a candle if done forcibly, an indistinct *f* is produced; if more weakly, a *v*. But the more usual way and more perfect, of pronouncing both is by pressing the edge of the upper teeth against the underlip. (p.127)

Here Douglas seems to recognise the voiced and voiceless bilabial fricatives [β] and [Φ] as well as their labio-dental congeners [v] and

[f], but the former he sees as 'imperfect' pronunciations 'as when the *f* and *v* are pronounced by the compression of the lips instead of that of the upper teeth and upper [sic] lip' (p.134). The bulk of Douglas' comments on the voicing discrepancy occur under the entry for the item ‹calf› (p.180) where he notes how the possessive and plural morphology convert the voiceless syllable final [f] in items like ‹calf›, ‹wife› and ‹knife› to a voiced [v] in the speech of 'most English people'. Scottish vernacular speakers, on the other hand, and 'some English' retain the [f] form throughout the paradigm of these items. Likewise, the Scotch [s] pronunciation of the first syllable final in ‹houses› 'ought to be' [z] (p.202) as also in the ‹spouse›/‹spouses› pair, while in ‹nephew› the ‹ph› is represented by [v] in the pure dialect, by [f] in the Scotch (p.210).

2 Palatal and Velar Fricatives

These 'guttural semivowels' or strong gutturals 'so disagreeable to the English ear' (p.160) attract Douglas' opprobrium as 'barbarous pronounciation' to be 'got rid of' (p.176).[83] Elphinston too seems to share this dislike of the segments:

> Dhe guttural aspirate (*ch* or *gh*), essencial to evvery primmitive language, haz lost dhe aspiracion in dhe smoodhnes (or dhe softnes) ov dhe French and Inglish tungs. (1795:5)

Their pronunciation is like that of 'all the semivowels, aspiration is in some degree performed. The fauces are made to approach, yet not so as to preclude entirely the passage of the breath' (p.122). One such 'guttural semivowel' which 'has affinity to *k*' is exemplified in the item *Achilles* and probably represents the palatal fricative [ç], while a voiceless labial [x] fricative is to be assumed for the 'barbarous' Scotch realisation of the ‹gh› in items like ‹sought›, ‹bought›, ‹thought›, ‹fought› and ‹drought›; while 'the Germans and Dutch make the *g* a guttural semivowel, analogous to their *ch*, but softer in the same proportion as our hard *g* is softer than *k*' (p.127). Douglas also records [ç]/[θ] alternations in the item ‹technical›; the pure [k] for ‹ch› realised as [θ] in the Scottish dialect, Douglas sceptically (but probably correctly) surmises as arising from a 'resemblance between the Scotch guttural sound of *ch*, and the English sound of *th*' (p.227). [θ]/[ç] substitutes are, of course, commonplace in the history of English phonology, as we can see from such Middle English spellings as ‹michty›/‹mithty› '*mighty*' and presumably arise from the similarity in the acoustic 'fingerprint' of the two segments. Nares (1784) notes both the Northern-ness of the 'guttural' as well as its association with the interdental fricative:

> many words terminate in *gh*, in which situation those letters doubtless were originally the mark of the guttural aspirate, a

sound long lost entirely among the inhabitants of the southern parts of Britain. It is still retained by our northern neighbours, who utter these letters, especially when followed by *t*, with a sound which we cannot readily imitate. For this reason, *gh*, is wholly silent with us in general, as in *daughter*, *dough*, *high*, *night*, *slough*, *taught*, etc.

Sigh is by some persons pronounced as if written with *th*; a pronunciation which our theatres have adopted. Spenser has written it *sythe*, and rhymed it to *blythe*. (pp.105–6)[84]

The perhaps more commonly attested [ç]/[x]/[f] alternation (Walker, 1791:§391) is also recorded by Douglas, especially under his observations on the syllable final [f] in items like ‹rough›, ‹cough› and ‹laughter› in the pure dialect, 'while it is a provincial pronounciation in some counties of the west of England to say *oft*, and *thoft*, for *ought*, and *thought*. I known one instance of a man of education and eminence in a learned profession who retains this mode of sounding these words' (p.127): an observation paralleled by the ‹Buff› anecdote (p.176):

I know a schoolmaster in Scotland who was fond of general rules, and thought because *tough* was pronounced like *stuff*, *ruff*, *huff*, that *bough* should be pronounced likewise. He taught his school-children to pronounce it in that manner. But this sounded so ridiculous, even in their ears, that they gave him the nick-name of *Buff*, which, if alive, he probably retains to this day.

Two other fricative alternations with [ç] are noted by Douglas; the first with his observation that for the pure [ʧ] in the item ‹Rachel›, the Scots use the 'vernacular and guttural' [ç], but that in its turn is substituted by many of them by the voiceless [k] obstruent (f.246); an intervocalic [k]/[ç]/[ʧ] alternation suggesting an increased level of vocalicness for the obstruent in different dialectal contexts. Secondly, the pure English 'diphthongal' [hw] in items like ‹when› and ‹why› is pronounced in Scotland, Douglas claims, with the 'guttural *ch*, followed ... by a *u*, losing itself in the succeeding vowel' (p.141), thus possibly [xw-]; in its turn, this [xw] combination is, not unsurprisingly in the light of our observations above, realised 'in the North of Scotland ... like *f*; so that *what*, and *fat*, *why* and *fie*, form to the ear in that part of the Island, the very same words' (p.141). But we shall return to syllable initial [hw] combinations below.

3 [l] Vocalisation

Douglas' remarks on [l] effacement as the first element in [lk], [lm], [lf] and [lp] syllable final clusters are brief and fairly conventional. 'This semivowel and liquid' he regards as 'the most pleasing to the ear of all consonants' (p.132) and records it as 'mute' in items like ‹half›, ‹walk›, ‹stalk›, ‹talk›, ‹salmon›, ‹psalm›, while it is 'generally sounded' in the pure dialect in ‹scalp›, ‹calm›, ‹balm› and ‹psalmody› (p.221). He makes comment neither upon the peculiarities of the stressed vowel under conditions of [l] deletion/vocalisation nor of any idiosysncratic Scottish behaviour; but concerning pure dialect behaviour, under the ‹almost› entry comments: 'most good speakers sound the *l* in *almost*. In familiar conversation there are some who do not'. While Elphinston records *ammond* '*almond*', *sammon* '*salmon*' and *Annic* '*Alnwick*' (with *would/wood* as homophones), he suggests Scottish pronunciations in *aw* '*all*', *baw* '*ball*', *bow* '*boll*', *fou* '*full*' and *poo*, '*pull*', which hint at a vocalisation of the [l] segment to some labial or relatively labial shape, resulting in a diphthongal stressed vowel space in some instances.[85] At the beginning of the nineteenth century, Smith (1816:16–17) seems to suggest that [l] vocalisation (with concomitant stressed vowel and even sonorant lengthening) as well as simple effacement could take place. We shall see in the next section how he identifies two 'types' of [r] segment; the rough, as in *rogue*, and the smooth, which he associates with the sound of the last syllable of *Messiah*, and therefore probably as some kind of centralised [ə] vowel. He comments on [l] effacement that '*L* is changed into *m* in *salmon*; into smooth *r* in *almond*, *alm*, *calf*, *psalm*, &c, but in *could*, *should*, *would*, &c it is entirely silent', suggesting possible pronunciations as [ɑəm] '*alm*' and [kæəf] '*calf*', and so on. Douglas seems to make no comment on the social significance of [l] effacement, although Walker (1791:47) observes that:

> In *soldier*, likewise, the *l* is sometimes suppressed, and the word pronounced *so-jer*; but this is far from being the most correct pronunciation: *l* ought always to be heard in this word, and its compounds, *soldierly*, *soldiership*, &c.

4 [r] Segments

Douglas' comment that the English pronounce this sound ('the harshest of all letters', p.135)[86] 'more softly' than the Scotch might infer a greater degree of voicing, but it is just possible that Douglas uses the hard/soft distinction on occasion not as an indication of voicing co-efficient, but as a signal of obstruency versus (mainly affricative) continuancy. For instance, under the discussion in the ‹exaggerate› entry, he informs us that 'Some English people pronounce the *gg* hard, as in *waggon*, but the most general pronounciation is like *dg* in *badger*' (p.192).

While a hard/soft contrast, as it is usually used in the *Treatise*, might suggest an [ɛgzætʃəret] rather than [ɛgzædʒəret] pronunciation for this item, the prospect of a [wækən] realisation for ‹wagon› is a daunting one; perhaps Douglas infers by *hard* an obstruent [ɛgzægəret] as against a continuant [ɛgzæʤərct]. If this is at all a possible interpretation, then we might see the two [r] sounds as a 'hard' obstruent like [r] as against the alveolar voiced frictionless continuant [ɹ] (Anderson and Ewen, 1987:159–60); a viewpoint perhaps supported by Douglas' assertion under the ‹Architect› entry that 'the *ch* has its soft sound, though some English people pronounce it hard as in *arch-angel*' suggesting an [ærʃitɛkt]/[ærkɪtɛkt] contrast. Elphinston too uses the 'hard g' terminology as he records *exadgerate* and *sudgest* for ‹exaggerate› and ‹suggest› (1786:110). Again, in describing the [ŋ]/[ŋg] difference, Douglas says that in the former type 'the simple hard sound of the *g* is not heard at the beginning of the next syllable', e.g. ‹hanger›, ‹singer›, while in ‹Bangor› the hard *g* is distinctly to be perceived (p.132).

That some kind of [ʁ] or perhaps [ʀ] segment is recognised by Douglas in the contemporary language seems clear from his statement that:

> What by the French is termed *grassayment*, in England the *burr*, and by the Scotch a *rattle* proceeds from pronouncing the *r* in the throat, without applying the tongue to the upper jaw, as must be done in the proper pronounciation. This guttural *r* it is that resembles the snarl of a dog. (p.134)[87]

It is not too clear whether Douglas intends to suggest that the [ʁ] is a pure or Scottish dialect characteristic,[88] or both, although the use of the 'epenthetic' [r] at syllable boundaries is the saliant characteristic of Londoners, 'at least many of them, [who] make a very extraordinary use of this letter' (pp.134–5) Savage, 1833; Matthews, 1936; Flasdieck, 1900. Observing that [r] is inserted between vocalic syllable terminations and initials at syllable and word boundary points, he condemns it as a 'barbarous pronounciation' nevertheless to be found 'in the mouths of some persons of education' (p.135); it gives rise to such realisations as 'that is not my *idear* of the matter' and 'I shall be obliged to take the *lawr* of you'. Such a phonological 'sandhi' stratagem (along with others listed by Douglas on p.135) to 'avoid hiatus', is well attested in contemporary grammars, notably Elphinston (1787:264) who records the pronunciation of 'low Londoners' like 'a low feller of the causey'[89] (Jones, 1989:300–1; Rohlfing, 1984:318) and in the modern London and South East England dialect: cf.[læst tæŋgər ɪn pærts] in an otherwise non-rhotic phonology (Wells, 1982:§§3.2.3, 4.1.4). Note too expressions like ‹your will be pleased› and ‹we hear your are among the best people in England› in the contemporary Black American English recorded in the *Sierra Leone Letters*, 1793–98 (Fyfe 1991).

Perhaps in this context too we might mention the alternation between the 'generality of the English, both in speaking and reading' and 'some low people from vulgarity and some few persons of learning from affectation' in the pronunciation of the items ‹medicine› and ‹venison›, disyllabic [mɛdsən] and trisyllabic [mɛdɪsən] shapes produced by both groups of speakers. We can argue that the origin of this alternation, like that of the epenthetic [r] types above, stems from the speaker's desire to achieve a bi-syllabic status for segments at syllable boundary. A proper, discrete or non-overlapping configuration such as, for instance:

$$\{_1lɔ_1\}\{_2ænd_2\}$$

is made to appear, with the insertion of [r] at syllable boundary, with an ambisyllabic characteristic, such that

$$\{_1lɔ\{_2r_1\}ænd_2\}$$

results. In the same way, we might claim, the epenthetic [ə] in the ‹medicine› item, transforms a non-syllable overlapping boundary like

$$\{_1mɛd_1\}\{_2sɪn_2\}$$

to one like

$$\{_1mɛ\{_2d_1\}ə\{_3s_2\}ɪn_3\}$$

(see Jones, 1989:§3.5.1; 1976).

Douglas rarely comments directly upon the possible effacement of syllable final [r] in the pure dialect, despite the fact that, according to Walker (1791:50) at least, the phenomenon was current in London (Hill, 1940):

> In England, and particularly in London, the *r* in *bard*, *lard*, *card*, *regard*, &c is pronounced so much in the throat as to be little more than the middle or Italian *a*, lengthened into *baa*, *baad*, *caad*, *regaad* ... But if this letter is too forcibly pronounced in Ireland, it is often too feebly sounded in England, and particularly in London, where it is sometimes entirely sunk.

While disavowing ‹verse›/‹success› as a perfect rhyme (p.152), Douglas nevertheless clearly recognises the possibility of post-vocalic [r] effacement (albeit by 'the English' only) in his observation of the near alike homophony of ‹ass› and another item, giving 'occasion to numerous ambiguities of a very coarse nature', which is presumably ‹arse› (p.165). Elphinston (1786:141) notes syllable final [r] effacement (perhaps accompanied by vocalisation producing an [ɑu] diphthong) for the item ‹Malburough›:

> Nay *marl* wood yield to *maul* ... and show herself onnestly *Maulburrough*; but for fear ov dhe learned laffers ov London, hoo so duly decide in difficult cases.

Certainly by the early nineteenth century, there is increasing evidence of the effacement, and even the vocalisation, of syllable final [r]. Smith (1816), for instance, distinguishes two kinds of *r*, the rough sound, as in ‹rogue› and the smooth sound, in ‹hard›. That some phonetic difference between [r] types is not intended by this terminology is clear from his observation that the aspirate *h* 'when it is final, and succeeds a vowel ... has the sound of smooth *r*, as in *Messiah*' (1816:17), suggesting both [r] effacement and possibly vocalisation: see above, p. 70. Likewise, in his *Grammar and Rhetoric* ('being the First and Third Volumes of the Circle of Sciences' 1776:14) we find the statement that:

> The letter *r* has no variety of sound, is commonly pronounced, except in the first syllable of *Marlburough*. Some people sound it obscurely, or quite omit it, in the words *marsh*, *harsh*, and a few others.

We recall Douglas' assertion concerning [r] that 'In England it is pronounced more softly in general than by the Scotch' (p. 134). If we choose to interpret his 'softly' nomenclature as equivalent to Smith's 'smooth', then the p. 134 statement might just be used as evidence for his recognition of syllable final [r] effacement/vocalisation in the pure, and to a lesser extent in the Scottish, dialect.

5 Nasal Segments

Both the vowel-like qualities of nasal segments and their gesture relationship to a set of 'corresponding' stops, is clearly understood by Douglas:

> It is a common circumstance relative to these two letters *m* and *n*, that if you stop the nostrils by pressing them together with your finger and then pronounce either the one or the other, it becomes a *mute* instead of a semivowel: that is, you can commence or terminate a vocal sound with it, as with *b*, *p*, *d* or *t*, but you cannot protract its own sound without a vowel, as you may when the nostrils are open. (p. 132)

While Douglas has little of interest to say on the bilabial [m] nasal, he makes many observations on [n] and especially on [ŋ] with which it can, on occasion, alternate. Essentially he recognises two types of non-bilabial nasal, the first, [n] 'is formed by applying the tongue just above the roots of the upper teeth, as in performing *d*, or *t*, and suffering a slight expiration to be performed through the nostrils' (p. 132). The second, clearly [ŋ], he describes as 'more nasal', has a contemporary [ŋg] variant (Elphinston's 'ringing' or 'clinking' sound; 1765:7), exemplified respectively by the lexical pairs ‹singer› and ‹anger›. The set of items in the pure dialect showing the velar nasal pronounced 'softly' as [ŋ] and 'strongly' as [ŋg] are set out in some detail under the ⟨Anger, Angry⟩ entry (p.163), and we might list them as follows:[90]

[ŋ]	[ŋg]
⟨singer⟩	⟨anger⟩
⟨hanger⟩	⟨angle⟩
⟨ringer⟩	⟨angry⟩
⟨hanging⟩	⟨dangle⟩
⟨bringing⟩	⟨dingle⟩
⟨length⟩	⟨finger⟩
⟨lengthen⟩	⟨hunger⟩
⟨strength⟩	⟨single⟩
⟨hang'd⟩	⟨stronger⟩
⟨wing'd⟩	⟨surcingle⟩
	⟨wrangle⟩
	⟨mangle⟩
	⟨linger⟩
	⟨longer⟩
	⟨clanger⟩

where ⟨clanger⟩ would appear to be the only exception to what is current standard British English usage, although Douglas does observe that 'some vulgar persons in England, from a sort of affectation, sound the hard *g* at the end of *sing, thing, king,* etc. and rest their voice upon it. But this is to be carefully avoided' (p.163; Dobson, 1968;§412). However, late eighteenth-century Scottish vernacular usage seems to have been considerably at variance with this since 'In almost all cases where *ng* is found in the middle of a word, the Scotch sound it as in *singer*. Thus they make *finger* and *singer* a perfect rhyme, and *anger* and *hanger*' (p.163). Likewise, in the Scotch vernacular ⟨longer⟩ is pronounced as the pure ⟨singer⟩, i.e. with [ŋ], not [ŋg] (p.207). At the same time, Douglas observes an [ŋ]/[n] contrast under his discussion of the ⟨length, lengthen⟩ items. The pure dialect he records as showing [ŋ], but the Scotch 'and inaccurate speakers among the English sound both words as if written *lenth, strenth*' (p.205); indeed, Elphinston (1787:15ff) calls this feature of the phonology 'dhe Scottish Shibboleth' and records *lenth, strenth* shapes for that dialect, as well as [ŋg] in *hanger, singer, longed, hanging, longing* in contemporary polite London speech (Rohlfing, 1984:329).

A single (and traditional) instance of [n]~[l] alternation is recorded under ⟨chimney⟩, where both Scotch and English 'vulgar people' pronounce the word 'very inaccurately' as if written *chimley* (Jones, 1989:123ff).

6 Cluster Simplifications

Many of Douglas' observations concerning word initial cluster simplifications stem from his desire to point to orthographic inappro-
priateness (itself the product of earlier phonological change). For
instance in ‹gnat› and ‹gnaw› the syllable initial obstruent is effaced
(although in ‹gnome› and ‹gnomon› he records it as pronounced 'by
most English people' (p.127)). Likewise, *k* is mute in items like
‹knell›, ‹knight› and ‹knowledge› (Kökeritz, 1950), while even the
Scots (unlike the pure dialect speaker) suppress the [k] obstruent
syllable initially in ‹acknowledge›. Elphinston (1787:14) notes too:

> If dhe Inglish keep an impracticabel *k*, *g* or *w* in *know*, *gnaw*, and
> *write*; hware dhe onnest Scots hav long labored (widh hwatevver
> succes) to render dhose iniscials effective.

Again, in the pure dialect, word initial [sk] clusters are (with the
exception of the item ‹sceptic› realised as [s], thus in ‹schism›,
‹Scipio›, ‹scite› and ‹Scythia› (pp.136–7). An [sk] to [š] change for
the Scottish dialect is recorded by Douglas for the items ‹sceptic›, and
‹scepticism› and in 'all other words where *sc* are followed by *i*, or *e*'
(p.222). Word finally too, cluster simplification is sometimes recorded
by Douglas as an example of orthographic inconsistency; thus the
'mute' status of the syllable final [n] and [b] in such items as ‹damn›,
‹contemn›, ‹condemn› as well as ‹limb›, ‹womb› and ‹tomb›. Again
he records the mute status of *g* in the pure pronunciation of ‹sign›,
‹benign›, ‹assignee›, ‹consignee›, possibly reflecting an historical
process of a type where a syllable final [ç] or [ɣ] (orthographically
represented by ‹g›) is vocalised, resulting in a stressed [ii] vowel space
(Nares, 1784:104–5). Douglas notes, however, that in ‹cognizance›
the pure dialect also effaces the [g], pronouncing it 'as if written
conusance', while in the Scotch dialect the [g] is retained (p.185). In
items like ‹tremble› and ‹humble› 'the Scotch are apt to suppress the
b in this and other words ending in *ble* . . . But . . . in *member* . . . the *b*
is to be sounded, both in this, and all other words of the same kind'
(p.229): Elphinston records Scots *hemel* '*humble*', *tummel* '*tumble*',
nummer '*number*' and *temmer* '*timber*' (1787:7,18). Yet it is clear from
the observations of Douglas and others that in this area of the
phonology there was considerable lexical diffusion constraint on
these cluster 'simplification' phenomena, together with a degree of
sociophonetic sensitivity; under the item ‹London› we find the
observation that:

> The formal way of pronouncing this word, is to sound the *d*. The
> more usual and familiar method is to suppress it. Both are
> countenanced by the example of good, and unaffected speakers.
> (p.206)

Elphinston (1787:18) records *almond/ammond* ('raddher *ammon*') variations for the polite English dialect, while 'dhe northern Scots drop *d* final' (1787:18) as in *aul* '*old*', *shiel* '*shield*' and *Dunkel* '*Dunkeld*'; and Adams (1799:153) records the Scotch form ‹chil› '*child*'.

Syllable and word final [kt] and [pt] clusters are, but only in the Scots dialect, reducible to [k] and [p] respectively. Douglas observes that in the Scottish vernacular ‹fact› and ‹distinct› in turn rhyme to ‹attack› and ‹think›, rather than to ‹packt› and ‹linkt› (Dobson, 1968:§§404–407). He considers this Scotch phonological characteristic to be based upon considerations of *cacophonia* (p.159), but he is clearly not too attached to this idea since he asks: 'How shall we explain the different instances where certain sounds appear harsh and are avoided in some languages or dialects and yet are admitted without difficulty in others, although of a genius equally musical and sonorous' (p.160). In the item ‹apostle›, Douglas informs us (p.164) that 'the *t* is in a manner mute in both dialects.'

7 *[h] Dropping and Adding*

Douglas comments upon the syllable initial depletion of this 'modification of articulate sound, which is merely a strong aspiration' (p.128) or 'that effort to aspiration which precedes the pronounciation of the initial vowel in those syllables which are said to be aspirated' (*Of the Provincial Accentuation of Particular Words*, f.35). This [h] effacement and addition he describes as a 'most capricious defect' in some English individuals, one which is apparently randomly spread throughout the lexicon and inter-regionally, some people pronouncing the:

> *h* in as complete a manner as other people, in words where it should be mute and not written. Yet such is the power of habit that if you desire them to try to pronounce the *h* in *hungry* or any word of that sort, they cannot do it, nor avoid doing it in *heir*, or adding it to *air*,

going on to record the hairdresser anecdote (p.128). In the pure dialect Douglas records the [h] as 'mute' in the item ‹herb›, but 'pronounced' in ‹heron› (p.201). While the [h] is said to be mute in the pure dialect in ‹abhor›, ‹humble›, ‹humility› and ‹humbly›, it is realised in the same items in the Scotch vernacular; yet for the item ‹Leghorn›, the Scotch pronounce the [h], suppressed in the pure dialect. Douglas presents a picture of wholesale lexical diffusion with insufficient data to point to real conditioning factors or lexical trends in either dialect.[91] Elphinston's (1787:116) exemplification of the phenomenon smacks of parody:

> So hamiabbel howevver iz dhis yong Lady, dhat, widh her fine

air, sweet hies, quic hears, delicate harms, above all her tender art, she wood giuv anny man a ankering to halter iz condiscion.

A type of [h] dropping is perhaps also to be encountered in the Scottish treatment of the syllable initial [hw] cluster. We recall that this combination is said in the Scots dialect to be realised as a 'guttural *ch*' followed by a *u*, 'losing itself in the succeeding vowel'. Douglas notes that this pronunciation is a 'fault' corrected by the Scotch vernacular speaker by *h dropping*, so that ‹whit›/‹wit› and ‹whig›/‹wig› are homophonous in that dialect (p.141). Walker (1791:46) also views this kind of *h dropping* with some concern:

> This letter [*h*:ᴄᴊ] is often sunk after *w*, particularly in the capital, where we do not find the least distinction of sound between *while* and *wile*, *whet* and *wet*, *where* and *were*. Trifling as this difference may appear at first sight, it tends greatly to weaken and impoverish the pronunciation, as well as sometimes to confound words of a very different meaning.

Yet Smith (1816:17) still observes that the *h* 'has a weak sound in *where*, *when*, &c, as if written *hwere*, *hwhen*, etc. It is not sounded after *r*; as, *rheum*, *rhyme*, &c' and Douglas says that [hw-] pronunciations are 'the true English method of sounding these words', 'careless speakers' among the English falling into the 'same error' as the Scotch in [h] dropping (p.128).

8 Continuancy Adjustments

We have already commented above on what appears to be an alternation in the pure dialect between [d] and [ʤ] obstruent versus delayed release segments in the ‹exaggerate› item (p.192). A similar observation might be made for the ‹suggest› item (p.225) where in the pure dialect Douglas describes the intervocalic segment as a combination of the 'hard sound' (in the sense of non-continuant) *g* and the 'soft' *j* in *just*: [gʤ], 'in the same manner as in *ac-cent*; the first *c* is hard and the second soft', where the hard/soft dichotomy must again represent some continuancy differential, rather than some voicing contrast like *[ækgɛnt]. In the Scottish dialect only [syʤɛst] is countenanced, the obstruancy element being suppressed (perhaps to achieve segment overlap at syllable boundary). In syllable initial position, Douglas observes that in the Scotch dialect, items like ‹zeal›, ‹zone› and ‹zenith› show a 'combined sound of *d*, and the soft *s*' (p.142): [dz], compared to the more vocally sonorous [z] of the pure dialect. On the other hand, the voiceless obstruent [p] in the pure dialect item ‹trumps› is made continuant (more vowel like) in the Scotch version, pronounced 'as if written *trumphs*' (p.230). For the intervocalic [ʧ]/[k]/[ç] contrast, see our comments on the item ‹Rachel› on p.71 above.

9 Metathesis

Douglas, under his ‹hundred› enty (p.203) records the two classic contexts for [r] movement in the internal structure of syllables: the pre to post peak 'hopping' occurs in syllables whose rhyme component, when terminated by an obstruent consonant, is 'light', by this means achieving some kind of canonical configuration whereby maximal vowel prominence in the syllable is perceived as falling within the domain of the rhyme, thus [hyndrəd]/[hyndərd]. The corollary of this process occurs when rhyme terminations are 'too heavy' vocalically, i.e. when they comprise two or more highly sonorous segments to the right of the peak, as in the stressed syllable of ‹Birmingham›. One stratagem for the reduction of this 'over-vowelly' rhyme is the transposition of the [r] component of the rhyme into a pre-peak position: thus Douglas' ‹Briminjam› example (Jones, 1989:§3.2.3).[92]

NOTES TO THE INTRODUCTION

1 *Biographical Memoir Concerning Myself* (Bickley, 1928:vol.2;340).
2 Bickley (1928:Introduction, p.v).
3 Crompton Rhodes (1928:vol.III:261).
4 Crompton Rhodes (1928:vol.III:261).
5 Bickley, 1928:vol.2:213.
6 Bickley, 1928:vol.2:204;September 9th, 1811.
7 'By being *properly* pronounced, I would be always understood to mean, pronounced agreeable to the general practice of men of letters and polite speakers of the Metropolis; which is all the standard of propriety I concern myself about, respecting the arbitrary pronunciation or quality of sound given to monosyllables. Setting this caution aside, I know of no rule to determine, whether the provincial method of pronouncing such words be not as proper as that of the Metropolis.' (Kenrick, 1784:56n.) Perry (1776:Preface vii) in his *The Only Sure Guide to the English Tongue*, states unequivocally that the pronunciation target of his spelling book written especially for a Scottish audience is 'the present practice of polite speakers in the city of London.' While the Scots chauvinist Adams (1799:144) takes a less sanguine view of the English of the Capital: 'The *capital*, LONDON, the centre of refinement, like old Paris, is not the Athens of England; the native inhabitant has a very corrupt affected mode of speech; nothing is so remarkable as *v* changed to *w*, and *w* to *v*, and the suppression of *h* when it ought to be sounded after *w*.'
8 Sheridan (1781:142) indeed seems to suggest that the use of a London standard was unusual, even among the highest classes in Scotland: 'And yet there was still a more extraordinary instance which I met with at Edinburgh, in a Lord of Session (Lord Aylmoor), who, though he had never been out of Scotland, yet merely by his own pains, without rule or method, only conversing much with such English men as happened to be there, and reading regularly with some of the principal actors, arrived even at an accuracy of pronunciation, and had not the least tincture of the Scottish intonation.' Yet note the observation of

Cockburn (1856:10–11), a pupil at Edinburgh High School in 1780 (Bailey, 1987:131–142): 'among the boys, coarseness of language and manners was the only fashion. An English boy was so rare, that his accent was openly laughed at.'

9   spade a spade in margin (!).

10   But the difficulty of the task is fully recognised by Nares (1784:xix): 'The mutability of human speech has been perceived and lamented by every nation that has had a language worth improving . . . But the evil is perhaps too inherent in the nature of language to be removed entirely by any care; and the fate which attended Ennius at Rome, and has fallen upon Chaucer and his contemporaries in England, may perhaps overtake our later poets also; so that those sounds and that construction of words which delighted their own age, shall become obsolete and intolerable to some remote generation.'

11   Throughout this *Introduction* we shall, for the sake of convenience, adhere to Douglas' 'Scotch' and 'pure' terminology for the 'standard' Scottish vernacular and the 'proper English pronounciation' of those 'who are acknowledged to speak with propriety' (p.114).

12   In his usual uncompromising fashion, Adams (1799:158) does not see the Scottish vernacular as a mere dialectal form: 'In this favourable light we may place the origin of Scotch dialect, whilst *other dialects* of the English language are local corruptions, and carry with them the mark of defective education, and rustic ignorance. The provincial Englishman, who quits his country abode, and mixes with the polite world, is singled out as an unlettered, vulgar native, because pure classical English is the standard of polished society in English land, universally approved and received. The Scotch dialect does not carry with it this reproach; because refined English is neither the received standard of that country, and its most eminent scholars designedly retain the variation; retain it with dignity, subject to no real diminution of personal or national merit. It adds honour to their character, and weight to their words . . .'

13   Adams (1799:158) claims: 'Thus the Scotch dialect, as powerfully as opposing warriors, tended to preserve national right and equality. Thus it may rank with the dialects of Greece, which distinguished that great people, and preserved the different governments from sinking under the dominion of more polished Athens. These jarring variations of the Greek, some broad as the coarsest Scotch, were never deemed *vulgar, contemptible, laughable and casual* corruptions of the language, and much less proofs of uncultivated society.'

14   Cf. Wyld's (1953:179) condescending observation concerning Elphinston: 'The first thing which occurs to us with regard to Elphinston is that he was a Scot, not in itself a drawback in the ordinary affairs of life, but a fact which produces some misgivings in connexion with one who is to act as a guide to English speech in the second half of the eighteenth century.'

15   Angus (1800:4) too feels the necessity of excusing the pretentiousness of a Scot in writing about matters relating to the pronunciation of the standard English dialect: 'To those who, without examination, may object to this attempt, as being the production of a Native of North Britain, it may be sufficient to observe, 'That it makes no innovation in English Pronunciation; all the merit it claims (if it shall be found entitled to any merit) is that of exhibiting the Orthoepy of the Language, agreeably to the acknowledged Standards, in a manner more simple than has hitherto been done . . .' but Adams (1799:159) is unrepentantly nationalistic in matters linguistic: 'How ready are Englishmen to claim every affinitive perfection for their own; and how ready is a Scotchman to give up what genuinely appears not to be his own.' Yet, Wyld (1953:179) – citing *Roderick Random* – points to the relative popularity of Scottish teachers of English in London throughout the eighteenth century.

16 'My dear South Britons (for you are dear to me in the aggregate, and many among you are personally so) . . . I own I love my native country. I cannot love the man who does not love his; I love my native shire, my native parish, the silver stream near to whose verdant banks I first drew breath: but I also love and admire Old England. What other country can boast such military and naval skill and prowess as England can in her Malboroughs, her Nelsons, and her Wellingtons; such powers of intellect as she can in her Bacons, her Newtons, and her Shakespeares! (1822:112)

17 'Dunbar and Dunkeld, Douglas in *Virgilian* strains, and later poets, Ramsay, Ferguson, and Burns, awake from your graves, you have already immortalized the Scotch dialect in raptured melody!' (1799:157)

18 Cf. John Walker, *The Teacher's Assistant in English Composition, or Easy Rules for Writing Themes and Composing Exercises* (London, 1802); *Outlines of English Grammar Calculated for the use of Both Sexes at School* (London, 1805); John Hornsey, *A Short Grammar of the English Language: Simplified to the Capacities of Children with Notes and a Great Variety of Entertaining and Useful Exercises* (Newcastle, n.d.); D. Farroe, *The Royal Golden Instructor for Youth throughout the British Dominions* (Bristol, n.d.); Ellin Davies, *The Accidence, or First Rudiments of English Grammar Designed for the Use of Young Ladies* (London, 1777). A good example of the type of phonological analytical skills aimed at by some grammarians of the period is to be found in the *Orthographic Parsing* of Thomas Martin, set out in his *A Philological Grammar of the English Language* (London, 1814:198): '*Storminess*: a Trisyllabic Derivative; *Storm*, the Primitive; *ness*, the main termination, combining with the Primitive by means of the intercedent Vowel and Termination *I*. *Storm*, the principle syllable; *O* its Index; *St*, a consonant combination; *S* a simple palatal aspirate, agreeing with its attendant mute *I*; *O* a single vowel, sounded wide because it is succeeded by *R* and another consonant; *R* is a liquid of the first order, and consequently placed next to the Index . . .'

19 Yet the method had its supporters too; recall Adams' (1799:162) commendation of 'A learned and reverend Friend, native of Scotland': 'I yield with pleasure to that conciliatory medium his ingenuity has traced out, in the reform of the alphabet, though solely admissable in its application to Scotch orthography. His plan is a desideratum, and would at once proscribe the apparent inconsistency of the Scotch pronunciation, solely manifested by retaining our mode of spelling, and deviating from it in a manner not to be conceived by powers of English combination of the letters. How, in the name of wonder, can Scotch Schoolmasters teach poor children to read their Bible printed in the English way? They use no other. Hence every word is a stumbling block; and, from early youth, the Scotch are taught *that our pronunciation is anomalous and capricious . . .*'

20 Walker (1791:2:§§6–7) defines the vocalic/consonantal opposition in terms of continuancy/obstruency: 'The definition of a vowel, as little liable to exception as any, seems to be the following: A vowel is a simple sound formed by a continued effusion of the breath, and a certain conformation of the mouth, without any alteration in the position, or any motion of the organs of speech, from the moment the vocal sound commences till it ends. A consonant may be defined to be, an interruption of the effusion of vocal sound, arising from the application of the organs of speech to each other.'

21 Sheridan too (1781:9:§1) subdivides consonantal segment classes on the basis of a 'prolongation' criterion: 'Consonants may be divided into two classes, mutes and semivowels. The mutes are those whose sounds cannot be prolonged; the semivowels, such whose sounds can be continued at pleasure; partaking of the

nature of vowels from which they derive their name. There are six mutes, *eb, ed, eg, ek, ep, et*. And thirteen semivowels, *ef, el, em, en, er, es, ev, ez, eth, eth, esh, ezh, eng*.' Kenrick's (1784:39) distinction is less clear: 'The consonants also change their nature frequently by position: thus, *l, m, n, r, f*, and *s* are called half vowels, and are said to have a kind of obscure sound, while *b, c, d, g, k, p, q, t*, are said to have no sound at all. But let us place *m* at the beginning of a syllable, and it is nearly as mute as *b* . . . Again, the sound of *c* and *g* at the beginning of words is equally vocal with that of *s*.'

22 Kenrick (1784:6) observes: 'It is indeed on the celerity of utterance that all the difference in many cases between consonants and vowels depends; as in the *w* and *y*, in English; which being discharged quickly, perform the office of consonants, in giving form only to the succeeding vowel; but, when protracted and drawled out, acquire a tone, and become the vocal *oo* and *ee*.' (1784:6).

23 Walker (1791:21:§165) notes too that the vowel in such items is associated with a segment which is more, rather than less, labial: 'The fourth sound of this vowel [*o*:ᴄJ] is that which is found in *love, dove*, &c. and the long sound which seems the nearest relation to it, is the first sound of the *o* in *note, tone, rove*, &c.'

24 Kenrick (1784:55–60) seems to recognise three labial vowel types, a long *ou, oo, o*, in items like *soup, noon, who, boot, fool, food*; a short *o* in *stood, wood, wool, bull, could* and *good*; and an 'indistinct' sound (perhaps [ʌ] or [ə]) in *cur, blood* and *scourge*. 'The short *u* . . . as in *bull, could, good* . . . is not of the same quality as the former number ([ʌ]-type vowels in *cur, blood*:ᴄJ): *bull* and *trull, could* and *cud, good* and *blood*, being no rimes in London; where they have a very different and distinct quality of sound. I have said that this is only a contraction of the former long sound.'

He tells us, however, that the Irish, the inhabitants of Yorkshire and 'many provincials' frequently substitute the 'indistinct' sound for the short sound [u] in the items *blood, rut* and *rush*. On the other hand, Sheridan (1781:26,49) appears to see only a [u]/[ʌ] contrast in this area of the phonology: 'This vowel (*U*) has always its first sound as in the words *lull, pluck, hurl* &c; except in the following words, where it has the sound of u2; *bull, full, pull, bush, push*.' Nares (1784:75–77) differentiates [uu]/[u], the former in *cool, moon, doom*, the latter in *good, hood, wood, stood, foot, book, cook, bull, bullet, full, pull, bush, cushion, push, pulpit* and *put*. He also admits of a *u short* (pp.35ff) which 'has an obscurer sound' and is characteristic of *but, number, ultimate, blood, flood* and *foot*. The Scot Buchanan (1757:8–11) seems only to differentiate some kind of [u] sound in items like *move, prove, do, who, womb, tomb* (with no indication as to length differential) and what he calls a 'short or obscure' *u* sound (possibly [ʌ] or [ə]) in a long list of items which includes *but, cut, gun, rub, come, some, conjure, conduit, Monday, honey*.

25 Kenrick's (1781:95–6) observations on the duration of consonantal segments (under his *Rules to be observed in sounding the Consonants*) are worth recalling here: 'None of them are to be prolonged except when the accent is upon them; which can only happen when they are preceded by a short sounding vowel: as *tell, can, love*. When a long sound precedes, the voice must dwell upon the vowel, and take the consonant into the syllable in its shortest sound; otherwise, were they both dwelt upon, the syllable would take up the time of two long sounds, and would therefore seem to be two: as *vā-le, rāi-n, brā-ve, dāy-s*. This is an article very necessary to be attended to by the natives of Scotland, who are apt to prolong the sound of a semivowel after a long vowel. On the other hand, the people of England are to be cautioned against running the sound of the vowel too quickly into the following consonant, which is too generally the practice, to the great diminution of the number of our long syllables.'

26 Kenrick (1784:58) observes: 'The sound at present in question [the *long, ou, oo,* *o*:CJ] is generally expressed in English writing by the double *oo*, as in *boot, fool,* *food*, where it is long, and also in *stood, wood, wool*, where it is short; but care should be taken not to suffer the letters to mislead the reader, for *blood, flood,* &c. though written with two *oo*s, as well as some other words, have not this sound, but that of No. 16 of the Alphabet or I of the Dictionary (the indistinct *a,* *e, i, o, u, oo* or *ou*, are as in *earth, her, Sir, won, cur, blood, scourge* (p.55)); being pronounced as if written *blud, flud.* (Mr Ward mistakenly enumerates the words *blood, stood, wood*, as words of the same quality of sound).' See too Walker (1791:14–15).

27 Note his own rhyme in his *Imitation of the Namby-Pamby style*: written September, 1789 (*Occasional Verses*, 1820:36):
> 'I talk'd to my Deia of love;
> She blush'd, but confess'd it was sweet,
> So we wander'd about in the grove,
> And we sat upon every seat.'

28 Perhaps something like this [ɨ]-type vowel is referred to by Adams in his description of the *Scotch English Dialects* (1799:152) when he suggests as Scotch variants of *soon* and *moon* realisations rendered as ‹sain›, ‹main›, where he uses ‹ai› as a symbol for [e], perhaps perceived by him as being phonetically close to [ɨ].

29 Walker (1791:xi) observes under his *Rules to be observed by the Natives of Scotland* *for attaining a just Pronounciation of English*: 'In addition to what has been said, it may be observed, that *oo* in *food, mood, moon, soon,* &c. which ought always to have a long sound, is generally shortened in Scotland to that middle sound of the *u* in *bull*; and it must be remembered, that *wool, wood, good, hood, stood, foot*, are the only words where this sound of *oo* ought to take place.'

30 Almost all observers in the eighteenth century comment upon the shape of the stressed vowel in pre-[r] contexts, usually to the effect that it is 'obscure', 'indistinct' (even 'coarse Flemish' (Adams 1799:41)) and the like. Under his discussion of items like ‹bet› and ‹bell› with [ɛ]-type segments, Sheridan (1781:40) notes of the item ‹myrrh› that: 'This, and the two foregoing words [‹err›, ‹were›] are marked with short *u*, by Dr Kenrick and Mr Scott; but I choose rather, with Messrs Sheridan and Walker, to place them here'; and again, '*Herb,* *kerb, verb.* The same observation may be made with respect to these three words as the preceding, with this additional one, that both Dr Kenrick and Mr Scott seem confused in their marking of most of the following words as far as *squirt*: the one representing *girt* and *girth* by the short *i*, and *girl* by the short *u*; and the other describing the sound of *i*, in *mirth*, by *u*, in *cube*.' Once more, under his discussion of the *i* vowel, Sheridan observes (1781:48): 'When this vowel precedes *r* it never has its own sound, but it is always changed to that of first *e* [[ɛ]:CJ], or first *u* [[ʌ]:CJ]. To *e* in the following words: *birth, firth, girt, girth, gird,* *girl, mirth, skirt, squirt, quirk, chirp, firm, irk, smirk, dirge, whirl, twirl.* To *u* in *dirt,* *flirt, shirt, spirt, first, third, bird.*' Walker comments, under his discussion of 'the letter *i*' (1791:15:§§108–9): 'When this letter is succeeded by *r*, and another consonant not in a final syllable, it has exactly the sound of *e* in *vermin, vernal,* &c. as *virtue, virgin,* &c. which approaches to the sound of the short *u*; but when it comes before *r*, followed by another consonant in a final syllable, it acquires the sound of *u* exactly; as *bird, dirt, shirt, squirt,* &c. *Mirth, birth,* and *firm,* are the only exceptions to this rule; where *i* is pronounced like *e*, and as if the words were written, *merth, berth,* and *ferm* . . . In the same manner, the *i*, coming before either double *r* or single *r*, followed by a vowel, preserves its pure, short sound, as in *irritate, conspiracy,* &c., but when *r* is followed by another consonant, or is a

final letter of a word with the accent upon it, the *i* goes into a deeper and broader sound, equivalent to short *e*, as heard in *virgin*, *virtue*, &c. So *fir*, a tree, is perfectly similar to the first syllable of *ferment*, though often corruptly pronounced like *fur*, a skin. *Sir* and *stir* are exactly pronounced as if written *Sur* and *stur*'.

31 This claim for a high palatality level for the vowel segment in items like ‹pit›, ‹sit›in the late eighteenth century is perhaps borne out too in Kenrick's (1784:61) observation that: 'Grammarians have usually annexed two sounds of the *i*, which they have called the long and the short; but the sound given to the short *i*, for instance in *fit*, *give*, etc. is by no means a mere contraction of the sound given to the long *i* in *mine*, *life*, etc. It is a sound of a very different quality; being a contraction of the long sound of *e* or *ee*, in *me* or *meet*. This is plain by repeating the words *fit* and *feet*, *pit* and *peat*, *mit* and *meat*; in which the similarity of sound is very perceptible.'

32 Walker too, in his *Rules to be observed by the Natives of Scotland for attaining a just Pronunciation of English* (1791:xi) notes this lowering tendency in contemporary Scottish English: 'The short *e* in *bed*, *fed*, *red*, &c. borders too much upon the English sound of the *a* in *bad*, *lad*, *mad*, &c. and the short *i* in *bid*, *lid*, *rid*, too much on the English sound of *e* in *bed*, *led*, *red*', while Adams as well (1799:152) gives renderings like ‹mull›, ‹fust›, ‹sall›, ‹tall›/‹tull› for '*mill*', '*fist*', '*self*', '*tell*'.

33 Under his discussion of the symbol *EE*, Walker (1791:30:§246) notes: 'This diphthong, in all words, except for those that end in *r*, has a squeezed sound of long open *e*, formed by a closer application of the tongue to the roof of the mouth, than in that vowel singly, which is distinguishable to a nice ear, in the different sounds of the verbs to *flee* and to *meet*, and the nouns *flea* and *meat*. This has always been my opinion; but upon consulting some good speakers on the occasion, and in particular Mr. Garrick, who could find no difference in the sound of these words, I am less confident in giving it to the public. At any rate the difference is but very trifling . . .'

34 Note Adams (1799:152–3) who cites ‹see-ven› '*seven*'; ‹see-cond› '*second*'; ‹freend› '*friend*' and the items *bread*, *head* and *death* as showing 'e long', his [i]. He also records, for the Scotch vernacular, the opposite process, where items like *feet*, *sheep* and *deep*, manifest 'e short' and are possibly [fɪt], etc.

35 Recall here too Adams' (1799:152–3) observation on the Scotch dialect that it shows what he represents as ‹chil›, ‹meeld›, ‹weeld›, ‹heed›, ‹cree'd›, ‹bee› and ‹skee› shapes for '*child*', '*mild*', '*wild*', '*hide*', '*cried*', '*by*' and '*sky*'.

36 Recall Adams' (1799:152–3) Scotch versions of '*day*' and '*say*' as ‹dâi› and ‹sâi›, suggesting, superficially, some kind of [ɔi] diphthong: but see note 43 below.

37 Nares (1784:57) does not seem to attest an [ee]/[ɛɛ]-type contrast in pre-[r] contexts. He cites an *E short proper* (presumably [ɛ]) in items like *bed*, *bell*, *any*, *many*, *breath*, *dead*, *leopard*, etc., and an *a long improper*, equated with the *é* in the French *pais*, and possibly [e(e)] in the items: *ere*, *there*, *where*, *eight*, *their*, *vein*.

38 Recall Walker's (1791:30:§§241–242) phonaesthetically motivated comment to the effect that: 'The word *great* is sometimes pronounced as if written *greet*, generally by people of education, and almost universally in Ireland; but this is contrary to the fixed and settled practice in England. That this is an affected pronunciation, will be perceived in a moment by pronouncing this word in the phrase, *Alexander the great*; for those who pronounce the word *greet*, in other cases will generally in this rhyme it with *fate*. It is true the *ee* is the regular sound of this diphthong; but this slender sound of *e* has, in all probability, given way to that of *a* as deeper and more expressive of the epithet *great*. The same observations are applicable to the word *break*; which is much more expressive of the action when pronounced *brake* than *breek*, as it is sometimes affectedly pronounced.'

39 The contemporary debate over the palatality value of the stressed vowel in certain lexical items in standard and regional pronunciation is well captured in Kenrick (1784:64): 'It may here be necessary to advertise the speaker again of the mistaken practice of the provinces, in using the long sound of the *e*, or slender sound of the *a*, instead of the protracted sound of the short *i* . . . and the rather because I observe that Dr Bayly, and others, seem to authorize this corrupt method of pronunciation; "In words, says this last mentioned writer, having an *e* final, the *e* is mute, and serveth only to lengthen another vowel, thus *make* and *take*, are pronounced as if written *meak* and *teak*, as in *eat, break, speak*." I can yet hardly conceive, that this learned writer meant to say that *make* and *take* have the same quality of sound as *eat, break, speak*; and yet there must be some misconception, as the three words last exemplified are not usually pronounced by good speakers in the same manner. *Break* is generally sounded like *brake*, *make, take*, but few, except the natives of Ireland or the provinces, say *ate, spake*; but *eat, speak* . . .'

40 The observation by Walker (1791:xi) that in the Scottish dialect 'the short *e* in *bed, fed, red*, &c borders too much upon the English sound of *a* in *bad, mad, lad* &c' might suggest that the Scottish vernacular pronunciation was some kind of [ɛ⊤] rather than simply an [ɛ] shape.

41 Note here Adams' (1799:152–3) contention that, in the Scotch dialect, a palatalisation of [ɛ] to some kind of [ɨ] occurs in pre-nasal contexts, thus he represents '*send*' and '*end*' by ‹seend› and ‹eend›.

42 However, several examples are cited by Adams (ibid.), who represents the items *decent, thee, me, be* by ‹dai-cent›, ‹thai›, ‹mai›, ‹bai›, where his ‹ai› can mean an [e]-type vowel.

43 Adams (ibid.) records Scotch pronunciations of *day* and *say* as ‹dâi› and ‹sâi› (where ‹â› is his *broad a*, some kind of [ɔ] segment) suggesting, on face value, an extremely odd [ɔi] diphthong for the stressed vowel space in these items. However, given that he uses ‹ai› for [e], then it might just be possible to interpret ‹âi› as some kind of more open [e], i.e. [ɛ].

44 Adams (ibid.) records the Scotch ‹faither› '*father*', and also ‹airt› '*art*', ‹hait› '*hat*' showing Scotch [e] against English [ɑ] or [æ], even registering Scotch ‹waiter› '*water*'; ‹wais› '*was*'; ‹waint› '*want*'; ‹wair› '*war*' and ‹wairm› '*warm*' against English items characterised by the 'broad a', possibly [ɔ] or [ɒ].

45 For instance, Gray ('late of Peebles and Dundee') makes no distinction between what are either [ee] or [ɛɛ] vowels in pre-[r] and other contexts. He lists as words which are the 'same in Pronunciation, but different in Spelling and Significa- tion', items like *Air, E'er, Ere, Heir; Bare, Bear; grate, great, hare, hair;* and under words with the vowel in the item ‹clay›, he includes *bear, their, chair, where*, as well as *lace, race, yea, whey*, etc. (1794:9).

46 Note the following rhyme used by Douglas in his verses, written at Vienna (1768) and published in his *Occasional Verses* (1820:15):

If these, O, Prince! thy splendid merits are,
Shall spiteful satire lay thy foibles bare?

47 Kenrick (1784:54) observes that the items *door, floor* and *gold* can be pronounced 'without any imputation of a foreign or even provincial accent' either as his vowel 4 ([oo]) or vowel 8 ([uu]), perhaps suggesting too a [o⊥] value for the mid back vowel.

48 Walker (1791) has an [o] value for *revolt, oats, ford*, [ɔ] for *oatmeal, pod, log, sob* and [ɔɔ] for *groat, form*. For *knowledge* he provides an [o]/[ɔ] alternative, while Kenrick informs us concerning the sound associated with the ‹ou›, ‹ow› graph that: 'This sound is variously applied to particular words in different parts of

Great Britain and Ireland. Mr Ward gives us the words *foul, sound, grow, knowledge*, as being all of the same sound; whereas the two first only are alike in the sound: the two last differing not only from the first, but from each other, both in quality and quantity. Thus, *grow* is the long sound . . . as in the words, *no, toe, though*, &c. whereas the first syllable in *knowledge* is the short sound . . . as in *not, what*, and the like; which is not the same quality with either . . . *no, toe*, or . . . *how, thou*, &c' while Adams (1799:16) comments: 'Some modern variations, arising from simple combinations and analogy of rule, and sounds differently uttered and supported by the authority of practice of our Universities, are respectable and optional, as *Rome* per o long [[u]:CJ]. So most Cambridgians pronounce *know-ledge, kno-ledge*, others *knol-edge*, both by rule; *kno*, from the radical words to *know*; *knol* is guided by the shifting accent, which seizes the sound of simple *o* (found in *ow*) and unites it to the double consonant', and see note 50.

49   Cf. Walker (1791:22:§170): 'What was observed of the *a*, when followed by a liquid and a mute, may be observed of the *o* with equal justness. This letter, like *a*, has a tendency to lengthen, when followed by a liquid and another consonant, or by *s, ss*, or *s* and a mute. But this length of *o*, in this situation, seems every day growing more and more vulgar: and, as it would be gross to a degree to sound the *a* in *castle, mask*, and *plant*, like the *a* in *palm, psalm*, &c, so it would be equally exceptionable to pronounce the *o* in *moss, dross*, and *frost*, as if written *mauwse, drawse*, and *frawst*. The *o* in the compounds of *solve*, as *dissolve, absolve, resolve*, seem the only words where a somewhat longer sound of the *o* is agreeable to polite pronunciation.'

50   Walker (1791:37) observes: 'This dipthong, in the word *knowledge*, has of late years undergone a considerable revolution. Some speakers, who had the regularity of their language at heart, were grieved to see the compound depart so far from the sound of the simple, and with heroic fortitude had opposed the multitude by pronouncing the first syllable of this word as it is heard in the verb to *know*. The pulpit and the bar have for some years given a sanction to this pronunciation; but the senate and the stage hold out inflexibly against it; and the nation at large seem insensible of the improvement. They still continue to pronounce, as in the old ludicrous rhymes –

Among the mighty men of knowledge,
That are professors at Gresham College.

51   Buchanan (1762:18) includes the items *thought* and *sought* under his long *o* ('which makes the Mouth of an orbicular Form') classification.

52   Alexander Barrie (1799:xxvi), teacher of English, Writers Court, Edinburgh, in his section entitled 'Words in which the Natives of Scotland are most apt to err', tells us, regarding [o] and [ɔ], that: 'these two sounds of the vowel are particularly difficult to North Britons when occurring in the same word or near one another; as *post-office, coach-box, a long story, I thought so, not only, go on*, &c.'
Note Douglas' rhyme in his verse *Written from Hungary* to O.P, at Vienna 1768:
You pass your days at court
. . .
I make my letter short.
(*Occasional Verses*, 1820:21).

53   Adams (1799:152–3) notes a similar phenomenon, describing Scotch [ɔ] pronunciations for items like *ode, rose*, and also pointing to a timing difference in pre [ld], [rd] and [st] contexts where [o]-type vowels 'Are sounded long by us . . . Are sounded short in Scotch, & vice versa, or the vowel is changed ([o] alternating with [ɔ]:CJ).' Notice too Walker's assertion (1791:xi) concerning the Scotch dialect

to the effect that 'The short *o* in *not*, *lodge*, *got*, &c. is apt to slide into the short *u*, as if the words were written *nut*, *ludge*, *gut*, &c', suggesting perhaps that the Scotch vowel was a raised [oɹ].

54 Compare Kenrick's (1784:54) observation: 'By the addition of several distinctions, introduced by a multiplication of the vowels, it is true, that mankind have acquired a greater diversity in the matter of speech: but these vocal distinctions are by no means so forcible and precise as consonants. As in the mixture of colours in painting, there are many artificial varieties to be made, sufficiently distinguishable from each other by connoisseurs and artists; but the strongest and most precise distinctions of coloured lights and shades, do not come up to the full partition of black and white, or the divisions marked out by the primary colours of light. Thus, although there be more clearness and precision in the articulation of polished tongues, not withstanding their increase of vowels, than in the imperfect general languages; yet the nicer vocal distinctions, affected by fine speakers, tend not only to render their language enervate but indistinct'; while Douglas too observes (p.118): 'For, as in the rainbow, although the pure middle part of each of the different stripes of colours is clearly distinguishable from the others, yet, while the eye gradually passes outwards, to the edge of such stripe, on either side, it seems to die away insensibly into the neighbouring tint, and is at length so like it, that it is impossible for the mind to draw the line, or fix the limit where the one ends, and the other begins; so the same thing is observable in our perception of vocal sounds. Thus we may consider the long open *a* in *father* as a sound placed between *o* and the strong slender *a*, or Scotch Eta.'

55 Walker too (1791:10:§77) notes this tendency to describe this *a* sound as an intermediate entity: 'By some it is styled in the middle sound of *a*, as between the *a* in *pale*, and that in *wall*.' In all, his treatment of the [ɑ/ɑɑ] segment is much more detailed than Douglas'. He systematically distinguishes a long and short version of this 'middle sound' (which 'answers nearly to the Italian *a* in *Toscano*, *Romana*, &c. or to the final *a* in the naturalized Greek words, *papa* and *mama*).' Among the former he lists pre-[r] vowels in items like *tar*, *car*, *mar* and pre-continuant stressed vowels in *psalm*, *bath*, *past*, *aunt* and *glass*. Short [ɑ] vowels are to be found in *man*, *pan*, *hat*, *mat*, *wax*, etc, while the *father* item is listed as showing both long and short vowel forms. Although he states of the long [ɑɑ] vowel that 'We seldom find the long sound of this letter in our language' (§78), he nevertheless makes the claim that 'this pronunciation of *a* seems to have been for some years advancing to the short sound of this letter, as heard in *hand*, *land*, *grand*, &c and pronouncing the *a* in *after*, *answer*, *basket*, *plant*, *mast*, &c as long as in *half* . . . borders very closely on vulgarity' (§79).

56 Walker lists ‹father› as showing both long and short [ɑ] vowels.

57 Buchanan (1762:8) too perhaps suggests a more palatal possibility for the [æ] vowel: 'The short sound of (a) is expressed in *băd*, *băt*, *bănd*, *hănd*, *mănner*, *bătter*, &c. which Words are pronounced but a little more open than *bĕt*, *bĕd*, *bĕnd*, *hĕnd*, *mĕnner*, *bĕtter*'; and again (1757:8): 'The short sound of (e) differs but very little from short *a*; as *fet*, *set*, *bed* &c differ but little in their sounds from *fat*, *sad*, *bad*, only those with (a) have a little more opening.'

58 Walker (1791:11) recognises long and short versions of this 'deeper sound and still more open than *father*' (§77), the former in items like *fall*, *ball*, *gall*, *all*, *wall*, *call*, *salt*, *bald*, *false* (with the long sound of the deep broad German *a*); short versions are said to occur in syllable initial [w] contexts like *wallow*, *swallow*, *want*, *wasp*, *was*, *what* and since he also gives the same value for items like *not*, *got* and *lot*, sees it as homophonous with his second sound of the *o*, which is: 'called its short sound, and is found in *not*, *got*, *lot*, &c . . . corresponds exactly to

that of the *a* in *what*, with which the words *not*, *got*, *lot*, are perfect rhymes. The long sound, to which the *o* in *not* and *sot* are short ones, is found under the dipthong *au* in *naught*, and the *ou* in *fought*; corresponding exactly to the *a* in *hall*, *ball*, &c.' (§163). Sheridan too seems to see no difference between the short *o* and broad *a* types, listing all the following items under his *a3*: *call*, *talk*, *laud*, *taught*, *claw*, *broad*, *George*, *form*, *ought* (1781:25). However Buchanan's (1762) short *o* vowel in *got*, *rod*, *George*, is kept distinct from the 'guttural or broad sound' of *a* in *all*, *call*, *bald*, *ward*, *walk*, etc., and Nares (1784:31), under his discussion of Broad A, comments: 'though this sound is very like that of the short *o*, it is yet distinguishable from it; *moss* and *dross* are not the same as *cross* and *loss*.' Kenrick observes (1784:62–3): 'Expressed in letters by *a*, *au*, *ua*, short, as in *hand*, *barr'd*, and long as in *hard*, *guard*, *laugh*, is a sound common to most languages . . . It is somewhat surprising, that men of letters, and some of them even residing in the Metropolis, should mistake the simple and genuine applications of this sound. "The native sound of *a*, says Dr Bailey, is broad, deep, and long, as in *all*, *aw*, *war*, *daub*; but it hath generally a mixed sound, as in *man*, *Bath*, *Mary*, *fair*, which are sounded as if written *maen*, *baeth*, &c." But who, except flirting females and affected fops, pronounce *man*, and *Bath*, as if they were written *maen*, *baeth*, or like *Mary*, *fair*, &c.'

59   Adams (1799:152–3) has the items ‹wax› and ‹wagon› with Scotch pronunciations in [wɒks] and [wɒgən], while the English [e] stressed vowel in '*wafer*' and '*lady*' is realised in Scotch, he claims, by [ɒ].

60   Adams (ibid.) records what he claims are typically Scotch pronunciations of *bald*, *scald* as [bæld], [skæld].

61   Note the rhyme in Douglas' poem, *Written from Hungary*, and dedicated to O.P., in his *Occasional Verses* (1820:19):

> Unknown to sleeping trade,
>
> . . .
>
> In tattered garments clad.

62   Walker (1791:25) sees the diphthong as: 'a double vowel, or the union or mixture of two vowels pronounced together, so as only to make one syllable. This is the general definition of a diphthong; but if we examine it closely, we shall find in it a want of precision and accuracy. If a diphthong be two vowel sounds in succession, they must necessarily form two syllables, and therefore, by its very definition, cannot be a diphthong; if it be such a mixture of two vowels as to form but one simple sound, it is very improperly called a diphthong, nor can any such simple mixture exist.' Sheridan sees diphthongs generally as merely the 'junction of two vowels' (1781:16); Buchanan's definition (1762:14): 'What is a Diphthong? A Diphthong is the meeting of two vowels in one syllable' is immediately modified by: 'Some Writers absurdly define an English Diphthong to be the sounding of two Vowels in one Syllable; and make a bustle about dividing them into proper and improper, though they differ in the Method of their Division. They tell us a proper Diphthong is that which has a mixed or proper Sound of both the Vowels. According to this Definition there is not a proper Diphthong in the English Tongue, unless we allow (oi) to be one, to which some give the sound of the long (i) . . . It must be confessed that (oi) approaches the nearest of any combination in our Language to the Nature and Design of a Diphthong, as Diphthong imports the Coalition or Mixture of two Sounds in one.' Kenrick's scepticism for the wisdom of contemporary grammarians surfaces clearly in this area too: 'the very same Grammarians also tell us that *a diphthong or compound vowel, is the union of two or more vowels pronounced by a single impulse of the voice.* But how can there be *two* simple articulate sounds uttered by a *single impulse* of the *voice*? And that by *opening of the mouth only* in a particular

manner? If the mouth be opened only in one particular manner, it will admit only one vowel, not two; and if two are emitted there must be some change effected in the manner of opening the mouth.' (1784:38–9).

63 Of this diphthong Kenrick (1784:65) writes: 'This sound is typified by *i* or *y*, *ui*, or *ie*, as in *I*, *why*, *nigh*, *guide*, *fie*. As at present uttered by the best speakers in the Metropolis, it is the sharpest, shrillest, and clearest vowel in our language; altho' it has the appearance, when slowly pronounced, of being a compound of the *a* or *e* and *i*. I do not know that any other language has it equally clear, single and distinct. I have elsewhere observed that our Scottish linguists say it has the sound usually denoted by *awee*, but the errour of this is obvious to every Englishman,' referring to Buchanan's (1762:11) observation that: 'Long (i) has a double Sound, and is compounded of *aw* and *ee*, pronounced very quick, thus *ăweĕ*; as *fire*, *desire*, &c. is pronounced as if written *făweĕr*, *desăweĕr*; though it is not always so very open, but in many Words resembles the Greek ε'. Perhaps Walker's (1791:14–15) definition (under his discussion of the letter *I*) is most typical of the period: 'This letter is a perfect diphthong, composed of the sound of the *a* in *father*, and *e* in *be*, pronounced as closely together as possible. When these sounds are openly pronounced, they produce the familiar assent *ay*; which, by the old English dramatic writers, was often expressed by *I*.'

64 Adams (1799:152–3) records as typically Scotch [æi] vowel space in both ‹vicar› and ‹mist›, while for the items *hide*, *cried*, *by* and *sky* he uses ‹ee› representations (‹heed›, ‹cree'd›, ‹bee›, ‹skee›) suggesting a pure palatal [i]/[ii].

65 Kenrick's remark (1784:58) to the effect that this diphthong 'greatly resembles the barking of a full mouthed mastiff, and is perhaps so clearly and distinctly pronounced by no nation as by the English and Low-Dutch' is not particularly helpful.

66 Adams (1799:77–8) gives us little information about the phonetic value of the *ou* ('the most variable and difficult') diphthong other than that it resembles the 'coarse Dutch.' He does, however, provide a table of minimal pairs contrasting whatever is meant by this 'coarse Dutch' sound and [o]/[oo], which include *Bow* 'reverence'/*Bow* 'instrument'; *Bowl* 'globe'/*Bowl* 'cup'; *Crowd* 'numbers'/*Crow'd* 'crowing of fowl'; *Grows* 'a bird'/*Grows* 'he grows old'; *Enough* 'for number'/*Enough* 'enuff, quantity', etc.

67 Note the rhyme used by Douglas in his Imitation of Horace's Ode 25, Book 1, written in 1759:

> That youth prefers the vernal flower,
> Devoting, when the seasons lower,
> The wither'd leaf to floods that pour,
> Impetuous o'er the plain.
> (*Occasional Verses* 1820:4)

68 Telfair's *Town and Country Spelling Book*, published in Edinburgh in 1775 attempts to provide: 'a comprehensive view of the pronunciation of the best speakers in London; designed more particularly for the use of Schools at a distance from London', while Telfair himself (Curer of Impediments of Speech) advertises himself as one who: 'cures Dumbness, Stammering, and Other Impediments in Speech, at his home in Barranger's Close, Edinburgh. In Three years Deaf and Dumb persons are made capable of conversing in a plain and intelligent manner, and are taught reading, writing, arithmetic.'

69 Recall Kenrick (1784:59): 'Mr Ward says this sound [the [ɑu] in ‹town›] may be made more or less, close and deep, by making the mouth more or less hollow, and directing the breath more or less towards the palate. To instance this he falls into the errour countenanced by Johnson's Dictionary; saying that "a *bowl*,

meaning an orbicular body, requires a close sound; but a *bowl*, meaning a vessel, requires a more open sound." The people of Ireland, and perhaps those of some counties of England, do indeed pronounce *bowl*, meaning a vessel, in the same manner as we in London pronounce the words *howl*, *scrowl*, &c. but polite speakers in the metropolis pronounce the word *bowl*, whether meaning an orbicular body or vessel, exactly in the same manner; both long and open, as in the words *toll, hole, roll*, &c.'

70 Walker (1791:35) characterises this diphthong as composed of the '*a* in *water* [his *a3*; possibly [ɔ] or [ɒ]:CJ], and the first *e* in *me-tre*. This double sound is very distinguishable in *boil, toil, spoil, point, anoint*, &c. which sound ought to be carefully preserved, as there is a very prevalent practice among the vulgar of dropping the *o*, and pronouncing these words as if written *bile, tile, spile*, &c.' Sheridan (1781;16) sees this diphthong composed of the same elements as that in ‹time›, ‹mine›, etc, but with a discrepancy in the duration of the first component: 'The diphthong *oi* is formed by a union of the same vowels as of *i2*: that is *a3* [the vowel in *hall*:CJ] and *e3* [the vowel in *beer*:CJ]; with this difference, that the first vowel *a3*, being dwelt upon, is distinctly heard before its sound is changed by its junction with the latter vowel *e3*; as *oi*, *noise*.' Adams (1799:75) not very helpfully observes: '*oi*, *oy*, No. 1 open and broad *a-i*. – *Coil, foil, toil*. No. 3 it is sounded softer by some, – in *boil* (*bile*), *quoir, quire* or *kire*.'

71 Adams (1799:152–3) records Scotch pronunciations of '*coil*' and '*foil*' as ‹kile› and ‹file›; i.e. with [æi].

72 Perhaps some evidence for a monophthongal status developing for the [ɔi] diphthong can be read into the observations by Kenrick (1784:61): '*oil, toil*, are frequently pronounced exactly like *isle, tile*. This is a fault which the Poets are inexcusable for promoting, by making such words rhime to each other. And yet there are some words so written, which by long use, have almost lost their true sound, such are *boil, join*, and many others; which it would not appear affectation to pronounce otherwise than *bile, jine*. We find, indeed, that this mode of pronunciation becomes every day more general; a striking proof, among others, of the antipathy, if I may so call it, of speech to the use of diphthongs, or the utterance of the two sounds of different qualities, with one impulse of the voice.'

73 Sheridan (1791:20) gives a very similar definition of the diphthong: 'To Form it properly therefore, a foreigner is to be told that it is composed of the sounds *e3* [[i]:CJ] and *o3* [[u]:CJ], the first sound not completed but rapidly running into the last', although Walker (1791:22) is less precise: 'The first sound of *u*, heard in *tube*, or ending in an unaccented syllable, as in *cubic*, is a diphthongal sound, as if *e* were prefixed, and these words were spelt *tewbe* and *kewbic*.' Nares (1784:35) observes that: 'This sound certainly is a compounded one; it is the very same as is also expressed by the combination of three letters in the words *you* and *yew*. Yet that this is the regular long sound of the *u* with us is evident, by the manner in which we pronounce the vowel when we mean to name it alone, *u*. Dr Wallis says that this sound is compounded of *i* and *w*; but since, in English, the proper representative of the simple sound of *u* is the reduplication or false diphthong *oo*, I should rather say that it is compounded of *y* and *oo*'; and Elphinston (1765:14): 'The diphthongs inverted make *liquefactions*, where *y* and *w* become prepositive, and melt into vocal articulaters of the subjunctive vowel. The former thus virtually articulates *oo* in *u*, equal to *you* for *yoo*, as also to *yew* the tree.'

74 Walker (1791:§335) lists with [ju] the items: *clue, cue, due, blue, glue, hue, flue, rue, sue, true, mue, accrue, ensue, argue, imbue, imbrue, pursue, subdue, perdue, residue, avenue, revenue, continue, retinue, construe, statue, tissue, issue, virtue, value, argue.* Sheridan (1781:22) includes *cube, few, new, clue, view, beauty.* Nares (1784:62–3)

includes *dew*, *ewer*, *new*, *pew*, *deuce*, *Deuteronomy*, *feud*. Adams uses the [ú] symbol, his *yu* as in *Duke*, ‹diuuk›, for the Scotch rendering of '*poor*', '*door*' and '*moor*'.

75 The contemporary social, regional and lexical alternation between [uu] and [ju] vowel space is commented upon by almost all observers; Walker (1791:§462:178), for instance, noting the [t] → [ʧ] change in [ju] contexts, comments that: 'Though it is evident . . . that as the *u* is under the accent, the preceding *t* is preserved pure, and that the words ought to be pronounced as if written *tewtor*, *tewmult*, *tewmour*, &c. and neither *tshootur*, *tshoomult*, *tshoomour*, as Mr Sheridan writes them, nor *tootor*, *toomult*, *toomour*, as they are often pronounced by vulgar speakers.'

76 A characteristic of Scottish English also noted by Walker (1791:§178); 'But the strangest deviation of this letter [u] from its regular sound is in the words *busy*, *business*, and *bury*. We laugh at the Scotch for pronouncing these words *bewsy*, *bewsiness*, and *bewry*; but we ought rather to blush for ourselves in departing so wantonly from the general rule as to pronounce them *bizzy*, *bizness*, and *berry*.'

77 Walker (1791:§475) comments on syllable initial [w] segments that: 'In *swoon*, however, this letter is always heard; and pronouncing it *soon*, is vulgar. In *sword* and *answer*, it is always silent. In *two* it mingles with its kindred sound, and the number two is pronounced like the adverb *too*. The same thing may be observed of *toward* and *towards*, where the *w* is dropped, rhyming with *hoard* and *hoards*, but in the adjectives and adverbs *toward* and *towardly*, *froward* and *frowardly*, the *w* is heard distinctly. It is something dropped in the last syllable of *awkward*, as if written *awkard*; but this pronunciation is vulgar.' And again (1791:§334): 'This diphthong [*ue*], like *ua*, when it forms only one syllable, and both letters are pronounced, has the *u* sound like *w*; as *consuetude*, *dessuetude*, and *mansuetude*, which are pronounced *conswetude*, *desswetude*, and *manswetude*. Thus *conquest* is pronounced according to the general rule, as if written *conkwest*; but the verb to *conquer* has unaccountably deviated into *conker*, particularly upon the stage. This error, however, seems not to be rooted in the general ear as to be above correction; and analogy undoubtedly demands *conkwer*.'

78 'When the *a* is preceded by the gutturals, hard *g* or *c*, it is, in polite pronunciation, softened by the intervention of a sound like *e*, so that *card*, *cart*, *guard*, *regard*, are pronounced like *ke-ard*, *ke-art*, *ghe-ard*, *re-ghe-ard*. This sound of the *a* is taken notice of in Steele's Grammar, page 49, which proves it is not the offspring of the present day.' (1791:§92) 'The same might be said of the letter *i*: When this vowel is preceded by hard *g* or *k* . . . it is pronounced as if an *e* were inserted between the consonant and the vowel. Thus *sky*, *kind*, *guide*, *guise*, *disguise*, *guile*, *beguile*, *mankind*, are pronounced as if written *ske-y*, *ke-ind*, *gue-ise*, *disgue-ise*, *gue-ile*, *begue-ile*, *manke-ind*. From this view of the analogy we may form a judgement of the observation of a late writer on this subject, that "*ky ind* for *kind* is a monster of pronunciation, heard only on our stage." – Nare's Orth.' (1791:§160) Nares also comments (1784:138): 'It is observed by Dr Wallis, that the sounds of *w* and *y* creep in upon us unawares after the guttural consonants: thus, *can*, he says, is pronounced *cyan*; *get*, *gyet*, *begin*, *begyin*; and even *pot*, *pwot*; *boy*, *bwoy*; *boil*, *bwoile*. This strange corruption is now however, quite abolished, except in some instances already noticed.' (1784:138).

79 Discussing the voicing contrast between obstruents like [b]/[p], [d]/[t] etc. Walker seems to recognise some kind of laryngeal activity differential (1791:§41): 'It is certain the difference between them is very nice; the upper letters [the voiceless set:CJ] seeming only to have a smarter, brisker appulse of the organs than the latter; which may not improperly be distinguished by sharp and flat. The most marking distinction between them will be found to be a sort

of guttural murmur, which precedes the latter letters [the voiced set: cj] when we wish to pronounce them forcibly, but not the former. Thus, if we close the lips, and put the fingers on them to keep them shut, and strive to pronounce the *p*, no sound at all will be heard; but in striving to pronounce the *b* we shall find a murmuring sound from the throat, which seems the commencement of the letter.'

80 Sheridan (1781:35) sees post obstruent aspiration as a characteristic of non-standard pronunciation: 'In pronouncing this letter [*t*] the Irish and other provincials thicken the sound ... for *better*, they say *betther*; for *utter*, *utther*, and so on in all words of that structure.'

81 For detailed lists of [s]/[z] contrasts in nominal and verbal pairs, see Nares (1784:121ff) and Walker (1791:§437). Walker sees the [s] as 'sharp and hissing', Nares the [z] as 'the duller sound of *z*'.

82 For [θ]/[ð] alternants in the period, see Nares (1784:131ff); Walker (1791:§467), and Sheridan (1781:39) who sees the contrast as one of aspiration difference: 'In the beginning of the words, *th* has always its aspirated sound, or is formed wholly by the breath ... it always has its vocal sound when followed by a final mute *e* in the same syllable; as in *bathe*, *breathe*'.

83 The Scot, Adams (1799:153) comments that while English speakers either 'suppress the harsh gutturals, or convert them into single consonants': 'The Scotch retain them; and when they affect to soften them, the articulation or sound resembles that of a deep asthma, or last rattling of a fatal quinsey.'

84 '*GH* in this termination is always silent, as *fight*, *night*, *bought*, *fought*, &c. The only exception is *draught*; which, in poetry, is most frequently rhymed with *caught*, *taught*, &c. but, in prose, is so universally pronounced as if written *draft*, that the poetical sound of it grows uncooth, and is becoming obsolete ... *Drought* (dryness) is vulgarly pronounced *drowth*; it is even written so by Milton; but in this he is not to be imitated, having mistaken the analogy of this word, as well as that of *height*, which he spells *heighth*, and which is frequently so pronounced by the vulgar.' (Walker, 1791:§393).

85 Walker (1791:47:§§401–5) shows a similar set of items with [l] effacement, although he claims that '*l* is silent likewise between *a* and *m* in the same syllable, as *alms*, *balm*, *calm*, *palm*, *psalm*, *qualm*, *shalm*', and the conditions for [l] retention appear to hinge upon the ambisyllabicity condition on the syllable final nasal: 'but when the *m* is detached by the *l* by commencing another syllable, the *l* becomes audible. Thus, though the *l* is mute in *balm*, *palm*, and *psalm*, it is always heard in *bal-my*, *psal-mist*, *psal-mody*, and *psal-mistry*.' Nares (1784:111–12) gives a similar list of [l] effaced items as Walker, although his observation that *shalm* is 'written also *shawm*' may hint at diphthongisation concomitant with vocalisation. He suggests much lexical diffusion influence as well: 'In *fault*, the *l* is sometimes pronounced and sometimes dropped', while in the nominal forms of the items *vault* and *salve* the '*l* is sometimes suppressed' it is never so when they are used as verbs. Adams (1799:152–3) records both ‹caw›/‹ca› and ‹faw›/‹fa› for '*call*' and '*fall*' although his ‹aw› symbol probably represents [ɔ] or [ɒ] rather than a diphthong, with ‹a› realising [ɑ].

86 This phonaesthetic treatment of [r] is, of course, common in the period. Elphinston sees the segment as the 'harsh guttural' and the 'canine guttural' (1764:136;284), stemming from an 'irritated throat' as having an effect on the ear which is 'rough, harsh, horrid and grating' (1765:302). Walker too (1791:50) sees the sound as 'but a jar of the tongue' and 'the most imperfect of all the consonants'.

87 Cf. Kenrick (1784:48): 'the quibble of Abel Drugger in Ben Johnson's *Alchemist*, respecting the last syllable of his name, serving to shew that our ancestors considered it in the sense represented by Perius, who calls it *litera canina*; as

bearing a resemblance to the snarling of a dog'; and Buchanan (1792); '*R*, a palatal; it is expressed by a Concussion, or Quivering of the Extremity of the Tongue, which beating against the Breath as it goes out, produces this horrid dog-like Sound.'

88 Regional varieties of the *r* sound are commented upon by many grammarians in the period, notably Adams (1799:49): '*R*: this letter is singularly rough in the mouths of Normans, and the inhabitants of the county of Durham, who cannot pronounce these words, without a disagreeable rattling of the throat, *Rochus Rex Maurorum*'; and Kenrick (1784:49): 'In the northern parts of England, particularly in and about Newcastle, we find the *r* deprived of its tremulating sound, and aukwardly pronounced somewhat like a *w* or *eau*. *Round the rude rocks the ragged Rachel run*, is a line frequently put into the mouths of the Northumbrians, to expose their incapacity of pronouncing the *r*, as it is sounded by the inhabitants of the southern counties.' cf. Påhlsson (1972).

89 Note too Elphinston's (1786:116;1787:35) comments: 'Dhe same cauz (febel vocality in dhe end) haz made Grocenes assume *r* in (dhe colloquial) *idear* and *windowr*, for *idea* and *window*.' – 'But, nattural az it iz for a low Londoner to shut dhe febel vowel ov *fellow* or *window*, in *fellor* or *windor*.'

90 Walker (1791:48:§409;44;§381) uses the terminology 'finished, complete or perfect sound of *g*' and 'unfinished, incomplete or imperfect sound of *g*' for [ŋ] and [ŋg] respectively. Sheridan (1781:40) has little to say of interest on the [ŋg]/[ŋ] distribution, while Nares' account (1784:113–4) is not unlike Douglas', although (p.103) he does observe: 'In some provincial dialects, this final *g* is more distinctly spoken than it is among correct speakers; which mode of pronunciation sounds as if the *g* were doubled, thus, *sing-g*, *bring-g*.'

91 Nares (1784:108) observes: '*H* is a mere note of aspiration, and is irregular only in being sometimes without effect; as in these initials, *heir, honest, hospital, herb, hour, humour, hostler*. In *herbage* I think it is usually pronounced, though suppressed in *herb*: nor is it dropped in *horal, horary*, &c. though it is in *hour*, the origin of which is the same.' Very similarly, Walker (1791:46): 'This letter is no more than a breathing forcibly before the succeeding vowel is pronounced. At the beginning of words, it is always sounded, except in *heir, heiress, honest, honestly, honour, honourable, herb, herbage, hospital, hostler, hour, humble, humour, humourous, humoursome*'; and Smith (1816:16): '*H* is an aspirate sound; as in *house, horse*; but it is frequently silent, or nearly so; as in *humour, honour*; and an entire neglect of this distinction in the words *eat, heat; art, heart; ail, hail*, both in their primitive and derivative forms ... may possibly produce *ridiculous*, and even *serious* mistakes, through the omission or misapplication of the aspirate *h*.'

92 Adams (1799:153) sees this [r] movement not as some kind of non standard deviation, but as a conscious and deliberate innovation by the Scottish dialect: 'Artful contrivance, not ignorance, has also introduced another singular deformation of our sounds, backed with the usual change, corruption of vowels, and interposition of new letters; as *burn, pin, thistle; brin, prin, thrustle*, &c.' Elphinston (1787:38) records too that: '*Three* must be allowed dhe more ostensible parent ov *thred, thretteen* and *thretty*, dhan ov *third, thirteen*, and *thirty*'; and Walker (1791:50): 'The same transposition of *r* is perceived in the pronunciation of *apron, iron, citron, saffron*, as if written *apurn, irun* [sic], *citurn, saffurn*: nor do I think they can be pronounced otherwise without a disagreeable stiffness.'

A Treatise on the Provincial Dialect of Scotland

Being an attempt to assist persons of that country in
discovering and correcting the defects of their
pronounciation and expression.

Quare, si fieri potest, & verba omnia & vox, hujus alumnum
urbis oleant: ut oratio Romana plane videatur, non
civitate donata.

Quint. Inst. L.

by
SYLVESTER DOUGLAS
(Lord Glenbervie)

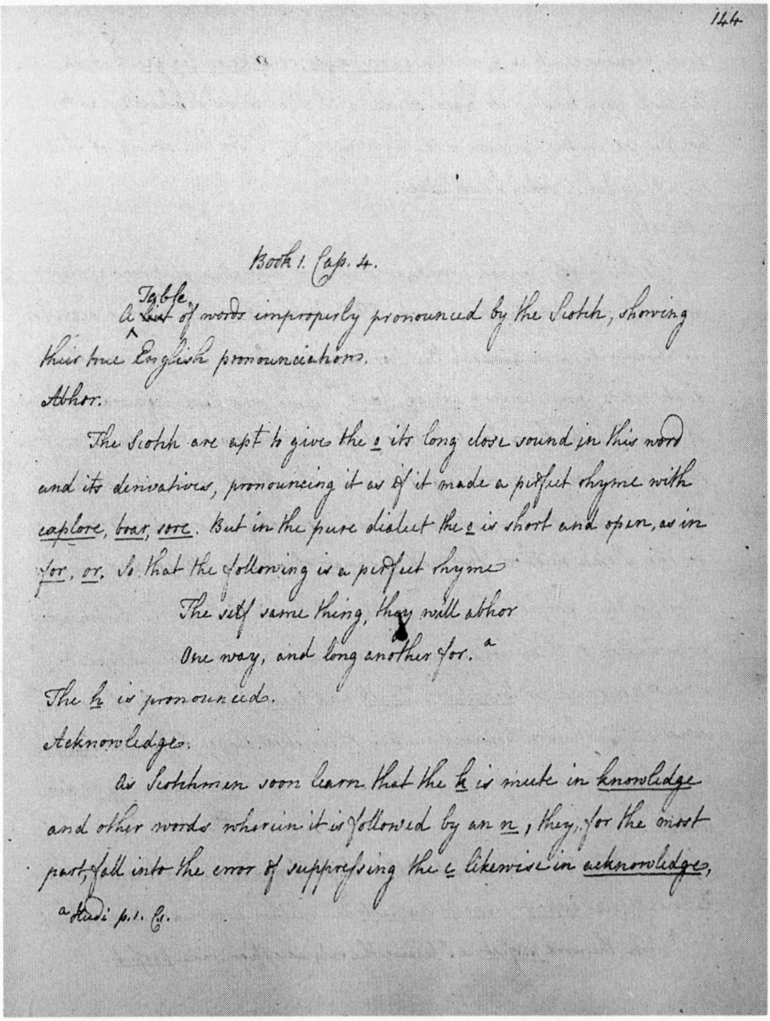

Book 1. Cap. 4.

A Table of words improperly pronounced by the Scotch, showing their true English pronounciations.

Abhor.

The Scotch are apt to give the o its long close sound in this word and its derivatives, pronouncing it as if it made a perfect rhyme with explore, boar, sore. But in the pure dialect the o is short and open, as in for, or. So that the following is a perfect rhyme

    The self same thing, they will abhor
    One way, and long another for. [a]

The h is pronounced.

Acknowledges.

As Scotchmen soon learn that the h is mute in knowledge and other words wherein it is followed by an n, they, for the most part, fall into the error of suppressing the c likewise in acknowledges,

[a] Vid. p. 1. C.

Plate 1: Reproduction of Folio 144 of the Signet Library Signals MS 106.41. (Reproduced by kind permission of the Curators of the Signet Library.)

Introduction

By a provincial dialect is understood, not strictly the dialect peculiar to any particular province or country of the same state, but rather that of a whole country or district where the common language is spoken with a barbarous and unclassical impurity. And it matters not whether there subsists any political connection between such district and that in which the standard idiom prevails, or any dependance of the one upon the other. The French of Languedoc is a provincial dialect of the language spoken[1] at Paris the Capital of the kingdom whereof Languedoc is a part.[2] But the Venetian and Neapolitan are equally considered as provincial dialects of the language common in Italy, although the Republic of Venice, and the Kingdom of Naples, are independent states, which neither are nor ever were provinces of Tuscany, where the pure and standard Italian is spoken. So the inhabitants of Westphalia and Austria make use of provincial dialects of German, of which the Saxon is generally allowed to be the standard. Yet Westphalia and Austria are perfectly independent of Saxony, although they are all members of the same empire. In this sense it is that I mean to treat of the idiom peculiar to Scotland as a provincial dialect of the English language, for in my opinion, (the grounds of which I shall presently explain) there are not sufficient reasons to justify the notion that it is so considered, merely on account of the political connection which now subsists between the two countries. It is unnecessary to mention that Erse, that particular dialect of Celtic, which is the mother tongue of the natives of the Highlands, makes no part of the subject of the following treatise. By a vulgar inaccuracy indeed this is often called Scotch in England; but the Scotch themselves never give it that name; and indeed it is as distinct a language from the dialect of English spoken in Scotland, and which is properly call'd Scotch, as Welsh is different from English, or the Patois, from the French, of Languedoc.

The Union of England and Scotland did not merely[3] give to the two nations[4] the same political constitution, and one common legislature. London thereby became the Metropolis of both countries. The laws by which the latter was to be governed as well as the former, were enacted in that Capital, by an assembly, of which the Scotch representatives made a very small part. The ultimate appeal in all law-suits was removed from Scotland. From the accession of James

1st to the crown of England until the reign of Queen Ann, Edinburgh had not only been the seat of Legislature, but also of an executive government, subordinate indeed, but such as bestowed on it in some degree the appearance of a court, and of the Capital of a Kingdom. After the Union, it sunk from that distinction, and became, at most, the first provincial town of Great Britain. These are often looked upon[5] as the chief causes which completely established the English dialect of our language as the standard of what is considered as classical, whether in composition or discourse. This effect indeed is supposed to have been already produced in some degree by the less perfect Union of the crowns, at the beginning of the last century. If the two kingdoms had continued as [6] distinct, as they had been[7] till the death of Queen Elizabeth, it has been thought probable, that two dialects might gradually have been formed, bearing that sort of relation to each other which subsisted between those of ancient Greece: that we might have possessed classical Authors in both: that the peculiarities of the Scotch idiom would not have been considered as defects and barbarisms at London, any more than those of the Ionic dialect were at Athens regarded as blemishes in the writings of Herodotus and Homer. But I question whether, in the history of languages, another instance is to be found, similar to that of the Greek dialects. Nor will the independence of the different states of Greece be sufficient to explain this singularity. It is true that as the various colonies and governments both in ancient Italy, and in the more distant provinces of the Roman empire into which the Latin tongue was introduced, were subordinate to Rome, the centre of power and eloquence, it was natural that in that tongue, *inter dominæ fastidia Romæ*, every deviation from the dialect of the Metropolis should be thought vicious and inelegant. The same observation applies to some of the modern languages, particularly the French.[8] But those states of Italy of which we have made mention[9] are as independent of one another as the Greek Republics were. Tasso's *Jerusalem deliver'd* has been translated into all the different dialects of Italy; In Venice the idiom of the country is spoken in the Senate and at the bar; the Neapolitan is said to be the only sort of Italian in which the present sovereign of Naples can express himself; Yet there is no Venetian, nor Lombard, nor Neapolitan who will say that the language of Pantaloon[10] or Harlequin, or the Dottore, or Tartaglio is to be viewed in the same light with the Ionic and Doric dialects of Greek. Those personages are introduced on the stage at Venice, Bergamo,[11] and Naples, and their particular Words, phrases and pronounciation, are there considered as adding to the buffoonery and ridicule of their characters, as well as at Rome or Florence. Tasso was a Neapolitan, and had long resided in Lombardy; Ariosto a Lombard;

Cardinal Bembo a Venetian. Yet they all employed the Tuscan dialect in their writings; and the enemies of the divine author of the *Gierusalemme Liberata* Jerusalem delivered endeavoured to detect him in the use of Lombard expressions, knowing that whatever was not Tuscan in his style must be and acknowledged to be impure and barbarous.[12]

The German language has of late merited the attention of all the lovers of polite literature in the different countries of Europe. Haller's genius as a poet was as sublime, as his learning and industry as an anatomist were extensive. Gellert is the successful rival of Phædrus and La Fontaine, Gesner of Virgil, Klopstock of Milton, Rabner of Swift. Have these celebrated writers, the natives and inhabitants of different [13] parts of Germany and Switzerland widely distant from each other[14] made use of the[15] idioms peculiar to the several countries where they were born and lived? No; their works are all composed in the only classical dialect of their language; and what renders the fact more striking and more difficult to explain is, that this classical dialect is not spoken at Vienna, which has so long been the seat of the Imperial Court: The worst of all the provincial dialects prevails in that Capital: But at Leipzig and Dresden, in Saxony, a state of the second order in the empire, and which does not seem entitled from its power, opulence, or elegance, to serve in any respect[16] as the rule and standard for its neighbours. Some other cause must therefore be assign'd for this peculiar property of the Greek tongue, besides the independency of the Grecian republics; and we cannot infer, from that single example, contradicted by so many others, that, if Scotland had not been incorporated with England, its idiom would have become classical, instead of being reckoned, (as I am inclined to think it always was from the days of Gawin Douglas downwards, and as it now certainly is) a provincial and vicious dialect of English.

There are I believe few natives of North-Britain, who have had occasion either to visit or reside in this country, that have not learned by experience the disadvantages which accompany their idiom and pronounciation. I appeal especially to those whose professions or situations oblige them to speak in public. In the pulpit, at the bar, or in parliament, a provincial phrase sullies the lustre of the brightest eloquence, and the most forcible reasoning loses half its effect when disguised in the awkwardness of a provincial dress. A certain cast of burlesque is thereby communicated from the manner of the speaker to his matter, and the misapplication or erroneous pronounciation of some particular word often produces a ludicrous ambiguity, which is not only fatal to his whole argument, but becomes the subject of an anecdote, and passing from mouth to mouth, stamps on himself a lasting ridicule, let his abilities in his station be never so respectable. I would, if it were proper, or necessary, produce examples[17] in proof of this assertion. The recollection of every reader will probably furnish him with instances,[18] that have fallen within his own observation. In short the effect is the same, though perhaps not quite so striking, as when a foreigner mutilates a language of which he is not completely master. This never fails to excite laughter in all countries, or if the French have a right to be considered as an exception to the universality of the observation, it is not that they do not feel the ridicule as strongly as other nations, when a stranger, according to their own [19]expression, [20]*flays their language alive*, but because from habit and education they acquire a greater controul over the muscles of their countenance. While the oppressive administration of Cardinal Mazarine rendered him the object of universal hatred; he was also an object of general ridicule from the blunders which as a foreigner, he often committed in the pronounciation of the French language.

But although it must be the serious aim of all Scotchmen of liberal education, and liberal pursuits, to divest themselves of the barbarisms of their native dialect, yet it is not difficult to assign the reasons why no successful attempt has hitherto been made to assist them in this design.

1. Minute discussions concerning pronounciation, or phraseology, are of a dry and forbidding nature. The principles of grammar itself, and the nature of language, though connected with some of the most curious and interesting branches of philosophy both natural and metaphysical, have in them I know not what which disinclines from either reading or writing about them. The ablest writers seem to be the best fitted for such enquiries: But the Poet or Historian, who commands all the power, and all the beauty[21] of style, finds in general as little entertainment in analysing the structure and component parts of language, the instrument of his art, as a painter or statuary would in examining the chemical ingredients of colours, or the natural history of marble.

2. The task of ascertaining and correcting the peculiarities of provincial pronounciation is as difficult as it is uninviting. If we suppose a person perfectly acquainted with all the vices of the Scotch, and perfectly master of the proper English pronounciation how is he to convey his knowledge to the others by the eyes? Can the shades and gradations of sound be painted? Or what adequate means can he employ to communicate a just idea of two different sounds which two different sets of men represent by the very same combination of letters?

3. Neither will it appear an easier matter to enumerate all the provincial singularities of diction; and to translate them into the equivalent expressions in the proper dialect. An Englishman when he

hears or reads a phrase which is not English discovers it immediately. One who is not fit to write an essay for the corner of a newspaper will detect such a blemish in a Hume, a Robertson or a Beattie. But an Englishman has no inducement to collect together, and form a catalogue of such barbarisms. Nor has he that experience which can enable him to discriminate such as may be peculiar to the Scotch dialect from others. A Scotchman, on the other hand, must be often at a loss to assign the English equivalent, and frequently may only substitute one barbarism for another. Many phrases, from false analogies, or the abuse of general rules, will appear to him provincial which in truth are not so; and others, which are, he will be unable to discover, or will not reject, because supported by the authority of some obscure or obsolete English author. Yet none of these reasons have detered me from the present attempt. They will be my apology if I fail, and where I fail. The following pages are the fruit of an uninterrupted attention and enquiry of many years. If they answer my wishes, I shall perhaps be entitled to the praise of having rendered an useful, though not a brilliant, service to my Countrymen.

Let it be understood[22] however that it is by no means my intention to observe upon[23] all the grosser barbarisms of the vulgar Scotch jargon. This would be an useless and an endless labour. I only mean to treat expressly of the impurities which generally stick with those whose language has already been in a great degree refined from the provincial dross, by frequenting English company, and studying the great masters of the English tongue in their writings: Of those *vestigia ruris* which are apt to remain so long; which scarce any of our most admired authors are entirely free from in their compositions; which, after the age of manhood, only one person in my experience has so got rid of in speech that the most critical ear cannot discover his country from his expression or pronounciation.

It is I hope [24] unnecessary to make any apology for the digressions which may occur in this work, or the length and number of the citations and illustrations. They will be of the same service to the reader as they have been to me. They will relieve his attention; and in some measure adorn the natural barrenness of the subject. He surely is not deserving of much censure, who having a journey to perform through a tedious and irksome road, deviates sometimes, though perhaps on slight pretences, to the right or left, in order to visit some beautiful structure or to enjoy the view of a fine landscape.

DIVISION OF THE SUBJECT

A provincial dialect is constituted by 1. A defective pronounciation. 2. A vicious phraseology. But pronounciation may be defective in three different respects; *viz.* 1. By a faulty manner of uttering the letters[25] and syllables of which certain words are composed. 2. By placing the accent improperly in particular words. 3. By what is called the provincial tone, brogue, or accent. And, in like manner, a vicious phraseology may also manifest itself in three ways; namely. 1. By the use of barbarous words not admitted into the pure dialect. 2. By the use of classical words in improper senses. 3. By the combination of words into barbarous and unclassical phrases. Each of these six heads furnishes in the following treatise the subject of a separate book.

Book 1

Of the Provincial Method of pronouncing the letters and syllables of certain words

Cap. 1

Of Articulate sounds, and orthography in general

Language is the peculiar[26] gift of Man. By this attribute the author of his being has raised him to a very distinguished eminence above all other animals; even those who approach the nearest to the confines of human nature. And though certain[27] philosophers have so far espoused the cause of some of the brute creation, as to express themselves with a kind of peevish resentment at their being treated as our inferiors, yet the superiority will appear very striking to any one who considers, on the one hand, the advantages we derive from the communications of speech, and, on the other, the physical inaptitude in the organs of all other animals, for the formation of articulate sounds. There is nothing perhaps more curious to a mind fond of speculation, nor whose origin seems more to triumph over the penetration of human researches, than that astonishing convention by which mankind have agreed from the earliest ages, in all countries, and in every state of society, to employ certain sounds, called words, as the signs of things to which they have not, in nature, the most distant relation. The sounds of βιβλιον, *Liber*, *Book*, have as little relation to the things so called as to any other object whatever; as little as the colour called Red, has to the taste of sugar. Yet the word βιβλιον was never heard by a Greek, *Liber* by a Roman, nor *Book* by an Englishman, without raising in his mind, if he attended to it, the idea of the thing. Written language is little less wonderful than speech. For what is the natural connection[28] between the sound of *book* or the thing itself, and that combination of figures or characters which, when presented to the eye, raises in the mind, either the idea of that sound, and, indirectly by the intervention of such idea of the sound, the idea of the thing itself, or directly (as it often does) the idea of the thing. If, in the same language, the same idea were always represented by the same sound, and such sound were never em-ployed as the sign of any other idea, inaccuracy of expression would be a thing unknown, and Logomachy, to which head the greater part of all controversy is reducible, would be at an end.[29] In like manner, if the same sound were always represented by the same character, or combination of characters, and such characters or combinations of characters never represented any other sound, false or provincial pronounciation would not exist. Uniformity in the former respect would indeed be a matter of much more important advantage than in the latter. It is not of very essential consequence perhaps whether of two Judges one in pronouncing the word 'Heir' uses the aspirate, and the other not, but it is very essential to the administration of justice, that[30] they should both employ it as the sign of the same idea. It is impossible for any person who attempts a scientific[31] discussion of any subject not sensibly to feel the inconvenience arising from the ambiguous and equivocal use of words. A nice and subtle multiplication of distinctions, divisions, and subdivisions, seems to have been the taste of the Philosophers of Greece and Rome. But true logical accuracy has been more pursued by the moderns. Hence it is that almost every modern book of science abounds with complaints of this ambiguity of language. Hence too many ingenious projects have been offered to remove this stumbling block out of the way[32] of philosophy. But all such projects hitherto have failed. Nor would it be difficult to show (were this the place for a disquisition of that sort) that, in consequence of the natural propensities of the mind of man, they always must prove abortive. The philosopher's language is, I am afraid, as chimerical a pursuit as the philosopher's stone.

The manner of expressing the two different sort of signs, which I have explained *viz* the audible, and written, affords an apposite and striking example of the ambiguity of language. Letter, syllable, word, are terms used indifferently either for the elementary or combined sounds of which audible language is comprised, or for the elementary or combined characters which constitute written language. The figure (*a*) is called a letter. So is the sound which that figure represents. This combination of four letters (*Book*) is called a word. So is the compound sound which it represents. Having no authority to supply this sterility of language I must like others submit to the inconvenience resulting from it. I must call both elementary sounds and elementary characters by the name of letters, and apply the term of word sometimes to the audible or direct sometimes to the written or indirect signs of ideas. By pointing out the ambiguities I have put the reader on his guard, and the context will always indicate when I use the terms in the one sense, and when in the other. Let me only add that, in this place, we have little or nothing to do with written words as the signs either mediate, or immediate, of ideas; but are merely to consider them, as well as their component parts the elementary characters, in the light of the representation of sound.

Language is composed of sentences; Sentences of words; words of one or more syllables; syllables of one or more letters. Letters are commonly divided into Vowells and consonants. The first are such as can be uttered by themselves. Consonants, as the name imports, can only be pronounced along with Vowells. Indeed pure consonants such as *p*, for example, or *t*, are not properly sounds themselves, but certain modes of commencing or terminating sound. You may begin, or you may close, the sound of *a* or *o*, with *t*, but you cannot utter *t* unaccompanied with a vowel. Hence in order to give names to each of the different consonants it has been necessary to compose those names of that particular consonant together with one of the vowels, as *Be, ce, de, Ge*. There is a third species of letters which hold a middle place between the vowells and perfect consonants, though generally ranked with the latter, but distinguished by the appellation of[33] semivowells. Such for example are the *f, l, m, s*. These, though they cannot, by themselves be uttered so clearly and audibly as the vowells, are yet capable of solitary pronounciation. Like the vowells, they may be protracted sensibly in the ear, either in singing or speaking, for any length of time. Some of them, which possess the last mentioned quality in a higher degree than the others, are on that account called liquids. The perfect consonants at the end of a syllable terminate the sound instantly. If we try to continue it the ear hears nothing farther, and the speaker perceives that in his ineffectual efforts he only retains by a certain muscular exertion,[34] his lips, teeth, tongue, or throat, in a particular position, and forces his breath outwards, without suffering it to pass, so as to compleat the act of expiration. In the following pages however it will be found con-venient to speak of consonantal, as opposed to vocal sounds, and to lead the mind to contemplate (though the senses cannot perceive) the consonants in themselves abstracted from all accompanying vowells.

Articulate sound, as distinguished from the song of birds, the cry of animals, or the scream of human passions, seems chiefly to depend on the interposition of the consonants. In the most diversified warblings of the [35]Lark and Nightingale we do not perceive any thing of that nature; and in Parrots, Starlings, and Canary Birds, that have learned to counterfeit the speech of men, it is in this respect that the imitation is most obviously deficient. I am not ignorant that a neat resemblance to some single consonant may be discover'd in the peculiar cries of certain animals, nor have there been wanting speculative enquirers into the origin of language, who have conjectured that it was by the imitation of those animals that such consonants were first adapted into the composition of human speech. That we learned the *b*, from sheep, the *m*, from oxen, the *r* from dogs, the *s* from serpents, the *th* from geese. But be that as it may, the utterance of these different consonants by those animals is very incomplete; and as none of them possess this sort of resemblance to above one consonant, they may be said to have been stopt short by nature at the very threshold of articulation. That the consonants have the principal share in distinct articulation, which constitutes as it were the essence of language, may be proved by the following experiment. Let us take a sentence in any language, as English, for instance the following,

> Curst be that verse, how well so e'er it flow
> That tends to make one worthy man my foe,[36]

and in every word let us change the vowels, substituting *e*, for *u* in the first, *o* for *e*, in the second, and so forth. We shall find that the words so metamorphosed will still continue tolerably intelligible to any person who understands the language. If on the contrary you should leave the vowells as they are, and alter the consonants it would be absolutely impossible to decipher the meaning. Not that the differences of vocal sounds have not their share in producing distinct articulation. It is possible to suppose a kind of language formed entirely of those ingredients, without any mixture of consonants. But such a language would be as defective, from a want of a sufficient discrimination of the different words, as most of the northern Teutonic dialects are, from the harsh, unsonorous, and difficult, pronounciation occasioned by too great a proportion of consonants. The most distinct and articulate words, and at the same time the most easy to pronounce, are those composed of single consonants and single vowels alternately succeeding one another, especially if the same vowell is not repeated in two adjoining syllables. Such are the following, φιλοτησις, solitudo, amicale, pathetique, titular.

It will appear evident, on an attentive consideration of the subject, that, to constitute a complete and rational alphabet, or series of written characters, in any language, there ought to be: 1. A distinct mark for every distinct vocal sound in the language, and the same for every simple consonant.[37] 2. There should be no synonymous letters (if they may be so called) that is[38] the same vocal sound, or consonant should never be represented in different words, sometimes by one character, sometimes by another. 3. Single characters should in no case be used for a combination of two or more vocal sounds (which is what is properly called a diphthong).[39] Or of two or more consonants. 4. A combination of two or more characters should never represent a simple vocal sound, or a single consonant. 5. There should be no characters in the written which correspond to nothing in the audible language; In other words, there should be no mute letters. Yet, though the propriety of these rules is unquestionable, there never has existed hitherto a language in which such an alphabet, and such a plan of orthography, have been observed. The Italians, by the modern improvements they have made, have brought their orthography[40] nearer to perfection, than any other with which I am acquainted; and this is one of the reasons why the pronounciation of Italian is so easily acquired by foreigners. Nevertheless it would not be a difficult task to point out deviations from most of the rules just mentioned even in the present mode of writing that language. We are, and, from the nature of the thing, must ever continue, extremely in the dark concerning the pronounciation of the Greek and Latin, but we may gather from some circumstances mentioned by ancient grammarians, that the Romans[41] were particularly inaccurate in the use of vocal characters. Priscian tells us that they pronounced the *a* in ten different ways. And though the Greek alphabet was more copious in the signs of vocal sound than either the Latin, or any of the modern European tongues, we have no reason to consider[42] that as affording a complete model of rational orthography. This will be manifest to anyone who reflects on their Ψ, Ξ and Z which are single characters that undoubtedly represent combinations of two consonants. The learned Haller justly observes that the German orthography is more uniform and accurate than that of most other modern nations, and considers this as the reason why Amman the famous teacher of dumb people, never made use of any other, and why his writings on that curious subject are more perspicuous and intelligible than those of Popham, Holder, and other Englishmen. The French orthography is extremely imperfect. It particularly abounds with mute letters, and with compound characters to represent simple sounds. But the most imperfect beyond question, is our own. How much it errs against every one of the five rules or canons I have mentioned may be rendered evident by a few examples.

1. The ear immediately perceives three different vocal sounds in the words, *all*, *pat*, and the first syllable of the word, *patriot*, yet these three different sounds are represented by one and the same character. The two names *Caius*, and *Cæsar*, begin with two different consonants in audible language, yet in writing the first character of both is the same.

2. The vocal sound in *Bud*[43] and *glove* is the same, but in the first word it is represented by *u*, in the other by *o*. The consonant at the beginning of *City*, and of *Sister* is to the ear the same, but it is represented to the eye by the two different figures, *C*, and *S*.

3. In the words *sigh*, and, the first syllable of the word *Unity*,[44] *Lute*, the vocal part is a compound sound, consisting of a combination, in the first of these words[45] of the two simple vowels, commonly represented by the characters *a*, and *e*, (or the Italian, French, German, and Scotch i) in the second, of the same sound of *e*, and that represented by the Italian, German, and Scotch *u*, or the English *u* in *put*, *pull*, and other words of that sort. Yet there is but one vocal character both in *sigh*, and the first syllable of *Unity*,[46] *Lute*. In *expect* and *auxiliary* the simple character *x* represents the combinations of

those two consonants to which the characters *ks* and *gs* generally correspond.

4. The instances where a combination of more than one vocal character is employed as the sign of a simple vocal sound are innumerable. In 1. *Bear, gain.* 2. *Spear, sneer.* 3. *Soul, Goal.* 4. *moon.* The vocal sounds represented by *ea*, and *ai*, *ea*, and *ee*, *ou* and *oa*, and by *oo*, are simple, and the same of which the signs on other occasions, are 1. *a*, as in *bare.* 2. *e*, as in *here*, 3. *o*, as in *roll*, 4. *u* as in *pull*. In like manner, in the words *Philosopher, thought, shatter*, the consonant is a simple one which the combined characters of *Ph*, *Th*, and *Sh* are employed to represent. 5. At the end of words the *e* is almost always a mute vocal character,[47] and the consonantal marks *g*, *k*, and *gh* are not the representatives of any consonantal[48] sound in the words *gnaw, know, knight, sigh, sight*.

The probability that such an alphabet and orthography as I have described is what in practice will never take place may be fairly inferred, both from the experience of what has hitherto happened and also, from the known caprice of mankind, in making continual variations in the pronounciation of words. To regulate or restrain this caprice is beyond the efforts of any authority, were it to be thought, in any country, a proper subject for the exertion of authority. And if this caprice continue daily to operate, unless a society of scholars were appointed to alter and adapt the written to the changes introduced into the audible[49] language, the sounds represented by the same characters must perpetually fluctuate and vary. But the fluctuations in pronounciation have their limits.[50] No man will seriously doubt but that the *o* and *a* of the Romans were pronounced by them two thousand years ago, in a manner much more resembling the sounds which we represent by these characters, than those represented now by *i* and *e*. It can admit of as little doubt that a systematical alphabet and orthography would tend greatly to render those limits much narrower. To contrive such an alphabet is therefore a speculation not unworthy of learning or genius; and if there is any where that sort of authority which can introduce[51] into general use all or part of the improvements a well directed consideration of the subject might suggest, no good reason can be given why it should not be attempted. Indeed the numerous and judicious alterations which have been made from time to time in Italian and French orthography, by the Academia della Crusca, and the French Academy, are sufficient to demonstrate that such improvements are both practical and advisable. To say that all old books would thereby be rendered useless,[52] is to assert that the original manuscripts of Dante and Boccace, and the first editions of Corneille and Racine, are unintelligible, and of no value. And to those who think improvement is not to be attempted, because perfection cannot be attained Horace has given the following humorous, but just answer.

Non possis oculo quantum contendere Lynceus;
Non tamen idcirco contemnas lippus incengi.

What in some measure, deserves the ridicule with which it has been treated, is the vain endeavour of some individuals to subvert by their arguments, or example, the whole established orthography of a language, and substitute in its room, together with a set of new characters, a mode of spelling entirely different from general usage. Should such characters and spelling happen to possess every imaginable advantage, the attempt merits the epithet of absurd, because a very slight insight into human nature might have shown the contriver that success was not to be expected. A few years ago some whimsical person imagined an innovation in the figures and characters of playing cards, not unlike the projects of those knights errant in orthography of whom I have been speaking; And with similar success. Shocked with the unmeaning marks, and grotesque images now in use, so little correspondent to the names they bear; He had engravings of Kings, Queens, Knights, hearts, *swords*, ([53]*spade* being a corruption of the Spanish or Italian word *spada*) well executed, and made up in packs for sale, [54] persuaded that in this gaming age so great a refinement in the very instruments of pleasure, would be immediately and universally adopted. But the event [55]disappointed his hopes for the old gothic dawbings still maintain their ground, and all this gentleman's elegant assortment has been left in obscurity in the corner of some stationers lumber room. Indeed in orthography one single alteration has often been attempted in vain by persons of the greatest power in the political and of the greatest weight in the literary worlds. The Emperor Claudius was not able to prevail on his subjects to make use of the Digamma in Latin.[56] Trissino in the 15th Century notwithstanding his reputation was high as a poet, a critic, and grammarian, endeavoured with as little success to introduce the *w* and *n* into Italian, though he had this improvement so much at heart, as to write to Clement VII to solicit the assistance of his authority and example. In our time Voltaire,[57] whose universal genius had enabled him to establish a sort of despotism in French literature, has prevailed on so few of his countrymen to substitute *ai* for *oi*, in *avoient, êtoil* &c. that there is very little probability in the practice becoming general. Lord Shaftesbury (if I am not mistaken), Hughes the editor of Spenser, and some others, rejected the *e* at the end of *judge, hedge*, and such words. Dr Middleton changed *claim, disclaim*, &c, to *clame, disclame*; But they have made no converts among subsequent writers. Such petty and partial alterations are truly ridiculous. Our great Lexicographer has spoken of them with a degree of cynical irony which they undoubtedly[58] merit. Yet (so difficult is it for the wisest men to be always consistent) even he has felt the itch of innovation in some instances. *Cesar*, *Edipus*, and *skeptick*, are by him substituted for *Cæsar*, *Œdipus*, and *sceptick*; nor has he been more fortunate in the number of his prosylites, than the others who have been just mentioned.

If there is so frequently a diversity of sounds, in one and the same language, represented, in the manner we have seen, by the same character, such diversity is much more frequent and remarkable among the different languages in which the same alphabet is in use. To exemplify what I mean, the *u* never represents the same vocal sound in French, as in English and Italian; nor does it in Italian ever represent the diphthong which is its more common sound with us. There is often not less diversity in this respect between the classical and provincial dialects of the same tongue. Thus *u*, *e*, and *i* in Scotland are scarcely ever employed as the signs of the same sounds as in this country. This is one source of the difficulty with which foreigners and provincials acquire the true pronounciation of any language. A Frenchman who from his earliest attempts to read[59] has been accustomed to consider *ou* as representing the simple sound of which *u* is always the sign in Italian, and *oo* generally in English, scarcely ever acquires a sufficient readiness in pronouncing it as we do in *our*. The ideas of the other sound and of these two combined characters are so firmly united in his mind, that he cannot, without a constant and persevering attention, habituate himself to this new association. By a similar habit, the idea of the *a* in the word *patriot* is associated in Scotland with the idea of the English sound in that character in *Father*, *fastidious*, &c. Hence it is not without some difficulty that a Scotchman can accustom himself to give it the proper sound in that word, notwithstanding he has always been used to pronounce it in that very manner in several others, as *pare*, *hasty* &c. Or, to mention another instance, how long is it before a Scotchman, when he [60]begins to correct the vices of his pronounciation, acquires the habitual practice of giving the proper sound to the *i*, in *idea*. Not that his organs are not all unqualified for uttering that sound, which they do with great facility in the Greek particle και, or in the words *fire*, *mire*, &c, but because, in *idea*, and a great many other words in his own dialect,[61] he has considered the *i* as the sign of that vowel which in English is commonly expressed by *ee* or *ea*. It may be doubted whether there ever was a language which comprehended all the simple vowels, all the diphthongal combinations, and all the consonantal modifications, which the human organs are capable of forming. In one, some of them are wanting; In another, others. The simple vowel represented by *u* in French is not found in the pure dialects of the English or Italian. The German and Dutch guttural and aspirated *g* is wanting both in French, and English. The semivowel of which *th* is the sign is almost peculiar to us. In this respect, likewise, there is frequently a difference of the same sort between the pure and provincial dialects of the same language. Here then we have a second, but a much more insurmountable obstacle in the way of foreigners and provincials. Of sounds which do not at all enter into the composition of our[62] own language and dialect we often find it impossible to catch the true pronounciation, at least after our organs have grown rigid, as it were, in that mould in which they have been cast by the constant use of our mother tongue. How few Englishmen, or Tuscans can the most experienced and able French master boast of having taught to pronounce his vernacular *u*; if they were men before they attempted to learn it? How few foreigners have ever attained to the proper pronounciation of our *th*? Not that it requires a more difficult exertion of the instruments of speech than many of their own letters. They indeed are apt to ascribe the difficulty to some peculiar harshness in this consonant. But this is very erroneous inference.[63] To an ear accustomed to it, there is something peculiarly mellow in its softer sound (for it has two) as in *thou*, and *though*. Another instance or two will serve to demonstrate the general fallacy of such conclusions. The guttural pronounciation of *ch*, and *gh* which still obtains in Scotland cannot be attained by the modern English. This is vulgarly thought to arise from the harshness of this letter,[64] to which the more delicate organs of the southern inhabitants of the Island are not by nature adapted. But those who assign that reason do not know, or do not consider, that the Tuscans, whose throats are at least of as delicate a structure, and their language as musical, as those of this country, have the same or nearly the same sound in their vicious manner of pronouncing the *c* before *a*, *o*, or *u*, and which seems to resemble that taken notice of by Catullus as a disagreeable singularity in the speech[65] of one Arrius.

Chommoda dicebat, siquando Commoda vellet
Dicere . . .[66]

The French sound *ch* as *sh* is pronounced by us, or *sc* before *i* and *e* by the Italians, and many of them consider our pronounciation of it in *choose*, *cherry* &c as barbarous and uncouth merely because, not being found in their language, that consonantal combination of the *t* and their *ch* is to their organs extremely difficult or unattainable. Yet in Italy, the country of music, and melodious language, no sound is more familiar to the voice and ear of the inhabitants than this, the *c* being always so pronounced in[67] that country, when it is followed by *e* or *i*. It is a general observation, confirmed by daily experience, that the more northern nations fall much more easily into the pronunciation of the southern language, than theirs are acquired by the natives of the south. Russians, Danes, Swedes, Poles, Germans, Scotch, and even English do often attain to a very correct pronounciation of French and Italian. The French and Italians hardly ever arrive at any degree of perfection in speaking the languages of those nations. The chief reason of which undoubted fact I take to be, that almost all the French and Italian sounds may be found in the northern tongues, but mixed with many others peculiar to those languages, and to which, therefore, the French and Italian organs of speech have not been accustomed.

Now, to bring this general enquiry, into the nature and causes of diversity of orthography and pronounciation, home to the more immediate subject of this treatise, I believe it will appear to every attentive observer of the Scotch pronounciation, that there is scarcely a single vocal or diphthongal sound, or consonant, in English, which is not also to be found in Scotch. The difference between the two dialects (with regard to that head to which this [68]part of our work is dedicated) consists in this. – That the same sound is seldom given by the Scotch and English to the vowels (and sometimes though not so generally, not to the consonants) of the same word; and that the Scotch have sounds in theirs not to be met with in the English dialect. From these premises two conclusions naturally follow, neither of which would have been easily admitted either by the English or Scotch reader if they had been abruptly announced. The first, that a Scotchman, at any time of life, may be taught, or may teach himself, the true English pronounciation of the letters, and syllables, of every word in the language. The second, that the proper instructions for this purpose, may be communicated in writing, without the interpretation of oral information or illustration. [69]A persuasion of the truth of the second of these propositions, has induced me to undertake this first branch of the present treatise, the least entertaining no doubt to me in the execution, and to others in the perusal; but which, should it answer the end proposed, will be found perhaps of more general utility than any of the others. The method I mean to pursue is so simple that it may be explained in the compass of a very few lines. Whenever one or more letters whether vowels or consonants are improperly pronounced in any given word in the Scotch dialect, I shall mention some other word in which such letter, or letters, have the true classical sound given to them, even by the Scotch. This will be a distinct, unequivocal, and infallible criterion to guide the Scotch reader to the just pronounciation of the word in question. [70]An example will put the matter out of all doubt. The Scotch make the proper name of *Cain*, a word of two syllables; and pronounce the *a* as the English do in [71]*Father*. If I mention that it is only a word of one syllable, and that the *ai* has the same sound as in *hair, pair, stain*, it is impossible for any man who reads such a rule, to have the smallest difficulty in discovering the true pronounciation. But if any assistance can be given to the memory so as to put it in the power of the reader to retain also with some degree of facility what he learns with ease, a still greater advantage will be gained. This sort of assistance I think may be procured by the selection of passages from our best poets, where the word whose pronounciation is to be ascertained happens to form a *perfect* rhyme with some other word which the Scotch and English pronounce in the same manner. Thus *complain* (by all but the most illiterate Scotch, or those who have the silly affectation of adhering to the grossest particularities of their provincial dialect) is pronounced in Scotland as in England. If then a couplet can be found where this word is made to rhyme to *Cain*, which happens to be the case in the following lines in the *Essay on Man*

> We just as wisely might of heav'n complain
> That righteous Abel was destroyed by Cain.

By telling the reader that this is a perfect rhyme, I not only give him as clear an idea of the true pronounciation of the word as by the former reference to *hair, pair, stain*, but also supply him with a couplet of verses, easily retained, which will serve him instead of what is called a *memoria technica* whenever he has occasion to pronounce the word. The only objection that can arise, as it seems to me, to this plan is this; that I, a Scotchman, may be very liable to mistake the true English pronounciation of many words. To this I can only answer that I have taken all the pains in my power to guard against errors of this sort. I have not only listened,[72] and with the utmost attention, to the pronounciation of every word whose proper sound I have attempted to ascertain, in the mouths of English persons of both sexes, who are acknowledged to speak with propriety: But I have also submitted what I have written as well in this as in the subsequent parts of my work to the perusal and correction of [73]several persons of a like description.[74] Still however I will not flatter myself but that some mistaken or erroneous pronounciations are inserted. In which case the worst that can happen will be, that the reader, among a great number of right rules, will be misled, in a few instances, where he will be taught to substitute one improper method of sounding some particular word or syllable, in the room of another. Let me however give him one caution. Not hastily to reject any of the pronounciations I shall point out merely because [75]some Englishman of his acquaintance may disapprove of them. This Englishman may be a person infected, himself, with the defects either of some county dialect, or of the vulgar idiom of the city of London.[76] He may be addicted to a particular system in the method of pronouncing certain words, not consonant to general usage; a fault too common with the professed masters of the art of reading. He may be one who takes his model only from the more solemn manner of the pulpit or the theatre, and who (when they differ from that model) considers the colloquial modes of pronounciation as vicious. In such a case, without entering into the question which is to be prefered, I shall only remark, that a Scotchman will make a good bargain who exchanges his own barbarous method of sounding any particular word, either for the one, or the other.

To arrange the false pronounciation of Scotland under heads and classes, according to any system of general rules, is what I not only have not attempted, but have purposely avoided. I have already made the reader observe how often the English represent the same sound, in different words, by different characters, and again, different sounds by the same characters. To endeavour to investigate the laws by which this unaccountable caprice may be supposed to be directed would savour of whim and extravagance; And would have besides this Disadvantage, that, when the system was once formed, the parental affection which all system makers feel to a certain degree, would naturally incline me, if it did not always accommodate itself easily to certain unlucky instances of anomalous pronounciation, to find some ingenious reason for imposing on the learner, instead of the true [77]sound, one more accordant with the pre established rules. It were well for philosophy and science if this effect of the love of system had never shown itself in [78]matters of infinitely greater importance than our present subject. To aim at the discovery of general rules is indeed extremely natural. It is an errour Scotchmen are continually running into, when they are trying, by their own observation, to correct the faults of their dialect. But I will venture to affirm that all that have ever yet been laid down for the proper method of pronouncing English, have produced ten false pronounciations for one just one.[79] I have therefore adopted the less scientific, but more useful plan, of arranging all the false pronounciations which come within my design in alphabetical order. There would have been a propriety perhaps in adapting the arrangement to the letters whose sound was to be ascertained; but it was easier to myself, and will be more convenient for the purpose of consulting the book for the pronounciation of particular words, to class them according to the initial letters. It still remains, before I proceed to this catalogue, to lay before my readers some observations on the powers and different sounds of the several letters of which our alphabet is composed, both in our own, and some of the more popular languages of the continent, and to subjoin to these some others, on the subject of rhyme. The first will be of considerable service by accustoming the mind to contemplate and distinguish, and the organs of speech to render with precision, the several varieties and gradations of articulate sound. The second will fix the attention on what, in time, might be rendered the [80]instrument of arresting, in some measure, the flitting, and evanescent nature of pronounciation; and might furnish the best helps of any towards conveying by the eyes, lessons meant for the use of the voice and ear.

Cap. 2d

Observations on the Alphabet

A

This vowel is not placed by chance at the beginning of every alphabet. The sound it represents in the word *Father*, *rather*, is, of all others, of the easiest utterance. This is however not its most common sound in the [81]pure dialect of our language; but that which both the Scotch and English give to it in the words *pare*, *stare*. According to this last mentioned sound therefore it is generally named in England in repeating the Alphabet. The Scotch and Foreigners name it according to the other, that being its most usual sound with them; and some few people affect to name it in that manner in England. It has besides these a third sound in the words *call*, *all*, *salt*, *malt*, which is also a sound very frequent in the south of Scotland; and is what the vulgar inhabitants of Edinburgh give to it in those very words *salt*, and *malt*. Of these three sounds[82] that in *father* has been called the open, that in *pare* the close or slender, and that in *all*[83] the broad. Mr Sheridan (whose lectures on this subject are well worth the readers perusal)[84, 85] takes notice of the same three fold variety of sounds ascribed to this letter, calling them first, second, and third. The broad or third sound is always long, but the first or [86]open, and second or [87]slender are sometimes long as in *father*, *glaze* sometimes short as in *hat*, [88]*race*, *grace*, *pace*. The open being however more commonly short than long, the slender more commonly long.[89] But, besides these differences of quantity, there are certainly two sorts of the slender *a*, differing in the quality of the sound. This will appear to any one who attentively listens first to the pronounciation of *hare* or *care*; and then to that of *grace* or *waste*; The *a* having a thinner, and feebler sound in the two last words, than in the two former. The distinction will be still more evident if we compare the usual manner of pronouncing *tail*, and *tale*; where *ai* in the first word represents the strong, and *a* in the second the thin, slender sound. It is necessary to remark that some good English speakers, either from affectation or habit, pronounce such words as *tail* and such as *tale* in the same manner viz with the strong slender *a*.[90] Those who do so from habit, will perhaps not understand, and therefore may probably dissent from, the distinction I have made.

The sound in *pare*, *stare*, and *tail* is exactely the same with that given to the Greek η in Scotland, and to the *e* in *bête*, *père*; or *oi* and *ai*, in *vouloit*, *pâitre*, by the French. The other in *waste*, *grace*, *tale* is the Scotch sound of the ε and the French sound of their *e* in *portér*, and *extrait* in which last word the two sounds are contrasted. We may therefore enumerate four sorts[91] of the *a* in English, differing in sound.[92] 1. The open *a* which is sometimes long as in *father*, sometimes short as in *hat*. 2. The strong slender *a*, as in *pare*, *stare*; The short quantity of this sound is never I believe represented by *a* in English, but often by *e* as in *pen*, *stern*, *rest*. 3. The thin or feeble slender *a*. Which is long, as in *phrase*, *waste*, or short as in *race*, *pace*, *chase*. 4. The broad *a* which is always long, as in *all*, *call*. Of these, certainly the broad[93] is as different from the slender, as [94]the open from the common sound of *o*, and therefore they would in a rational orthography be represented by different characters. But the broad and open are only to be considered as shades and gradations of the same sound, like the lighter and darker shades of the same colour; and the same is true, in a still stronger degree, of the two sorts of the slender.[95] Some philosophers think, notwithstanding the received opinion to the contrary, that there is an analogy between the laws of motion and communication of light, and of sound. There is certainly such an analogy in the manner in which they are perceived by our organs of hearing and of sight. For, as in the rainbow, although the pure middle part of each of the different stripes of colours is clearly distinguishable from the others, yet, while the eye gradually passes outwards, to the edge of such stripe, on either side, it seems to die away insensibly into the neighbouring tint, and is at length so like it, that it is impossible for the mind to draw the line, or fix the limit where the one ends, and the other begins; so the same thing is observable in our perception of vocal sounds. Thus we may consider the long open *a* in *father* as a sound placed between *o* and the strong slender *a*, or Scotch Eta. But its sound in *all* gradually approaches and seems, in some measure, to confound and lose itself in that of *o*, as, on the other side, in *hat*, it approaches to the limits of, and begins to mix itself with, the short and strong slender sound in *better*. The truth of this remark will become more sensible if we attend to the different figures and positions which the throat, mouth, and other organs of speech, assume in uttering these different sounds. It might perhaps be called a whimsical refinement were I to carry the analogy still farther, and say that, although the sound of *a* in *all*, is certainly simple, and not diphthongal; yet it is, in a manner, formed of a mixture of the long open *a*, and the *o*; in like manner as green, one of the simple primitive colours, is formed by the mixture of blue, and [96]yellow.

Some of the sounds of the *a*, are often represented by that, and another vocal character combined. Thus the broad is frequently expressed by *au*, as in *haul, paul.* – Sometimes by *aw*, as in *mawl, drawl.* The strong and slender sometimes by *ai*, as in *hair*, sometimes by *ea*, as in *bear, wear;* and the thin, and slender, also sometimes by *ai*, as in [97]*daisy, baize;* and sometimes by *ei*, as in *rein, weigh.* In the common [98]grammars *ai, ea,* and *ei,* are generally treated as Diphthongs, which proceeds from that poverty of language, of which we have complained; namely, there being but one set of names, for elementary sounds, and elementary characters. For hence it happens that because a combination of two vocal sounds into one syllable is properly termed a diphthong; a combination of two vocal characters which is the regular way of representing such combined sound, is also termed a diphthong, even in cases where (as in the instances before us) the sound it represents is only a simple vowel. In this respect the Italian orthography is particularly superior to ours, for I believe there is not in that language a single example, where a combination of more than one vocal character does not represent a true diphthongal sound.[99]

B

As *A* is the first vowel, so this is the first consonant in every alphabet, and its place is determined by the same reason; for it is manifestly the most easy uttered; and therefore is one of the first that children learn to pronounce, for which physiologists assign also this additional reason, that it is formed by the simple pressure of the lips together, and that those organs acquire a degree of vigour, and perfection, by their exercise in sucking, before the other instruments of speech. In confirmation of this opinion I think I have observed that children brought up by hand do not begin their first efforts of articulation by pronouncing *b, p* and *m,* (commonly called labial letters) as those which suck do; but that on the contrary they utter the gutteral *g* or *k* the first of any. If this fact should be fully supported by the observation of others, it may be explained from the circumstance of the throats of such children being exercised in deglutition long before they have occasion to exert in any degree of force the muscles of the lips. The reason we have given for the place which *a* and *b* hold in the alphabet, can be carried no farther. The arrangement of the other letters seems quite arbitrary. – If the same rule had prevailed throughout, *p* should be the next to *b,* being pronounced only by a more forcible exertion of the very same[100] sort of pressure of the lips. As the others are not placed according to any natural reason, we find their disposition differing in different languages. In Greek and

Hebrew *g* is the third letter. In Latin and modern European tongues *c*. We have already seen why it is necessary to join a vocal sound with the consonants in giving them a name. It seems perfectly indifferent whether in such name the vowel is made to precede (as some innovators have proposed) or to follow, as has been the general practice in all languages. According to either method one of the effects of the consonant viz, its mode of commencing or its mode of terminating vocal sound is exemplified. With regard to the semi-vowels indeed there is a particular propriety in prefixing the vowel as is done in English and several other languages. Thus *ef, el, em, en, ar, es*, because by that means their distinguishing quality by which they are capable of being protracted to any length after the cessation of the accompanying vocal sound is rendered more obvious; and to make this peculiarity in *them* still more perceptible is perhaps the reason why the vowel is made to follow in the names of the perfect or mute consonants. Yet so difficult is it to discover perfect uniformity in any thing relative to language that we have one semivowel in whose most common name the vowel is made to follow viz *v*, called vee; tho many with more propriety call this letter also *ev*. In Italian the names of the semivowels are formed by putting the vowel both before and after, thus *esse, elle, emme, enne*, &c

> Questa Fata del' popolo Boemme
> Hebbe per tanti secoli governo
> Che'il tempo non potria segnar'ion l'emme.[101]

and in Greek there is no vowel precedes. Indeed the Latin and modern European method of denominating the consonants in general, and the vowels also, have a considerable advantage over the greater part of the literal names of the Greeks, the most of these consist of two syllables, and contain an example of the pronounciation of one or more other letters besides that of which they are the name. For instance the names *Beta*, and *Delta*, not only exemplify the pronoun-ciation of *b* and *d*; but also the one, that of *t*, and the other, those of both *l* and *t*.

Let not these observations be condemned as the fruit of an over-curious and useless subtlety. I know by repeated experiments that, from the force of habit, most people, when they attempt to reason on the nature and power of the elementary sounds have the name they have been taught to give to any particular letter, so closely linked to the idea of the sound of such letter, that it is not without a considerable exertion of imagination that they can disjoin them. An Englishman is apt to think in the letter which he calls *bee*, the *ee* as essential a part of the name as the *b*. So I suppose many of the Greeks did the η, τ, & α. A discussion of the reason, and propriety of the different names naturally tends to destroy the effect of this habit, and to render familiar to the mind, what is palpable at all times on reflexion that in the name of any letter there is no necessary or peculiar connection between such letter, and the others which are accidentally joined with it.[102]

B is mute in *debt*, *subtle*, *limb*, and a few other words. The Scotch pronounce the name of the letter *b* as the English do the word *bay*. The English make it to the ear the same word with *bee* or *be*.

C

C is certainly an unnecessary character as it is used in our language. In all cases (except where it precedes an *h*) it represents the sounds which at other times are expressed either by *s*, or *k*. Before *a*, *o* and *u*, and all consonants it has the sound of *k*. As in *case*, *cost*, *custom*, *ecbatan*, *eccentric*, *eclipse*. Before *e*, *i*, and *y*, that of *s*, as in *cedar*, *city*, *cyder*. The same may be said of this letter as pronounced in French, and German; and, by us, in Latin. Many critics have supposed, not without great probability, that the ancient Romans always pronounced it like *k* or *kappa*. 1. Because in writing the Latin names in which we give the *c* the sound of *s*, the Greeks made use of their *kappa*, as καισαϱ for *Cæsar* Μαϱϰελλος for *Marcellus*, ϰιϰεϱων for *Cicero*. If the Romans had sounded the *c* as we do in those words they would have been written in Greek with a sigma.[103] 2. Suidas expressly calls it the Roman *Kappa*. To these arguments I think the two following may be added. viz. that *Keiser* is the German word for Emperor, which is evidently derived from *Cæsar*, and may be supposed to have been adopted into that language from the mouths of the ancient Romans, and transmitted down to modern times with very little change of Pronounciation. 2. Because according to our method of reading Latin, the sound of *k* never once occurs in the Latin tongue before *e*, *i*, and *y*; which we can scarcely believe to have been really the case in the living pronounciation. This is enough on a subject that can never be thoroughly ascertained, and if it could, would not repay the trouble the investigation would cost by any utility resulting from the discovery.[104, 105]

Ch in several words has (like *c* before *a*, *o* and *u*,) the sound of *k*, as in *Chymist*, *scheme*, *choler*, *Archangel*. In a few others [106]as *Chaise*, *Charlotte*, *machine*, *French*, *chicane*, *champaign*, *Champerty*, *machine*, *chagrin*, it represents that semivowel which the English generally express by *sh* as in *shower*, the Italians by *sc* before *e* and *i*, as *scernare*, *scintilla*, the Germans by *sch* as in *schon*, *scheyne*, and the French always by *ch*,[107] as in *chandelle*, *chemise*. But in the general pronounciation of the *ch*[108] in English it represents a combination of *t*, and *sh*; as in *church*, *chimney*, *Archbishop*. In some words the English prefix the *t*, as in *itch*, *ditch*, *dutch*, *crutch* &c. This consonantal combination the Italians represent before *e* and *i*, by the single character *c*; as in *citta*, *Francesco*, *placido*.

In the Scotch dialect, and in Dutch, and German, the *ch* often expresses a guttural semivowel, which has the same affinity to *k*, that we shall observe between several other semivowels and mutes.[109] This guttural semivowel is the sound given to the Greek *chi* by all the nations who admit it into their own language. According to the English and French method of pronouncing the *chi*, it is not distinguishable from *kappa*, and that circumstance affords a very strong presumption that those methods are wrong. But as those two nations are unaccustomed to the guttural in their own language, their organs are in general unable to express it. Since this sound of the *chi* is certainly a simple consonant, it is strange that the Latins chose rather to express it by two characters the *c* and the *h*, as in *Achilles*, than to imitate the example of the Greeks in using one appropriated mark. That it cannot be decomposed into the hard sound of *c* followed by the aspirate, as many people are apt to suppose merely because they are used to see it expressed by those two letters may be rendered evident in two different ways; either 1. by comparing the Scotch pronounciation of *ch* in *Chymist*, or *Achilles* with the contiguous sounds of *c* (or rather *k*) and *h* when they happen to meet in compound words like *Music-hall*, when each is clearly and distinctly uttered. Or 2. by attending to the particular exertion of the organs of speech in pronouncing the guttural *ch*. For then, as in the utterance of all the semivowels, expiration is in some degree performed. The fauces are made to approach, but yet not so as to preclude entirely the passage of the breath. Whereas to sound the hard *c* or *k*, before *h* or any other vowel or consonant the breath must be suddenly and totally stopt and the act of expiration suspended.

The Scotch name of *c* is, to the ear, the same word with *say* when pronounced in the English method. The English name is, to the ear, the same word with *see* or *sea*.

D

This character, like *b*, always represents the same consonantal modification. – I reserve the observations I have to make on it and *t* till I come to that letter.

The Scotch name of *d* is pronounced as the English sound *Day*. The English name is the same with *Dee*.

E

This vowel is named in England as the Scotch, and most foreign nations name the *i*. Yet though that is one of its sounds, as in *scene, he, the, she*, it is not the most common. It has three, which are easily distinguishable from one another. 1. That just taken notice of. 2. That which corresponds to the strong slender *a*,[110] and is found in *better, cellar, there, pen, stem, fell, debt*. This is the French *e* open, as in bête, ferme, and the sound given to the Greek η in Scotland: except that the Scotch make the η (as it should be) long and therefore exactly like the English *a* in *bare, stare, care*. I believe in France the Eta is now pronounced as in Scotland.[111] Formerly indeed there were two fashions in this subject among the French; one party standing up for the pronounciation last mentioned, the other for that which still prevails in England, namely the sound of *e* in *scene*. The advocates for the Scotch method cite that passage where Eustathius tells us that βηβη exactly expressed the bleat of sheep. Which sound certainly resembles the Scotch, more than the English, Eta. A great many other arguments are to be found in writers who have treated this weighty subject.[112] Both the Scotch and English are certainly right in one respect, viz, in making the Eta and Epsilon differ, not only in the quantity, but also the quality, of their sounds. When Simonides[113] introduced the η and ω, formerly wanting in the Greek alphabet, we must suppose he made that innovation in order to represent two sounds for which there were no appropriated characters at that time, and not merely to mark a prolongation of the very same sounds already represented by ε and ω. If that had been the case, there was precisely the same reason for contriving three more characters, to represent the α, ι, and υ in words where they happened to be long. [114]3. The *e* has a sort of obscure and smothered sound not unlike that of the French *e* in *le ce que le*vez-vous &c. Examples of this sound we have in the English method of pronouncing *clergy, earth*, [115]*impertinent*.

The first of these three different sounds of the *e* is often represented by *ee*, as in *thee, been*: or, by *ea*, as in *clear, spear*. Sometimes by *ie*, as in *mien, field*; by *ei*, as in *perceive, conceive*; and, in one word, by *eo*, viz, [116]*people*. The second (as we have seen above) by *a*, as in *pare, stare*, and by *ea*, as in *bear, pear*. The Scotch are extremely prone to substitute the thin slender sound of *a*, for the 2nd second of *e*, as in the words *dĕlicacy, Pĕdant*; and the strong slender *a* for the third as in *Clĕrgyman*. But they *have* this third sound, as in perceive.

The thin slender sound of *a*, or *ay*, as in *state, pay*, is the most usual sound of the *e* in the Scotch dialect. It takes its name from thence; and that is the sound the Scotch give to the Greek E.

The mute *e* in English has generally the effect of lengthening, and often at the same time of altering, the sound of the vocal part of the preceding syllable. Thus in the word *star* the *a* has its short open sound; add the mute *e*, and you form the word *stare*, in which the strong protracted slender *a* prevails. In *theif* the *ei* has the first sound of the *e* shortened. Add the *e* at the end and as in *theive* (where indeed the consonant is also altered) and the *ei* retains the same sound, but is protracted. There are several instances however where the preceding syllable remains short, as in *gŏne, shŏne, sĕive, lĭve, gĭve*. It is extremely probable that our mute *e* was once sounded in every word where it is used. The arguments for this opinion are to be found in all the books of English grammar. I need not repeat them here. But it is now the only instance, in any language I am acquainted with, of a single[117] vocal character preceded by a consonant which either at the end, or in the middle, of words, does not form a distinct syllable. As in the following lines of Milton,

> Other creatur*e* in this plac*e*
> Living or lif*e*less to be found was non*e*.

Where every body knows that the *e*'s printed in the Italics do not form syllables in scanning the verse. The feminine *e* in the French language is indeed scarcely audible (except in the pronounciation of the southern provinces) and accordingly some of their own grammarians call it the *mute e, e muet*. Yet in the measure of their verse it invariably forms a syllable. I say invariably, because the instances where, at the end of a word, it is followed by a vowel in the next, as, for example, in these lines of Voltaire in his invocation to truth,

> Viens parlé, et s'il est vrai que la Fable autrefois
> Scut a tes fiers accens meler sa *douce* voix
> Si sa main delicate orna la tête altiere
> Si son ombre embellit les traits de la lumiere.

are not to be considered as exceptions to the rule. For there the feminine *e* is entirely suppressed by the figure called *synalephe*. – A figure, used by the Greeks and Latins, with regard to all vowels, but by the French in the instance of the *e* feminine only.

One of those very lines I have cited, viz the 2d, affords an example where the feminine *e* forms one of the twelve syllables of which that line is composed. The following happy imitation, by the same author, in his tragedy of Zaire,[118] of the last speech in Othello, will serve to show how constantly the rule must be adhered to

> Et toi
> Guerrier infortuné, mais encore,[119] que moi
> Quitt*e* ces lieux sanglans, remporte en ta patri*e*

Cet objêt que ma rage a privé de la vi*e*
Ton Roi, tous tes Chretiens aprenant tes malheurs
M'en parleront jamais sans reprandr*e* des pleurs
Mais si la verité par toi se fait connaitr*e*
En detestant mon crime, ils me plaindront peutetr*e*
Porte aux tiens ce poignard que mon bras egaré
A plongé dans un sein qui dit n'êtr*e* sacré
Di-leur que j'ai donne la mort la plus affreus*e*
A la plus dign*e* femme, a la plus vertueus*e*
Dont le ciel ait formé les innocens appas.
Di-leur qu'à ses pieds j'avais mis mes etâts
Di-leur que dans son sang cett*e* main s'est plongé*e*
Di, que j*e* l'adorais, et que je l'ai vengé*e*.

In French singing the feminine *e* is generally rendered as audibly as the other vowels, and, even in conversation, all good speakers make its effect sensible by a sort of rest or pause of the voice. The rule of French verse, which requires, when they write in couplets whether of Alexandrines or shorter lines, that every other couplet should terminate with supernumerary syllables formed by this *e* and therefore called feminine verses, has certainly a good effect to *their* ears. 'Je faisais voir' says Voltaire 'à la lettre *e*, que nos *e* muets qui nous sont reprochés par un Italien sont précisément ce qui fait la délicieuse harmonie de nôtre langue. Empir*e*, Couronn*e*, diadêm*e*, epouvant-abl*e*, sensibl*e*, cet *e* muet qu'on fait sentir sans l'articuler, laisse dans l'oreille un son melodieux, comme celui d'un timbre qui resonne encore quand il n'est plus frappé. C'est que nous avons déja repondu a un Italien, homme de lettres, qui était venu a Paris pour enseigner sa langue, et qui ne devait pas y décrier la nôtre. Il ne sentait pas la beauté & la nécessité de nos rimes feminines. Elles ne sont que des *e* muets. Cet entrelassement de rimes masculines et feminines fait le charme de nos vers.' It may be observed that in all the words he has mentioned the *e* feminine is preceded by a semivowel, and I suspect the pleasure he mentions (of which I even though a foreigner am very sensible) arises from the prolongation of those semivowels. When the verse in French is alternate like Elegaic measure, every other line is feminine, and when the rhymes are irregularly mixed the proportion of the masculine and feminine is preserved as nearly equal as possible.

It is remarkable that the Germans (and also the Dutch, for they too have their poets[120]) have subjected themselves to the same sort of restraint. For with them as with the French every alternate couplet, or alternate line, must end with a supernumerary syllable; and the vocal part of this syllable is generally formed by a final *e* which with them too has a very obscure sound not much more perceptible than in French. Sometimes this thirteenth syllable consists of other obscurely uttered[121] letters; but it is never accented.

The following two passages from Haller will serve as examples. The first is taken from his justly celebrated poem called the Alps, which is written in stanzas. The other, from an [122]Epistle in couplets.

> Versuchts, ihr Sterbliche, macht euern Zustand bess*er*
> Braucht was die kunst, ernfand, und die natur euch gab,
> Belebt die blumenflur mit steigendem gewaass*er*,
> Theilt nach Corinths gesetz, gehaune felsen ab;
> Umhangt die marmorwand mit Persichen Tapet*en*
> Speist Tunkins nest aus gold, trinkt perlen aus Smaragd;
> Schlaft ein beym saitenspiel, erwachet bey trompet*en*,
> Räumt klippen aus der Bahn, schliest länder ein zur Jagd;
> Wird schon, was ihr gewünscht, das schichsal under schreib*en*
> Ihr werdet arm im Glück, im Reichthum elend bleib*en*

> O Freund der fern von mir im Schoss der Vater stadt
> Noch itzt ein schatzlar herz mir vorbehalten hat
> Wie soll dein lied mein leid, mein ewig leid vermind*ern*?
> Kann eines freundes schmerz des andern schmerzen hind*ern*?
> Nein, mein noch wundes herz von langer weymuth weich,
> Fühlt alles was du sagst, und weint mit dir zubleich.
> Er, wünsche, wer da will, ein herz das wie sich bind*et*,
> Das von der liebe nichts, als den genuss empfind*et*,
> Das Vorige vergisst, ans Künftige nicht denkt,
> Und nur ans Jetzige sich, klug wie thiere, henckt;
> Das giebt die Weisheit nicht. &c[123]

The verses I have just cited are Alexandrines, which is the Heroic measure both of the Germans and French; and I am apt to believe that, in them, the feminine rhymes[124] operate to a degree in counteracting the monotony occasioned by the pause which by the versification of the language, is absolutely necessary after the sixth syllable, and which divides each line into two Hemistichs.

If an excuse is necessary for the length of this article Dr Johnson furnishes me with one; For he tells us, that the *e* is the letter which occurs most frequently in our language. – From its importance therefore it seemed to require a fuller discussion than the others.

F

This semivowel has the same analogy to *p*, that *v* has to *b*. In words derived from the Greek, we, in imitation of the Romans represent it by *ph*. It may be pronounced by the pressure of the lips together as in uttering *p*, or *b*, but so as to leave some slight issue for the breath. In the act of blowing out a candle if done forcibly, an indistinct *f* is produced; if more weakly a *v*. But the more usual, and more perfect, way of pronouncing both, is by pressing the edge of the upper teeth against the underlip. *F*, in *of*, is commonly pronounced like *v*; and in *rough* and in some other words, it is represented by *gh*. The name of this letter as those of *k*, *l*, *m*, *g*, *s*, *x* and *y*, are the same in Scotland, as in England.

G

This letter has two very distinct sounds, which seem to have little or no relation or analogy to one another. 1. What is called the hard sound, which it has always before *a*, *o*, *u*, and before consonants. This is a simple consonant formed by the organs of speech in the very same manner with *k*; except that the last mentioned letter requires a stronger exertion. 2. A complex sound composed of *d*, and the semivowel expressed by *z*, in the word *azure*; and by *g* itself before *e* or *i* in the French language, and by *s* in *pleasure*. This sound *g* has in most words before *e* and *i*, but not in all, for it is hard in *give*, *gelding* and several others. In Italian it always has this complex sound before *e* and *i*, – as in *gente*, *giro*. When in that language they mean to prefix the hard sound to those two vowels they interpose an *h*,[125] as in *ghirlanda*. As the French do an *u*, as in the word *guerre*. On the other hand when the Italians want to produce the soft sound of *g* before *a*, *o*, *or u* they interpose an *i*. As in *giallo*, *giogo*, *giusto*.[126] The Germans and Dutch make the *g* a guttural semivowel, analagous to their *ch*, but softer in the same proportion as our hard *g* is softer than *k*. One would expect to find this softer guttural in the Scotch manner of pronouncing *gh* in *light*, *thought*, *sight*, but I cannot, by my ear, discover any difference between the Scotch *ch*, and *gh*. *G* in English is mute before *n* in all words of Saxon origin, and most, if not all, others, as *gnat*, *gnaw*, *sign*, *benign*. I believe in *Gnome*, and in *gnomon* and its derivatives, it is pronounced by most English people. *Gh*, and *gu* at the beginning of words have the sound of the hard *g*, as *ghost*, *guest*, *guardian*. In the middle of words *gh* is mute, as in *sight*, *sought*, and, often, at the end; as *plough*, *bough*, *though*. Sometimes at the end *gh* has the sound of *f*, as *rough*, *cough*, *laugh* and in the middle, in the word *laughter*. It is a provincial pronunciation in some counties of the west of England to say *oft*, and *thoft*, for *ought* and *thought*. I know one instance of a man of education and eminence in a learned profession who retains this mode of sounding those words. The Scotch name the *g* like the English word *jay*. The English name rhymes to *bee*.

H

This modification of articulate sound, which is merely a strong aspiration, as when we sigh, is no longer in use in any one instance in the Italian language. [127]And the most modern Italian orthography has rejected the character in writing except in *hai*, and *hanno*, where it is still retained to distinguish those words to the eye (for to the ear there is no distinction) from *ai* the plural of the indefinite article, and *anno* a year. With us, and the French, it is mute at the beginning of many words, but pronounced in others. Thus in *honnête*, *homme*, *humble*, *honesty* it is mute, in *Heros*, *hardi*, *hungry*, *hazard*, it is pronounced. It is never mute in German, or Dutch.

In the speech of some individuals in England there is this most capricious defect, that in words where others pronounce the *h*, at the beginning, they do not; and where others suppress it, or where it is not written, they pronounce it. This is one of the most unaccountable singularities I have ever observed. It does not seem to arise from imitation for I have not been able to trace it as a general habit among all the inhabitants of any place or district.[128] Neither can it be attributed to any particular configuration of the organs of speech, because these persons pronounce the *h* in as complete a manner as other people, in words where it should be mute or is not written. Yet such is the power of habit that if you desire them to try to pronounce the *h* in *hungry* or any word of that sort, they cannot do it, nor avoid doing it in *heir*, or adding it to *air*. I know a hair-dresser who has this singularity of pronounciation, and who often lays it down as a maxim to his customers, that nothing is do destructive to the *air*, as exposing it too much to the *hair*. I likewise know a Portuguese Lady who has been long enough in England to speak the language with great fluency, and to pronounce it in general tolerably well; but who has this extraordinary habit with respect to the *h*.

It is not very easy to account for the introduction of the *h* by the Romans in the guttural and labial semivowels *ch*, and *ph*, in words taken from the Greek. Nor for our employing it in those other semivowels which we represent by *sh*, and *th*. – That they are all simple consonants, and not a combination of the contiguous but distinct sounds of the preceding consonants and the *h* will appear by comparing the following words. *Achilles* (in the Scotch manner of pronouncing it), [129]*Usher*, *Athelstan*, *although*, with *music-hall*, *sheep-hook*, *brass-handle*, *pot-hook*, *God-head*. The best reason I can discover for the use of the two characters is, that these semivowels are, (or, at least in the case of the *ph* or *f*, may be) formed by nearly the same position of the organs as the mutes prefixed to the *h*; viz *c*, *p*, *s*, and *t*; with this difference only that room must be left for the passage of part of the breath, which is made to issue with the same sort of exertion as when we pronounce the *h*.

Although the *v* has exactly the same analogy to the *b* that *f* has to *p*. Yet that letter has never been expressed by *bh*. But to show that its sound is not a combination of those two consonants [130]a more striking proof cannot be had than by joining the two Greek words λαβε & ηυια, thus λαβ'η'υια. If the *v* were a union of *b* and *h*, those two words pronounced together in the English way would be the same in all respects as *Lavinia*, which every body's ear will tell them is not the case.

The Scotch name of the *h* is to the ear, the same word with *each*. But the English form the name, of the thin slender *a* as in *slate* prefixed to the sound of *ch*, in *each*. This name ... rhymes exactly with the first syllable of the legal word *laches*.

I

There are three distinct sounds represented by this letter in the English language.

1. What I would call its diphthongal sound, being in truth a diphthong composed of the short open *a*, and the first sound of *e*. Although a diphthong this sound is sometimes short, as in *dice*; often long, as in *wise*. When it is long [131]the ear can with the greatest facility discriminate the two vocal sounds, of which it is composed. When short, this cannot be done without a considerable effort of attention. It is from this sound that the English give it its name.

2. The very same which I have called the first sound of the *e*. This is its universal sound in Italian, and is what it is named from by foreign nations, and by the Scotch, but it is not found in many English words. In none I believe that have been completely naturalized or that are of a Teutonic origin.[132] The following are instances of it; which occur to me at present *Eloïsa*, *Clementīna*, *Virginia*, *Racīne*,[133] *marine*, *magazine*, and *caprice*.

3. Its short close sound, as in *picture*, *fixture*, *sin*. This sound is I believe almost peculiar to our language, and the other northern descendants of the Gothic Stock. Two different shades of it are easily perceived by an attentive ear.[134] One, in words in which an *r* follows, as *first*, *thirst*, where it approaches nearly to, but seems not entirely the same with, the short *u*. This any person may judge of who will take the trouble to make an Englishman pronounce the words *burst*, and *thirst* one after the other. The other shade approaches, on the other side, to the first sound of *e* shortened. This is most sensibly perceived before a semivowel as in the words *fin*, *sin*, *will*, *ill*, *is*, *his*, *Lizard*.[135] The Scotch are apt to substitute the other shade for this, in

many words, and before *n*, *l* and *t*, scarcely ever hit this exactly. Hence the English in caricaturing their pronounciation will say *wull*, *full*, *spull*, for *will*, &c.

It is curious to observe with regard to almost all our words of *Teutonic*, or *Gothic* derivation where the *i* has its diphthongal sound, that in the corresponding German word a diphthongal combination of letters is used. Not indeed *ai* but *ei*. As for instance, *schein*, *to shine*; *wein*, *wine*; *weiss*, *white*; *weit*, *wide*; *leicht*, *light*; *fein*, *fine*; *mein*, *mine*; *dein*, *thine*; *Rhein*, *Rhine*; *Eis*, *Ice*; *Leim*, *Lime* &c. The pronounciation of the vocal part of these words is also very nearly the same in German and in English. It is only more slender in the former language, being composed of the short slender, instead of the open, *a*, and the first sound of *e*. Many Scotch people pronounce the diphthongal *i*, exactly like the German *ei*. This perhaps may afford a solution (in this instance) of the seeming absurdity of representing a compound sound by a single character. These two letters were perhaps employed by our early ancestors as now by the Germans; but one of them came to be gradually dropt while the diphthongal sound was still retained. If such a deviation from the original orthography did ever in fact take place, it must have been at a very remote period; for in the Anglo-Saxon the words where *i* has now its diphthongal sound were written as in modern English with that character by itself as *Scinan*, *to shine*, Þid, *wide*, Hþit, *white*, Fir, *fire*, Þin, *wine*, Þis, *wise*, &c. When once the practice was introduced of representing the diphthongal sound by *i*, it was natural to extend that sound to that letter in the case of words not Teutonic, as they were gradually adopted from the French, or other languages.

Y is in English, only another character for *i*; In the middle or at the end of words it often represents the diphthongal sound. As in *by*, *cyder*, sometimes the third short sound, as in *dynasty*, *Dysentry*. Joined to *a*, it represents the thin slender sound of *a*, as in *hay*, *day*, *say*, as *ai* often does, viz in *raise*, *praise*. *Y* has this effect also when it follows *e* as in *they*, *Day*.[136] At the beginning of a word before a vowel it has the first sound of *e*, or the second of *i* shortened and running into the succeeding vowel, so as to form a proper diphthong, but in which the sound of the next vowel predominates. Thus in *yes*, *your*, *yard* the *ye*, *your* and *ya* form diphthongs which might be equally well written *ie*, *iou*, and *ia*. No one will call this in question who is acquainted with the Italian language, and will compare the pronounciation of the first syllable of the words *piange*, *diede*, *piede*, *piange*, *mietitore*, *pioggia*, *piu*, with *yard*, *yes*, *yesterday*, *Yorick*, *you*.

This being the case, there is certainly great impropriety in the common arrangement of the *y* among the consonants. An impropriety which has not escaped several writers on orthography. Yet it must be confessed that when *y* is followed by the first sound of *e* as in *yield*, *year*, it has a sound something between a vowel and a semivowel, and approaching to the German and Dutch semivocal sound of *g* but extremely softened. Certainly it has not in the words in question the first sound of *e*; for as a vowel twice repeated must either form only one long syllable, or two distinct ones of the very same vocal sound; if *y*, had the same sound with the *ei*, and the *ea* in *yield* and *year*, they might be spelt thus *eeld*, *eer*, or *ee-eeld*, *ee-eer*. Now every body perceives that the true pronounciation of *year* and *yield* is something different, being clearly monosyllabic, and distinguishable from *eer* and *eeld*.

J

The consonantal mark *J* in our language is only a synonymous character with the soft *g*. The Italians have not this letter in their Alphabet. The Germans, and Dutch use it at the beginning of words before a vowel, and pronounce it as we do *y*. As in *jaar, jahr, year*; *ja, yes*. The Italians as well as the Dutch and Germans pronounce it so in reading Latin. Yet in the Italian words derived from Latin in which this consonant *J* occurs they have substituted *gi*, which they pronounce like our sound of the *J*. A plain proof that they once pronounced that letter even in Latin, in the English manner. Thus in Latin they read *Julius* as we should if it were written Yulius; but in their own language they say *Giulio*, and so *giustizia, Giesie, Giordano*, &c. This circumstance furnishes a reason for believing that ours is the proper pronounciation of the Latin *J*. The French pronounce the *J* both in their own language, and in Latin, like their soft *g*.

The common English name of *J*, is, what the Scotch give to *g*.

K

This consonant, like its correspondent letter the hard *g*, is silent before *n*. Thus *knell* is to the ear the same word with the proper name *Nell*, and *knight* the same with *night*. The word *knight* may furnish a very proper example to show how fallacious an argument to prove harshness in our language is that which foreigners draw from the number of consonants in our orthography. *Knight* is indeed, to the eye, a syllable consisting of only one vowel, and no less than five consonants, but this very word, in its pronounciation, and indeed according to the Italian orthography, consists only of two consonants, and of the like number of vowels.[137]

131

L

This semivowel and liquid is the most pleasing to the ear of all consonants. I believe in all languages it has the same sound. In ours it is often mute, as in *walk*, *talk*, *salmon*.

M

This nasal semivowel has also the same sound in all languages, except that in some words as *temps*, *champ*, *nom*,[138] the French pronounce it like their *n*.

N

1. The proper sound of the *n* is also uniformly the same in all languages, and is formed by applying the tongue just above the roots of the upper teeth, as in pronouncing *d*, and *t*, and suffering a slight expiration to be performed through the nostrils.

But 2. the *n* has another sound when it precedes a *g*, or *k* in our language, as in *singer*, *ink*. This is more nasal than the other, and in forming it the tongue is not employed in the same manner. People are apt to consider this particular sound of the *n* as occasioned by the *g* or *k*, which follow; but that it is not will appear by comparing the difference of sound in *singer*, and in *anger*. For in both words the *n* has the sound of which I am speaking, but in the first the *g* is not pronounced. In the second it is. In French the *n* when followed by a vowel has its general, or first sound; but when followed by a consonant of whatever sort, it has the second or more nasal sound. Not entirely however like ours; for the French make it (if I may so speak) less consonantal, and leave almost a free expiration by the nostrils. A common fault of foreigners in speaking French is that they pronounce this *n* exactly like ours in *singer*. The difference cannot thoroughly be explained in words, but it is extremely sensible to the ear. This second sound we give to the γ in Greek, when it is followed by another γ or an ϰ, as in ἀγγελος & ἐγϰωμιον, and we are probably right, since when a word ending with γ was compounded with one beginning with γ or ϰ the Greeks themselves in their orthography substituted another γ for the ϰ as ἐγγραφω, ἐγϰεφαλος and in Latin, words like ἀγγελος & ἐγϰωμιον were rendered *Angelus* and *Encomium*.

It is a curious circumstance relative to these two letters *m* and *n*, that if you stop the nostrils by pressing them together with your finger and then pronounce either the one or the other, it becomes a mute instead of a semivowel: that is, you can commence or terminate a vocal sound with it, as with *b*, *p*, *d* or *t*, but you cannot protract its own sound without a vowel, as you may when the nostrils are open: or as you can that of the other semivowels,[139] even when they are shut. The French second sound of the *n* may be protracted when the nostrils are closed.

The *n* is mute at the end of words after *m* as in *damn*, *contemn*, *condemn*.

O

This letter has two distinct sounds differing in quality from each other.[140] The one is open and commonly short, as in *not*, *lost*, *cross*, *horse*. The other close, and usually long, as in *bone*, *stone*, *post*, *hoarse*, *toll*. The first we give to the Greek *o*,[141] and the other to the *ω*. It is evident that the sounds we give to those two vowels differ in quality, and we have mentioned under the letter *e* a reason for supposing that such a difference subsisted in the living pronounciation of Greece. There is in our language a long sound of the open *o*, as in *Corn*, *Horn*. It is seldom however represented by this single character, But sometimes by *ou* as in *bought*, *thought*; or by *oa*, as in *groat*, *broad*. This sound, if not the same, is near the confines, or the external edge, if I may so speak, of the broad *a* in *all*. [142]Some writers think them the same. I imagine I can perceive a[143] difference.

The close *o* which verges towards the vowel represented by *oo*, is, in like manner, sometimes short: especially before the soft mutes *b*, *d*, & *g*, as in *sob*, *pod*, *log*. The long close *o* is often represented by *ow*, as *bowl*, *sow*, or also by *ou* as in *soul*, *though*, or *oa*, as in *road*, or *oe* as in *woe*, *toe*, *foe*, By *eau*, in *beau*; and, in one instance, by *ew* viz *shew*.

The combinations of *o* and *u*, and *o* and *w*[144] very frequently represent a proper diphthong (as in *foul*, *howl*, *now*) composed of the close *o*, and the simple vowel sound of the *u* in *full*, *pull*. *O* and *i* also form a proper diphthong composed of the same sound of the *o*, and the first sound of *e*, as in *boil*, *foil*. Some observations will be made in the catalogue on a diversity in the English method of pronouncing this last diphthong.

P

Has but one uniform sound, being formed in the same manner with *b*, but with a more forceful exertion of the lips. For some further observations on the analogy between this letter and *b*, *f* and *v*; between the hard *g*, *k*, and the Scotch *ch* and between *d* and *t*, and the two sounds of *th*, I must refer to the article *v*. The Scotch name of *p*, is the same with the word *pay* as pronounced in England. Its name in England is, to the ear, the same with *pea*.

Q

This letter in our language and in Italian is exactly the same with *k* only it is never used except before an *u* when that vowel forms a diphthong with some other that follows it. *Quarter, question, quick, Quorum*. In Italian *qu* is only used before *a, e* and *i*, as in *quadro, questo, acquisto*; the *cu* answering the purpose before *o*, as *cuore*. The French use *qu* before *e* and *i* to represent the hard *c* or *k*; as *querelle, exquis*.

In one English word (*Quoit*) the *u* is silent so that the pronounciation is the same as if it were written *coit* or *koit*.

R

The English in naming this letter prefix the open *a*, so as to form to the ear the same word with *are*. The Scotch and Foreigners use the same vowel as before the other semivowels; so that their name is the same sound with the French word *erre* (Wander) as *J'erre* (I wander). In England it is pronounced more softly in general than by the Scotch.[145] What by the French is termed *grassayment*, in England the *burr* and by the Scotch a rattle proceeds from pronouncing the *r* in the throat, without applying the tongue to the upper jaw, as must be done in the proper pronounciation. This guttural *r* it is that resembles the snarl of a dog. We have already observed other instances of a sort of imperfect pronounciation of semivowels by a different manner of employing the organs of speech from that which is necessary to a perfect utterance of them. As when the *f* and *v* are pronounced by the compression of the lips instead of that of the upper teeth and upper lip; and when the *n* is pronounced as in *sing*, without applying the tongue to the upper jaw. The Londoners, as least many of them, make a very extraordinary use of this letter. They introduce it in their pronounciation at the end of almost every word with a vocal termination, when such word is followed by another that begins with a vowel. Thus they say 'that is not my *idear* of the matter.' 'I shall be obliged to take the *lawr* of you.' 'That *fellowr* ought to be punished'.

> I could a tale unfold whose lightest word
> Would harrowr up thy soul.

I have been astonished to hear this barbarous pronounciation in the mouths of some persons of education. One particularly occurs to me at present who has a critical knowledge of his own and several other languages, and who yet constantly inserts the *r* in this manner, between two concurring vowels. I remember when I first read Pope and Swift's Miscellanies I could not understand the reason why the old Woman in the humorous account of the madness of Dennis is made to call Cato *Cator*: but when I came to be acquainted with the Cockney dialect I discovered that the author's meaning was to turn this barbarous habit into ridicule.[146] To account for such a peculiarity we must suppose a sort of local dislike, stronger than in other places, and among other nations, to that concurrence of vowels which grammarians have termed a hiatus. In a few instances the French, even in their pure dialect, have a similar contrivance.[147] Thus they always interpose a *t* between a verb which ends, and a pronoun that begins, with a vowel. *Qu'a-t-il fait, Qu'a-t-elle ecrit, Que dira-t-on, Que fera-t-elle, Ou ira-t-on.* For the same purpose too they employ the masculine possessive pronoun even before feminine words if they begin with a vowel, As *mon* amie, *son* innocence.[148] Nor is our own pure language entirely without examples of the same sort. Before a noun beginning with a vowel *n* is always added to the indefinite article *a*. As *an Orchard, an Arbour*. In like manner in the phrase *says-I* which is certainly classical (if authority can entitle any expression to be so called,) the final *s* seems to be employed to avoid the hiatus. Some over-scrupulous puritans in language even in their familiar conversation use *said-I*, and (that they may be uniform) *said-he*, where others would have said, *says I* and *says he*; but how stiff this appears in discourse, let the unaffected reader judge: The substitution of the present, for the past, tense[149] is a figure which animates and enlivens colloquial narration, and is lost by this supposed improvement. But as the general use of the *r* to prevent the hiatus is confined to the vulgar dialect of London, every man who wishes to speak with propriety will carefully avoid it, as every foreigner whose aim is to speak pure French will shun the general introduction of the *t* between the vocal terminations of verbs, and all words indifferently which begin with a vowel, although that manner of speaking is common among some of the lower class of Frenchmen. As, *mon Maitre m'a-t-ordonne: Il sera-t-arrive.*

R, though a semivowel is often considered as the harshest of all letters. The poets therefore when they mean to express something extremely dissonant and unpleasing to the ear make choice of words in which the *r* abounds.

> Non tu in trivijs indocte solebas
> Stridente mise*r*um stipula despe*r*de*r*e ca*r*men.[150]

Chiama gli abitato*r* de l'omb*r*e ete*r*ne
Il rauco suon de la ta*r*ta*r*ea *tr*omba
*Tr*eman le spaziose at*r*e cave*r*ne
E l'ae*r* cieco a quel *r*umor *r*imbomba.[151]

Their lean and flashy songs
G*r*ate on their sc*r*annel pipes of w*r*etched st*r*aw.[152]

Or like Si*r* *R*icha*r*d *r*umbling *r*ough and fie*r*ce
With a*r*ms, and Geo*r*ge, and B*r*unswick c*r*oud the ve*r*se
*R*end with t*r*emendous sounds you*r* ea*r*s as unde*r*
With Gun, d*r*um, t*r*umpet, blunde*r*buss and thunde*r*.[153]

S

S has two distinct sounds. The one hard, which it always has at the beginning of words, and at the end, or in the middle, when the *s* is doubled. As in *slaughter, soul, ass, passing*.[154] The other[155] is the sound sometimes represented by *z* as in *Zeal*. *S* has this sound in *has, as, was, Pheasant, wise*. The Scotch are apt to pronounce it always in this manner when it is followed by a mute *e*; But according to the pure dialect it has often its hard sound in such cases, as in *erase, base, grease*. The preceding vowel is generally made short when it has the first sound, and long when it has the second. *Erăse, grĕase, băse, Wīse, prāise, rāise.*

In the county of Somerset, the inhabitants are remarkable for using the second sound in all words where *s* occurs. Thus they pronounce the name of their own county as if written *Zomerzet*. We have seen that *sh* (as in *sheet*) represents a simple semivowel sound, and that the French soft *g*, their *j* and our *z* and *s* in many words, as *pleasure, azure* represent another semivowel bearing the same relation to the first that the [156]second sound of *s* does to the first, or that *v* does to *f*. *Ti, ci, ce, ssi* and *si* in the middle of words also represent the *sh* as in *nation, relation, circumstantial, special, Dacia, sociable, ocean, passion, Asia.*

To consider *ti* as a syllable, so as to make *nation* for instance a trisyllabic word, is a solecism common to all the vulgar writers on English grammar. One is surprised that Dr Johnson should have adopted it. He considers the coalescence of the *ia* and *io* into one syllable in the words *question, and special* as caused by a poetical licence, or figure, to which the learned have given the name synaeresis. Now my idea of a poetical licence is some deviation from the common mode of speech, or of writing in prose. If so, it is a poetical licence to divide the *tion* and *cial* into two syllables; This never is done in conversation, or in reading prose, but it is sometimes practised by our [157]earliest poets; As Milton

> Yet not terrible
> That I should fear, nor sociably mild
> As Raphael . . .[158]

And by Spenser in the following Alexandrine

> It seeme'd the Ocean could not contain them there.[159]

More modern writers have used it very seldom in verse, and the ear is now so unaccustomed to it, that in reading or speaking those lines of Shakespear (which are many in number) where the verse requires *tion* at the end of a line to be considered as two syllables it is usual to sacrifice the measure to the established method of pronounciation. In the following lines

> O for a muse of fire that would ascend
> The brightest heav'n of inven*tion*.

No modern reader, or actor, would divide the word *invention* into four syllables, although, in scanning, this is necessary to complete the regular number of feet. One of the circumstances that throws a ridicule on the vulgar verse translation of the psalms is, that the music to which they are set as well as the measure of the verse requiring the division of *tion*, in *salvation* and such words, into two syllables, it is usual for parish Clerks to read them in that manner. When this figure is used which is the opposite of synæresis, and is called diæresis, we are obliged to sound the *i* after the semivocal sound,[160] whether that[161] be represented by *sh* as in *fa-sh-ion*, or by any of the other substitutes, as *ti* in *na-ti-on*, *ssi* in *passion* &c.

It is singular that this semivowel which we represent[162] by *sh*, *ti*, &c and the French by *ch*, should have been in Anglo-Saxon expressed by the same character as in Italian. viz *sc*. Thus is Anglo-Saxon, *Ship*, *Shire*, and numberless words of the same sort, were written *scip*, and *scire*. In reading Latin the Scotch likewise pronounce the *Sc* in that manner. As in *Scipio*, *Scilicet*. Another singular relation may be remarked between our language and the Italian with regard to this semivowel; To almost all our verbs which end with *sh*, there is a corresponding Italian verb in which the oblique persons of the present tense have the same sound. The following are examples. He banishes, *bandisce*, he punishes, *punisce*, he ravishes, *rapisce*, he polishes, *pulisce*, he vanishes, *vanisce*, he languishes, *languisce*, he perishes, *perisce*, he finishes, *finisce*, he flourishes, *fiorisce*, he nourishes, *nudrisce*.

T

T is formed in the same manner with *d*, and only differs from it by being uttered with more energy, as *k* does from the hard *g*, and *p* from *b*. The two semivocal sounds of *th* have been already sufficiently explained. The French, Dutch, Germans and Italians pronounce the *th* in their own languages, and in Latin, and the θ in Greek like *t*. It is certainly nothing but want of habit that renders its semivocal sound so unattainable by those nations.[163] Children with us pronounce it as early as most consonants. There are several letters which persons who have defective organs of speech cannot sound, but I never knew an Inhabitant of this Island who could not utter the *th*. Many Irishmen indeed cannot, but make it a *t* as the foreigners I have mentioned. In Portuguese the *d* has often the soft sound of our *th*. So far is this sound from being difficult to British[164] organs, that by those who have a very strong lisp (as it is called) it is substituted for *s*. The Anglo-Saxon like the Greeks had a distinct single character for *th* viz Ð & ð. A complete orthography would demand a separate character for each of its sounds, which are as distinct from one another as those of their co-relative mutes *d* and *t*. The Greeks originally wrote *th* as we do before the invention of the simple characters Θ & θ.

We have mentioned under *s* the common pronounciation of *ti*, it is proper in this place to add that when it is preceded by an *s* the *t* retains its proper sound. As in *question*, *bastion*. But even then the *tion* forms but one syllable.

Th in some words, as *Thames*, *Thanet*, *Chatham*, *Thomas*, *Thyme*, has only the mute sound of *t*.

U

This letter has three leading and distinct sounds.

1.[165] A simple vocal sound the same with that which it has in Italian, which the French represent by *ou*, and the English most commonly by *oo*. This sound it has in *pull*, *full*, *pulpit*; and it is from this sound that the Scotch give it its name. The *W* (so improperly ranked in our language at least among the consonants) is nothing but a character expressive of this sound of the *u*, when it is followed by another vowel, with which it unites into a diphthong. Let any one who wants to satisfy himself of this, pronounce the Italian words *buono*, *tuono* and immediately afterwards the English words *won*, *wont*, and he will perceive directly that *uo* in the first, and *wo* in the second words form exactly the same diphthong consisting of the first sound of *u* and *o* conjoined; in which that of the latter predominates.

There is indeed one case where the *w* seems to have something of a consonantal effect; namely before this first sound of *u*, as in *wood*, *worsted*. That it has not in such cases the exact first sound of the *u* may be proved in the same manner as we showed that *y* had not the first sound of *ee* in such words as *yield* and *year*. The Scotch pronounce the Greek ου, or γ, with the first sound of *u*. The English more properly like *ou* in *sour, hour*.

2. The second sound of *u* is a sort of smothered vocal sound, as in *Tully, scull, rut*. There is another shade of this second sound which approaches nearer the first in such words as *punt, hulk, rump, dub, mud*. As the first sound of the *u*[166] is represented by *oo* in many words such as *stool, good, brood*, so is this shade of the second, in others, represented also by *oo*, as in *flood, blood*. In the northern counties of England *oo* is always pronounced in this latter manner, as much in *stood* and *good*, as in *flood* and *blood*. And so is the *u* in words like *scull, Tully, rut* where it has the first shade of the second sound in the pure dialect. This second shade of the second sound is also sometimes expressed by a single *o*, as in *love, dove, glove, come*.[167] Sometimes *ou* has that sound as in *couplet*. Sometimes *o* has the first sound of the *u*, as in *move, prove, Tomb*. In *two, wo* has this first sound of *u*.

3. The third sound of *u*, and that from which it takes its name in England, is diphthongal; consisting of the first sound of the *e* followed by the first of the *u*; but so as that the *e* is hurried over, and leaves the *u* to predominate. Of this we have examples in *usage* (which some old authors have written *yusage*) *curious, unity, pure*. To be convinced that this sound of the *u* is compounded in the manner I have described, let the reader compare the pronounciation of the Italian word *piu* with that of the English words just mentioned; or with the first syllable of the word *puling*. The Italian Grammarians call this sort of diphthong, where the first vocal sound is hurried over, and the voice rests on the second; *Dittongi raccolti*, in opposition to those like our *ou* in *hour*, and *oy* in *boy*: where both vowels are more equally and distinctly heard; and which they term *Dittongi distesi*. When an *s* precedes this sound it is not easy to distinguish the *s* from the semivowel *sh*, as may be seen by comparing the first syllables of the French word *chouette* and the English *surely*. *Ew* often represents this sound, as in *pew, dew*; and *ue* sometimes, as in *hue*.[168] In many words the *ue* represents the first sound of *u* where the Scotch give it this diphthongal sound, such as *blue, pursue*. In the pronounciation however of this sort of words, good speakers among the English differ. In *beauty*, the *eau* has the diphthongal sound of *u*.

U being properly the last of the vowels, it may be proper to make in this place, one general observation. viz. That in words where the accent is not on the last but some preceding syllable, the words of the succeeding unaccented syllable, are always pronounced in an obscure indistinct manner, so as to be scarcely distinguishable. Thus in the following words – *Dýsentry, dispénsary, exécutory, hándily, prómontary, systolé,* the *e, a, o* and *i* can hardly be distinguished from each other by the ear. So in *patience,* and *nations* the two syllables though so different to the eye, are, to the ear almost the same.

V

I have reserved to the article of this letter which ought in strictness to be considered as the last of our alphabet, some observations on the analogy and relations which subsist between the various mutes and semivowels. – *B,* and *p* are pronounced by the same position of the organs of speech, and are as much entitled to be considered as one letter as the two sounds of *s* or of *th* are. The same is true of the hard *g* and *k.* And of *d* and *t.* Now each of these has a corresponding semivowel, which have the same sort of affinity together as the co-relative mutes. The semivowel of *b* is *v*; of *p, f*; of the hard *g,* the Dutch and German *g*; of *k,* the Scotch and German *ch*; of *d,* the soft *th.*[169] It is to this affinity between these different sets of consonants that we are to ascribe the frequent changes from one of them to another, in words which have been transplanted out of one language into another. Thus for the *d* of the German *du, dein* and *das* we have substituted the soft *th,* in *thou, thine,* & *that,* and the hard *th* in *think* for *d* in *denk*; and, on the contrary for their *t* in *thun, taub, gut, blut,* we have substituted *d* in *do, dove, good, blood.* For their *b* in *sterben, liebe* and *taub,* we have put *v* in *starve, love, dove.* In like manner the Romans changed the Greek β often into *v,* as in βις, *vis,* βολω, *volo,* βαινω, *venio,* βοβαιω, *voveo.* Not that I would rely much upon such instances in the dead languages, because it is impossible for us to ascertain exactly what differences the ancients made in their pronunciation between the correspondent consonants. We are apt to consider the φ, and *f* of the Greeks and Romans, to have had exactly the same sound, yet there is a passage in Quintillian which proves the contrary. He tells us that Cicero laughed at a Greek who pronounced *Fundanius,* as if it had been written φ*undanius.* In the Italian language, whose distinguishing characteristic is a peculiar softness and liquidity of sound, the harder mutes *k* and *t* of the Latin are frequently exchanged for the corresponding softer ones of *g* and *d*; And the *b* again is often altered to its semivowel *v.* Thus from *Acus, Lacus, Locus, explicare,* have been formed *Ago, lago, Luogo, spiegare.* From *caritate, virtute, civitate, nutrire, latrone, strata; caritade virtude, cittade, nudrire,* *ladrone, strada.* From *laudabilis, favorabilis, habere, labor*; *lodevole, favorevole, avere, lavoro.*

The analogy between the *b* and *v* might serve to explain the peculiarity in the speech of the Gascons, by which they always give the sound of *b*, to *v*. Saying *je l'ai bu* for *je l'ai vu. Bérité* for *vérité.* But if my memory does not deceive me they also pronounce like a *v* what is written with a *b*. As *veaux yeux* for *beaux yeaux.* This sort of exchange of the two sounds, is equally unaccountable with the habit of those people of whom I have already made mention, who pronounce the *h* where it is mute and suppress it where it ought to be pronounced. The continual substitution of *v* for *w*, and *w* for *v*, by the inferior class of citizens in London is an inexplicable phenomenon of speech, of the same nature with the two others of which I have just taken notice. I have known some individuals in Scotland have this last habit, and (if I am not mistaken) it is common to all the inhabitants of a small district of one of the Northern counties of that kingdom.

W

In the Anglo-Saxon the *h* was prefixed to the *w* in words where it follows it in modern English. Thus they wrote *Hþæt* for *what, Hþelp* for *whelp, Hþi* for *why*. This, as Dr Johnson, Mr Tyrrwhit, and several other writers have observed, is more consonant to the modern pronounciation. For, by the true English method of sounding these words, the *h* is first heard, and then a diphthong composed of the first sound of *u* rapidly run into, and lost, in the open *a* in *what*, in the second sound of *e* in *when*, and in the diphthongal sound of *i* in *why*. The Scotch pronounce the *wh* like their guttural *ch*, followed in like manner by a *u*, losing itself in the succeeding vowel. When they endeavour to correct this fault they are apt to omit the *h*, so as to pronounce *whit*, and *wit*, *whig* and *wig* in the very same manner. Careless speakers among the English very commonly fall into the same error. In the North of Scotland *wh* is pronounced like *f*; so that *what*, and *fat*, *why*, and *fie*, form to the ear in that part of the Island, the very same words.

X

Is a character which expresses 1. The sound of the hard *g* followed by the soft *s*, or *z* as in *exact*, which might be written *egzact.* 2. The sound of *k*, followed by the hard *s*, as in *extreme* which might be written *ekstreme.* The Italians have rejected this letter entirely.

Y

Concerning this letter we have nothing to add to what has been said under *I*.

Z

In English the *z* has always the second or soft sound of *s*. As in *gaze*, *baize*, *zeal*. The Scotch, at the beginning of words, as *zeal*, *zone*, *zenith* pronounce it with the combined sound of *d*, and the soft *s*. This is its most common sound in Italian. It may be proper to remark that Dr Johnson calls the sound of *z*, or the second of *s*, the hard *s*; Whereas I have applied the epithet soft to that sound, and have called the other hard. It matters little which is used. Both expressions are metaphorical. But according to my ear and to the ears of those whom I have consulted on the subject, there is more propriety in calling the *s* in *praise* soft, than that in *past*. We may observe that what we have called soft, is the sound given by the Venetians to the *c* in *piase* for *piace*, and their dialect is thought to derive much of its acknowledged softness from this circumstance.

Cap. 3

Of Rhyme considered as contributing to ascertain the pronounciation of words[170]

There are four striking features in all the languages of modern Europe, by which they are distinguished from those of the Greeks and Romans. The first, is the use of particles, instead of a variety of termination, to mark the different cases of nouns. The second, the use of auxiliary verbs in the place of a similar variety of termination in verbs. The third, the construction of verse, by a certain determinate mixture of accented, and unaccented instead of long and short syllables. And the fourth, the use of rhyme. Yet traces of every one of these, are to be met with in the ancient languages.

The disquisitions of some learned men have rendered it highly probable that particles or prepositions were not infrequently used instead of diversified termination in the vulgar colloquial Latin, while yet a living language.[171] Many instances where *habeo* is used as an auxiliary verb with a[172] participle passive, have been collected; and in all the common grammars there are tenses marked where *sum* is employed in the same manner.

Accent had usurped the place of quantity in the Versus Politici of the Greeks of Constantinople[173] at an earlier period than the date of the most ancient verses formed upon that model which are to be found in any of the modern vernacular tongues. Instances of such verses are met with in the works of the Patriarch Photius, who wrote in the 9th century, And in various other writers of that country down to the time of Tzetzes, who lived in the 12th.[174]

It was an opinion hastily taken up about the time of the revival of letters, and long blindly adhered to, that rhyme had its origin in the dialects of those northern tribes who overthrew the Roman empire. In like manner the style of architecture which prevailed in the middle ages, and differed so essentially from that of the Greeks and Romans, was attributed to the same rude invaders, and it is usually called Gothic to this day. But of late years the history of literature and the arts, has been more accurately investigated. The species of architecture improperly named Gothic has been traced to another source, and the following short deduction will satisfy the reader that the Goths had as little share in the invention of rhyme.

Examples of rhyming verses in the best Greek and Latin poets are not infrequent.[175] The reader, by turning his eye to the passages cited at the bottom of the page, will find this assertion fully justified, & such instances seem[176] to show that Rhyme was not so anxiously avoided by the ancients as some have imagined. It is impossible to believe that so many like endings escaped the correct and polished ear of Virgil without being perceived by him. Among the passages I have taken from him it is observable that the sense often ends with the second line of the rhyme. In these the correspondence of sound could not but strike the most inattentive reader or hearer. If they had been thought a blemish the Poet would have altered them with the same scrupulous care as he would have done a false quantity, and of this there is not an example in the whole *Eneid*,[177] though it had not received its last polish when he died. I am far from thinking that he, or any other antient Poet ever used rhyme by design. Probably it was neither shun'd, nor sought after. It was a sort of accident, which of course happened but seldom, and was not thought of as a thing that might be produced in a regular and constant manner, so as to form one of the uniform requisites in the structure of verse. But in the succession of ages men became satiated with established modes of versification. Then it was that Writers who did not feel themselves endowed with genius and invention capable of gratifying that restless appetite for novelty which is so strongly implanted in the human breast, by the creative effusions of the imagination, in which true poetry consists, struck out an humbler path, more suited to their own limited talents and to the tame and finical taste of their cotemporaries.[178] Having remarked that the accidental chiming of some scattered lines in the works of the early poets, produced rather an agreeable effect to the ear, they resolved to try how[179] an intentional and frequent use of such lines would be received. After the idea had suggested itself, the execution was easy; and the experiment was attended with success. The uninterrupted and increasing employment of rhymes from the time of their first introduction sufficiently proves that they met with the approbation of the public of those days. They abound in the writings of St Ambrosius, and Damasus, Ecclesiastical poets of the fourth century. Sedulus and Fortunatus in the 5th and 6th use them frequently in their hymns, and they came into very general use among the Latin poets, or, if you will versifiers, in the 6th 7th 8th and 9th. It was in Latin therefore that Rhyme as a designed modification in the structure of Metre had its commencement. After very learned researches it appears that Osfrid of Wüssemberg was the first who employed it in any of the modern European tongues; and he did not write till towards the end of the 9th century.[180] It never seems to have been introduced into the Anglo-Saxon, at least not before the

Conquest. A very accurate and learned Critic[181] has discovered that the first example of Rhyme that can be found in our language is a couplet mentioned in William of Malmesbury. It was dictated by the spleen of Aldred Archbishop of York, soon after the Norman Invasion, against one Urse sheriff of Worcestershire.

> Hatest thou (i.e. hightest, art thou called) *Urse?*
> Have thou God's *curse*

That is (as the Historian renders it) 'Vocaris Urse – Habeas Dei Maledictionem.'[182] God knows the only advantage this curious distich has over the worst modern doggerel is derived from the circumstance of its priority in point of date.

This is not the place to enquire whether rhyme is really such a deformity to modern poetry, as some great masters of the art have asserted. Milton calls it 'a thing to all judicious ears trivial, and of no true musical delight;' and Dryden says that it debases the majesty[183] of verse. Armed with such authority the numerous race of lesser critics treat it as a puerile contrivance that not only cannot afford pleasure to the ear, but must disgust every person of a refined and cultivated taste. If this is so, I would ask those gentlemen how they will account for the continued, voluntary, and almost universal, submission to the shackles of rhyme by the best poets of all the nations of modern Europe. Exclusive of tragedies, we cannot reckon up in English, above three or four poems of sterling merit written in blank verse. In Italian the number is still smaller. In French, there are none. Milton himself employed rhyme in his lesser compositions. Dryden in[184] almost all his poetical works, tragedies not excepted. In discussing this problem perhaps it would be more philosophical to argue from the practise of those great men, than from their loose assertions; especially as those assertions were the result of temporary impressions[185] and adapted to particular occasions. Milton, in his short preface to *Paradise Lost*, thought it necessary to prepare the reader for the singularity of an heroic poem in English blank verse, by the degradation of rhyme; and the passage of Dryden to which I have referred is contained in a copy of verses addressed to Lord Roscommon in commendation of his blank verse (or rather prose) translation of Horace's *Art of Poetry*. It is not sufficient to say that rhyme is tolerated by the reader, and submitted to by the poet, because [186]'*without any other assistance, it throws the language off from prose.*' The best prose is not indeed so grateful to the ear as harmonious verse. But good prose has great claims to those who have a taste for literature, and surely a writer never could find his account in substituting in its room a species of composition wherein he, with no small trouble to himself, had introduced an absolute blemish whose

145

necessary tendency must be to nauseate and disgust, for no other purpose but '*to throw it off from prose*'. In short this proposition, when stated to its full extent, involves the greatest absurdity, and though it may be difficult to say why, it is impossible to consider the long and general prevalence of rhyme without admitting, that there is something in it, which heightens the pleasure derived from modern versification. The chief objection to it with some, is the supposed uniformity attending it. But this is easily confuted; for there is much more uniformity in the regular and unvaried return of two long syllables at the end of every line, than in the varied succession of different rhymes. The constant conclusion of every line by a spondee was never however considered as a source of a disgust in the *Iliad* and *Æneid*.

It would not be difficult, methinks, to trace the origin of the common censure and declamation which has so long been echoed from Critic to Critic against rhyme. When the study of the Greek and Roman literature was revived it excited a degree of admiration approaching to enthusiasm and idolatry. Every thing of which there was no model to be found in ancient authors was disgraced with the appellations of Gothick and barbarous. Accented verse and rhyme, the inventions of what were called the monkish times, could not but share the common fate. Many of the best geniuses scorned to write in the languages of their respective countries; and those who did, strove to bend them to every rule of composition which had been deduced from the writings of Homer, Sophocles, Demosthenes, Cicero, and Virgil. Hence that inverted order of the words which we observe in early prose authors during the reigns of Elizabeth, and James. Hence the attempt in almost every country of Europe, to adapt the vernacular tongue to the Hexameter, and other antient schemes of versification. Among the adventurers in this last-mentioned field of reformation were Alberti among the Italians, Desportes among the French, and Sir Philip Sidney in England. This gallant soldier, and polite scholar had '*almost drawn over Spenser to his faction*', for so we learn by one of that poet's own letters. But he soon found out that the genius of the English language opposed itself to their design. The same discovery was made in Italy and France, and it is surprising that what had been tried and exploded so long ago among the other nations of Europe should have been renewed in our days in German by Klopstock, who has written his poem of the Messiah in Hexameters. I would not pretend upon my own judgment to affirm that his verse, like Sydney's '*halts ill in Roman feet*' but I know this to be the general opinion of the best writers[187] among his Countrymen; and I am satisfied from what I have collected from some of them, that the reign of this sort of metre will not be of much longer duration in Germany than it was in England. After it was discovered that verse regulated by quantity, and not by accent was incompatible with the nature of modern language, it was still thought that the accented verse would lose one badge of its unclassical origin if it were divested of rhyme. Accordingly blank verse, or *versi sciolti* were introduced into all the languages of Europe. Their fate has been different in different countries. In France they never gained any footing. Trissino, who had more learning than genius, was their great patron among the Italians, both by precept and example; having composed[188] his tedious poem called *Italia Liberata*, in blank verse. Such a work was not likely to make many converts, and his followers have not been numerous. Tasso indeed towards the end of his life is said to have come into the opinion that this sort of verse was in their language the most proper for heroic poetry. But it is well known, (and to prove it, it is only necessary to compare his *Gierusalemme Conquistata*, and his *Gierusalemme Liberata* together) that the taste of that divine author had degenerated before his death. How few are there, even in Italy, who have read his *Giornate* (which are written in blank verse) compared with the number of those who know the greatest part of his *Gierusalemme Liberata* by heart. With us the example of Shakespear, the most wonderful genius that ever adorned human nature, and that of Milton, not much beneath him in genius, and in learning superior to all our English poets, have stamped a value on blank verse which has enabled it to hold, ever since their time, a sort of divided empire with rhyme. In tragedy, it certainly approaches nearer the natural language of discourse, and that reason (which perhaps might be proved to be rather plausible than solid) has totally banished rhyme from our stage. The beautiful[189] and matchless variety of cadence, and pauses in the *Paradise Lost*, and the monotony which prevails too generally in the works of our best writers in rhyme, but especially in Pope, have contributed to establish a notion that blank verse has a necessary advantage in this respect over rhyme. Yet particular passages might be selected from the writings even of Pope, and many more from some of Milton's rhymed poems, and from those of Dryden and Prior, which would show that this is but a hasty and ill founded conclusion.

But whatever may be thought of the advantages or disadvantages arising to modern poetry from the use of rhyme, it will readily be admitted that those who adopt it ought to study to render that part of their versification as correct and perfect as possible. If this had been sufficiently attended to the modern languages would have possessed one considerable advantage over the ancient. Rhyme then would have served to ascertain, in a degree perhaps to fix, the true pronounciation of words. The inaccuracies and caprice of orthography, would not have misled foreigners, provincials, and posterity. Thus, for example, the words *there, care, hair, bear*, are, except in the beginning consonants, exactly the same in sound. If they had never been made to rhyme with others, which though agreeing with them in orthography differ in sound, as *bear* and *appear*, or which differ from them both in orthography and sound, as *care* and *war* the pronounciation of one of them would have served as a key to that of all the rest. Our English poets have been far from adhering scrupulously to the exactness of rhyme. The French cannot boast of greater accuracy. Even of the Italians it can only be said that they have approached nearer to perfection in this respect than other nations; not that they have attained it. The restraint such nicety would have laid the poet under, is not perhaps a sufficient apology for the neglect of it. For when he undertakes to write in verse he necessarily lays himself under other similar restraints, and greater. Could Homer or Virgil have excused themselves for the introduction of an Iambus sometimes at the end of a line, by alledging that they could not bear the restraint of terminating every verse with a spondee? It is one of the chief praises of a poet, and what adds much to the pleasure we derive from the perusal of his works, that while he has complied with the strictest rules, he has been able to express himself in a manner as free and flowing as if he had written in prose. Those rules indeed must be in themselves rational, and such as are known by experience to produce a pleasing effect. Not like the frigid and ridiculous conceits of acrosticks, wings, and altars. Subject to that qualification I am persuaded that much of the delight good verse affords, flows from the sense of admiration excited in our minds by what the French critics call *la difficulté vaincue*. This cannot be more happily expressed than in the words which Mr Mason has put into the mouth of Milton in the supposed address to that great poet by Pope.

> I such bonds
> Aimed to destroy, mistaking: bonds like these
> T'were greater art t'ennoble, and refine.
> For this superior part Museus came.
> Thou cam'st, and at thy magic touch the chains
> Off dropt, and (passing strange!) soft wreathed bands
> Of flow'rs, their place supply'd, Which well the muse
> Might wear for choice, not force: obstruction none
> But loveliest ornament.

The authority of every one of our poets, even the most correct, has now given a sanction to a great number of rhymes that are far from perfect and which some have chosen to distinguish by the epithet *allowable*. By this means we are deprived of the advantage of using their verses as authorities to ascertain the sound of words. If Pope does not scruple to make *bears* rhyme with *appears*, *care* with *war*, and *vice* with *caprice*, it cannot be a conclusive inference in any case because two words are found rhyming together in *his* writings, that they correspond exactly in pronounciation. The only advantage therefore to be expected from the poets in correcting the vices of this branch of provincial pronounciation is, when the word whose sound is to be described occurs in a perfect rhyme, to employ such rhyme in the way of illustration. The benefit which will accrue from thence, I have pointed out in another place. It will be expedient here to give the analysis of the different circumstances which must concur in its formation.[190] In regular verse rhyme consists in a certain resemblance between the last syllables of corresponding lines; and in our language the rhyme is not perfect unless it possesses the following requisites.[191]

1. If both the rhyming syllables begin with one or more consonants, those consonants must not be the same in each

> But now secure the painted vessel *g*lides
> The sun-beams trembling on the floating *t*ides;
> While melting music steals upon the *sk*y
> And soften'd sounds along the waters *d*ie;
> Smooth flow the waves, the Zephirs gently *p*lay
> Belinda smiled and all the world was *g*ay.[192]
> All but the Sylph – with careful thoughts op*p*rest,
> Th' impending woe sat heavy on his *b*reast.[193]

These rhymes possess this, as well as all the other requisites which I am about to mention. Indeed this one is more seldom dispensed with by any of our poets than the others. In the Rape of the Lock there is not one instance where Pope has broke through it. Unless perhaps in the two following couplets

> The doubtful beam long nods from side to *s*ide
> At length the wits mount up, the hairs sub*s*ide.
> But this bold Lord, with manly strength en*d*ued
> She with a finger and a thumb sub*d*ued.

But even in these, although according to the common manner of dividing the syllable, the rhyming part begins with the same consonant. viz. *s* and *d*, yet the ear is not dissatisfied for the following reasons. In the one case, the *s* in *subside* is immediately preceded by another consonant (*b*) which is not found in the corresponding word, *side*. And therefore the rhyme is in this respect analogous to the following.[194]

> O say, what stranger cause, yet unex*pl*ored,
> Could make a gentle belle reject a *L*ord.[195]

which is certainly as perfect, as any of those first cited. In the other case the *d* is immediately preceded by different consonants in the corresponding words, viz. by *n* in the one, & by *b* in the other, and therefore this is likewise rendered analogous to the following which will be allowed by every ear to be a perfect rhyme.

> And sullen Mole, that hides his diving *flood*
> And silent Davent stain'd with Danish *blood*.[196]

Still however these two rhymes it must be confessed, are in some slight degree defective. If *represst* and *presst*, *reply* and *ply* or *apply*, *dress* and *redress*, *deface* and *efface* were made to rhyme together the most slovenly ear would perceive something in them not complete, though a person who had not accustomed himself to reflect on the subject, might be puzzled at first to say in what they differed from other perfect rhymes.

2. If one of the rhyming words is a monosyllable and begins with a vowel, the corresponding syllable must begin with one or more consonants.

> He summons strait his Denizens of *air*
> The lucid squadrons round the sails re*pair*.[197]

> He takes the gift with rev'rence and ex*tends*
> The little engine on his finger *ends*[198]

> He springs to vengeance with an eager *pace*
> And falls like thunder on the prostrate *ace*[199]

This rule admits of an exception in the case of syllables beginning with *y* or *w*. For such syllables may form a perfect rhyme with monosyllables beginning with a vowel, although we have shown that *y* and *w* might themselves be considered as vowels. Thus *ear* and *year*, *wore* and *ore* are perfect rhymes. I am apt to think a syllable beginning with the diphthongal *u* will also form a perfect rhyme with one which commences with the long vocal *u*. As *use* a verb (*utere*) and *oose*.

3. The vocal part of the two rhyming syllables must be to the ear exactly the same, both in the nature of the sound, and in the *quantity*.

> Not with more glories on th' etherial *plain*
> The sun first rises o'er the purpled *main*.[200]

> On her white breast a sparkling cross she *wore*
> Which Jews might kiss, and infidels *adore*[201]

> Bright as the sun her eyes the gazers *strike*
> And like the sun, they shine on all *alike*.[202]

In those examples, not only the sound, but the orthography is the same. But the following which disagree in the vocal characters are however equally perfect.

> What, Godess! this unusual favour *draws?*
> All hail and welcome! whatso'er the *cause*;
> Till now a stranger, in a happy *hour*
> Approach, and taste the dainties of the *bow'r*.[203]

> The fanning wind upon her bosom *blows*
> To meet the fanning wind her bosom *rose*.[204]

Nor does a conformity of vocal characters render a rhyme perfect in which the vocal sound is not the same. In the following instances,

> That counteracts each folly and cap*rice*
> That disappoints th'effect of every *vice*[205]

> Criticks, of less judgment than cap*rice*
> Curious, not knowing, not exact, but *nice*.[206]

> Now looking downwards, just as grieved app*ears*
> To want the strength of bulls, the fur of b*ears*[207]

The Rhymes are as imperfect as where both sound and orthography disagree, of which sort our best poets will furnish innumerable instances.

> Or, as Ixion fix'd, the wretch shall *feel*
> The giddy motion of the whirling *mill*[208]

> Tomorrow she assumes a softer *air*
> Forsakes the pomp, and pageantry of *war*.[209]

> The form of peaceful Abigail assumes
> And from the village with the present comes.
> Awakes the sleepy vigour of the *soul*,
> And brushing o'er, adds motion to the *pool*.[210]

The following rhymes have all the other requisites and agree in the quality of their vocal sound, but are imperfect because they differ in quantity.

> These swell their prospects and exalt their *pride*
> When offers are disdained and love *deny'd*[211]

Here the vocal part of each of the corresponding syllables consists of the 1st or diphthongal sound of *i*; but in *pride* that sound is shortened, and protracted in *deny'd*.

> Fair Nymphs, and well drest youths around her *shone*
> But ev'ry eye was fix'd on her *alone*.[212]

151

> He is gone, He is *gone*
> And we cast away *moan*.[213]

In the first line of each of these rhymes the *o* has its short close sound and in the second of each the *o* and *oa* have the same sound but protracted. But these rhymes are less imperfect than where a sound different in quality[214] of the same vowel is employ'd in each line, and these sounds also differ in quantity.

> Nine years kept secret, in the dark *abode*
> Secure I lay, conceal'd from Man and *God*[215]

Here the *o* has its long close sound in *abode*, and its open and short sound in *God*.

With regard to rhymes which terminate with vowels there is nothing more necessary to render them perfect than what I have already mentioned. But it at least as frequently happens that the vocal part is closed by one or more consonants. This is the case with almost all the examples I have given, and to such rhymes there is another circumstance more indispensably necessary than any of the foregoing. For

4. The closing consonantal part of the two rhyming syllables must be to the ear exactly the same.

Here too a similar orthography is not sufficient to justify, nor does a difference in orthography vitiate, the rhyme. *Tricks*, and *mix*; *decks* and *vex*, are perfect rhymes. So are *tough* and *snuff*, *cough* and *scoff*, *laugh* and *quaff*. And the following

> Is this a dinner, this a genial *room*?
> No 'tis a temple and a hecat*omb*.[216]

A deviation from this 4th rule is not pardonable in the most careless or the longest compositions. I doubt if more than one instance is to be found in all the writings of Pope[217] where he has departed from it. But several other great Poets have suffered such blemishes to remain in their works. In Spenser who though not a correct is a most sweet and harmonious versifier, I could point out many instances of this sort

> Whiles all her sisters did for her lament
> With yelling outcries and with shrieking sound
> And every one did tear her garland from her crown.[218]

The concluding couplet of Addison's epistle on the English poets is become proverbial for the badness of the rhyme.

> I leave the arts of poetry and *verse*
> To those who practise them with more *success*.

And although the sound of the *e* in *verse* and *success* is not the same, the most offensive circumstance in this passage is the disagreement of the terminating consonants. Nor is the following rhyme in the *Dunciad* more justifiable

> Prompt or to guard, or stab, to saint, or *damn*
> Heavn's Serifs who fight for any god or *man*.[219]

This is the instance to which I have alluded. We however pardon more easily a defect of versification where the sense is so spirited, than where, as in the former instance, the meaning is cold and languid, as the rhyme is bald and[220] irregular.

But I have no where met so gross a fault of this kind as in two lines of Dryden's translation of the sixth satire of Juvenal

> The gaudy gossip, when she's set agog
> In jewel's dress'd and in each ear a bob,
> Goes flaunting out

Who would believe that this wretched doggerel could ever in the most hasty and careless moment have fallen from the pen of the author of *Alexanders Feast*.

From the four rules that I have already mentioned it follows that a word never can rhyme to itself, and accordingly I do not believe that such an instance is to be met with in any classical English writer since the Restoration.[221] The Italian and French poets are not so scrupulous in this respect. With them if the same word has two different senses & is used in the corresponding lines in those different senses it may rhyme to itself. The Italians in some instances will even admit of such a rhyme tho the sense of the word is not varied. I shall produce a few instances from both languages beginning with the Italian.

> Ne Guasco né Ridolofo a dietro lasso;
> Ne l'un, ne l'alto Guido, ambo famosi;
> Non Eberardo, e non Gernier trapasso
> Sotto silenzio ingratamente ascosi.
> Ove voi me, di numerar gia lasso,
> Gildippe, et Odoardo, amanti e sposi
> Rapite? O ne la guerra anco consorti!
> Non sarete disgiunti, ancor che morti.[222]

In the first and fifth lines of this stanza *lasso* is used in a different sense.[223]

> Ma Tancredi grido, che se n'accorse
> E con la spada a quel gran colpo occorse.[224]

153

In the first of these lines *accorse* belongs to the verb *accorgere*, in the second to *accorrere*

> Or si volge, or rivolge, or fugge, or fuga,
> Ne si puo dir la sua, caccia, ne fuga.[225]

In the first line *fuga* is a verb; in the second a substantive.[226]

> Come per acqua, o per cristallo intero
> Trapassa il raggio, e no 'l divide, o parte,
> Per entro il chiuso manto osa il pensiero
> Si penetrar ne la vietata parte.
> Ivi si spazia, ivi contempla il vero
> Di tante meraviglie a parte, a parte
> Poscia al desio, le narra e le descrive
> E ne fa le sue fiamme in lui piu vive.[227]

Here *parte* is repeated three times, and in the 4th and 6th lines it may be considered as bearing the same sense.

The rule of the Italian *Terzetti* (a species of verse invented by Dante, and in which he wrote his *comedia*) is this; – that there must always be three lines to rhyme together; but having an intervening line of a different termination between each; And this intervening line makes also one of three that rhyme together. Ariosto's satires, and the famous *Capitoli* of Beni, and other poets his contemporaries are in *Terzetti*. Sydney, who tried every sort of verse, has used this in his dialogue of Plangus and Basilius in the second book of the *Arcadia*. It is also adopted by Milton (who was deeply versed in Italian literature, And a great admirer of it) in his translation of the second Psalm. But they have no followers, and indeed the rhymes so intermixed have not an agreeable effect to an English ear. In the following and two other passages of the *Paradiso*, Dante has made *Cristo* the rhyming word of the three corresponding lines of a *Terzetto*.

> A questo regno
> Non sali mai chi non credette 'n *Cristo*
> Ne pria, ne poi che'l si chiavasse al legno
> Ma vedi molti gridan *Cristo Cristo*
> Che saranno al giudizio assai men prope
> A lui, che tal che non conosce *Cristo*[228, 229]

The other two passages are in the 12, and 14, Cantos of the *Paradiso*. Rhymes of this sort are not so common in French verse, and as was already observed it is absolutely necessary in that language that a word when it rhymes to itself should be used in two different senses

> Mon erreur me deplait, et je me plains *pas*
> Qu'au bords du precipice on arrete mes *pas*.

L'Intendant:

Henri, qui fait sur nous briller des jours heureuse
Veut que la loi gouverne, et non par qu'on la *brave*

Julie:

Non le brave Henri ne peut punir un *brave*[230]

Si me faut-il trouver, n'en fut-il *point*
Tempe rament pour accorder ce *point*[231]

The older English poets thought themselves at liberty to employ
rhymes of this kind; as the following passages taken from Chaucer,
Spenser, and Milton, will show

They ben so true, and therewithal so wise
For which if thou wilt werchen as the wif
Do alway so as women will thee rēde[232]

I recke never when that they be *beried*
Though that hir soules gon a black *beried*[233]

He lulleth hire, he kisseth hire full *soft*
With thicke bristles of his berd un*soft*[234]

But how long time said then the elfin knight
Are you in this misformed house to dwell?
We may not chaunge (quoth he) this evil plight
Til we be bathed in a living *well*.
That is the term presented by the spell.
O how, said he, mote I that well out find
That may restore you to your wonted *well?*[235]

Most sacred fire that burneth mightily
In living breasts, ykindled first above
Emongst th'eternal spheres, and lamping sky,
And thence poured into men, which men call *love*.
Not that same which doth base affectations move
In brutish minds, and filthy lust inflame;
But that sweet fit that doth true beauty *love*,
And chuseth virtue for his dearest dame,
Whence spring all noble deeds, and never-dying fame.[236]

The better part with Mary and with *Ruth*
Chosen thou hast; and they that over-ween,
And at thy growing virtues fret their spleen,
No anger find in thee, but pity and *ruth*.[237]

In one of the finest passages of Mr Prior's *Solomon* we are shocked to meet with a couplet, in which, if we were to pronounce *ear* as the Irish do, the same word (in sound) would be made to rhyme to itself. And if we pronounce it properly, the third of the above mentioned rules is transgressed.

> Perhaps the jest that charm'd the sprightly croud,
> And made the jovial table laugh so loud,
> To some false notion owed its poor pretence;
> To an ambiguous word's perverted sense;
> To a wild sonnet, or a wanton *air*,
> Offence, and torture, to the sober *ear*.[238]

Thus I have analysed, and by examples illustrated, the circumstances which occur to form a perfect rhyme, in our regular verse. But as our poetry admits of one, or sometimes two[239] supernumerary syllables at the end of a line, it is necessary to add that in such cases,

5. The supernumerary syllables in the corresponding lines, must be exactly the same, both in their vocal and consonantal part.

> The meeting points the sacred hair diss*ever*
> From the fair head, for ever, and for *ever*.[240]

> To sigh for ribbands if thou art so silly
> Mark how they grace Lord Umbra or Sir Billy.[241]

> But clear thy wrinkled front and quit thy *sorrow*
> I'd scorn your 'prentice should you die to-*morrow*.[242]

> Whether the Godless sinner it, or *saint it*
> If folly grow romantic – I must *paint it*.[243]

> Lucretius keeps a mighty *pother*
> With Cupid, and his fancy'd *Mother*
> And while her humour he re*hearses*
> Implores her to inspire his v*erses*.[244]

These are called double rhymes and are only used in familiar poetry; and because (which will appear afterwards) the supernumerary syllables are never accented, and the vowels which follow the accented syllable are pronounced in a sort of smothered indistinct manner, (vide supra) the most scrupulous ear hardly requires that the vocal part of the corresponding syllables should be exactly the same.

> Worth makes the man, and want of it the f*ellow*
> The rest is all but leather and pr*unella*.[245]

> He ranged his tropes and preached up pat*ience*
> Back'd his opinion with quo*tations*.[246]

When there are two supernumerary syllables, (in which case the rhyme should be called triplet) it is almost impossible that the vowels should exactly agree.

> Thence to the right and moving through there[247]

A variance to the ear in the consonantal part of the supernumerary syllables has a much worse effect. The following couplet is greatly defective on that account.

> As soon as Phoebus' rays inspect us,
> First, Sir, I read, and then I breakfast.[248]

The several foregoing rules of perfect rhyme may all be reduced to two. viz

1. If both the members of the rhyme begin with consonants they must disagree in those consonants, and in every other respect be entirely the same.

2. If one of the members of the rhyme begin with a vowel, the other must begin with a consonant. Or with *y*, *w*, or the diphthongal *u*.

Cap. 4

A Table[249] of words improperly pronounced by the Scotch, showing their true English pronounciation

ABHOR[250]

The Scotch are apt to[251] give the *o* its long close sound in this word and its derivatives, pronouncing it as if it made a perfect rhyme with *explore*, *boar*, *sore*. But in the pure dialect the *o* is short and open, as in *for*, *or*. So that the following is a perfect rhyme

> The self same thing, they will abhor
> One way, and long another for.[252]

The *h* is pronounced.

ACKNOWLEDGE

As Scotchmen soon learn that the *k* is mute in *knowledge* and other words wherein it is followed by an *n*, they, for the most part, fall into the error of suppressing the *c* likewise in *acknowledge*,[253] and pronounce it as if it were written *anowledge*, or *aknowledge*. But the English give this *c* its hard sound, and utter it as distinctly as they do the *κ* in the Greek word *εὐκνημιδες*. For the sound of the second syllable vide *knowledge*.

ABJECT

Is the first English word, according to alphabetical arrangement which has its termination in *ct*. This is therefore the proper occasion to observe that in general the Scotch suppress the *t* at the end of all such words, pronouncing *abjeck*, *fack*.[254] Some who have acquired the habit of sounding the *t* in some of this class of words omit it in others, or if they pronounce it in reading, they will often forget it in conversation. In pure speech the *t* is constantly and distinctly sounded. According to the Scotch method *fact* and *distinct* rhyme to *attack* and *think*, whereas they should rhyme to *packt* and *linkt*. Perhaps the Scotch pronounciation of these words, once prevailed in England. Shakespear writes *Benedick* for *Benedict*. *Track* and *tract* have nearly the same sense.

158

Dr Johnson however makes their etymology different. *Relick* and *relict* are[255] manifestly not the same, either in meaning or in derivation.

The French, in such of this class of words as are found in their language, viz, *aspect, respect, suspect* &c neither pronounce the *c* or the *t* in common discourse: but, in solemn speech, or on the stage, the *c* is sounded, without the *t*. So that *respect* (for instance) in the more accurate French pronounciation, has exactly the same sound as in the provincial dialect of Scotland.

ABOVE

The *o* has the second or short sound of *u*, exactly as in *rub, sunk*. The Scotch are very often apt to sound it like the long vocal[256] *u* or *oo*; so as to make *above*, rhyme to *groove*. There are a considerable number of words of this termination, and they are pronounced in three different ways. Some of them in the manner we have just described. In some, as *strove, rove, grove*, the *o* has its long close sound as in *abode*. And in some, as *move, prove*, it is sounded in the manner in which the Scotch pronounce it in *above*. As these three sounds are generally confounded in Scotland, so that the words pronounced in England in one way, are, in that country, pronounced in an other, it will be useful to attend to the following lists, where they are arranged according to their true pronounciation.[257] *Love* which they sound properly, and which rhymes to the true pronounciation of *above* will serve as the leading word in the first list. *Move* which rhymes to *groove* in the second and *Jove* (which is also properly pronounced by the Scotch) in the third.[258]

1. *Love, above* (pronounced by the Scotch like *move*) *dove* (by the Scotch like *Jove*) *shove*, noun and verb (by the Scotch like *Jove*) *glove*, *True-love*.

2.[259] *Move, amove, approve, behoove, disapprove, improve, prove,* (*remove, reprove*). All often pronounced by the Scotch like *love*.

3. *Jove, alcove, cove, clove* (verb and noun,) *drove* (verb and noun,) *grove, hove, rove, strove* verb and noun, *throve, wove*.[260] The following is a perfect rhyme.

> O! witness earth beneath, and heav'n *above*;
> For can I hide it? I am sick of *love*.[261]

ACCEPT

In words ending in *pt*, as [262] in those that end in *ct*, the Scotch in their pronounciation, suppress the *t*, which is never done by the English. This practice[263] among the Scotch must arise from a supposed *Cacophonia* in the junction either of the *p* or hard *c* with the *t* at the end of a word. How shall we explain the different instances where certain sounds appear harsh and are avoided in some languages or dialects

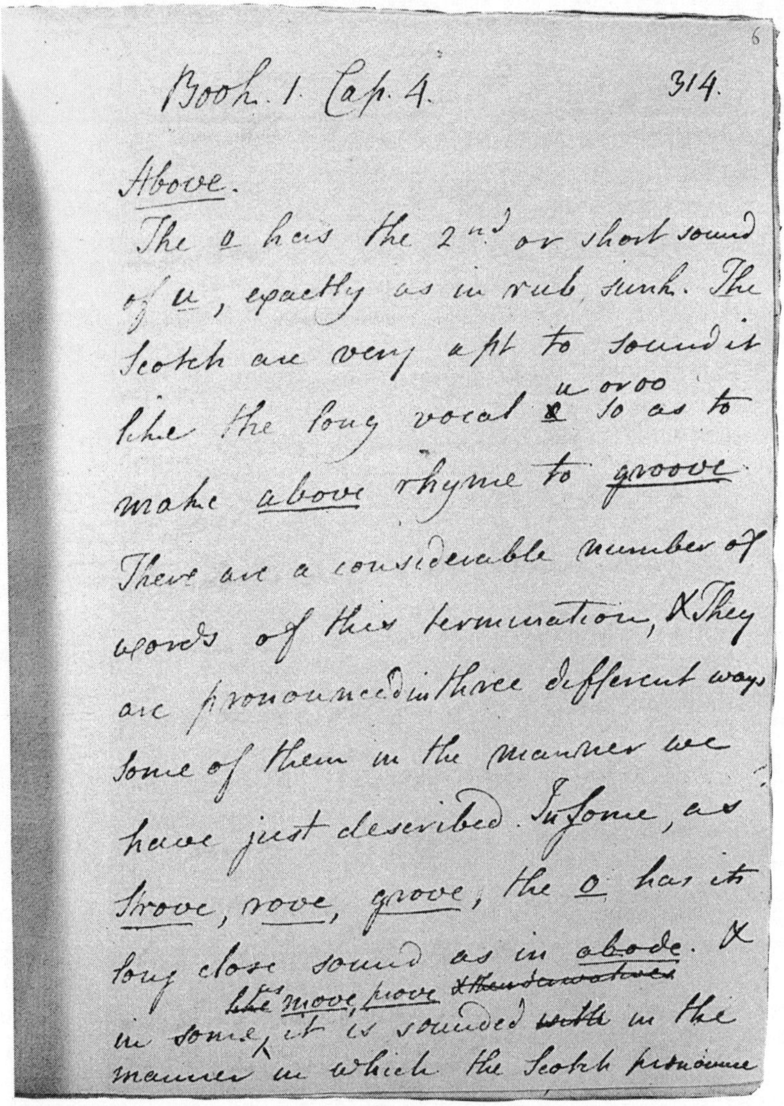

Book. 1. Cap. 4.   314.

Above.

The o has the 2ⁿᵈ or short sound of u, exactly as in rub, sunk. The Scotch are very apt to sound it like the long vocal u̱ (ᵘ ᵒʳ ᵒᵒ) so as to make *above* rhyme to *groove*. There are a considerable number of words of this termination, & They are pronounced in three different ways. Some of them in the manner we have just described. In some, as *trove, rove, grove*, the o has its long close sound as in *abode*. & in some, it is sounded (the *move, prove* & their derivatives) in the manner in which the Scotch pronounce

Plate 2: Reproduction of Folio 314 of the Advocates Miscel. 45, 23.7. (Reproduced by kind permission of the National Library of Scotland.)

and yet are admitted without difficulty in others, although of a genius equally musical and sonorous. The English pronounciation, in general, is certainly smoother than the Scotch, yet no English ear revolts at the true pronounciation of *accept*. Greek was a much more musical tongue than ours. But there is the greatest reason to believe that it admitted of the guttural sound of the χ which is so disagreeable to an English ear. On the other hand, an *n*, followed by an *r* was so intolerable to the Greeks that to prevent their meeting in the same word, they always interposed a *d* between them, while to an Englishman there is nothing in the least offensive in the sound of such words as *unripe, enrage, enroll.*

The Italians call an *s* followed by another consonant, as in *strano, spazio, Spagna, Scozia, S.sporio*; or impure, and think its concurrence with another consonant at the end of a preceding word so harsh, that to avoid it they in such case generally prefix an *i* to the *s* as thus. *E andato in Ispagna, Nacque in Iscozia, Per is-fuggirlo,*

> Che s'il nemico avra due mani, et una
> Anima solo, ancor ch'audace e fera,
> Temer non dei, per *isciagura* alcuna,
> Che la ragion da me difesa pera.[264]

The like assemblage of letters was not avoided by the Greeks, or Latins, nor is it by us[265]

> ἠδε και αὐτον
> Πρηνέα δος *Πεσεειν Σκαιων* προπαροιθε πυλαων
> Il. 6. 307[266]

> Inter spem curamque, timores inter & iras
> Hor.

That strain I heard was of a higher mood[267]

ACCUSATIVE
The Scotch give the *u* its second short sound, as in *buzzard*. It should be pronounced in this derivative as in the primitive *accuse*.

ACORN[268]
The *a* has its long slender sound as in *bake, rake*. The Scotch are apt to pronounce it as in *back*.

ACQUAINT, ACQUAINTANCE
The *ai* has the same sound as the *a* in the foregoing word. *Acquaint* rhymes to *paint*, not to *pant*, as it would by the common Scotch pronounciation.

AGAIN
Those Scotchmen who take pains to read and speak well generally make the last syllable of this word long, like *gain, stain, plain*. But the best speakers in England pronounce it short, as *pen, fen, den, men*. Some even write it *agēn*, as thinking that orthography more agreeable

to the pronounciation. It is so spelt by Mr Harris in his Hermes (pp.258, 259) and by Mr Pope in the following perfect rhyme.

> Then careful heav'n supplied two sorts of *men*
> To squander these, and those to hide *agen*.

ALGEBRA
The short open sound of the *a* as in *pallid*.[269]

ALMOST
Here[270] the *a* has its long broad open sound, as in *all*, or like the *aw* in *awl*, which two words are to the ear entirely the same. Most good speakers sound the *l* in *almost*. In familiar conversation there are some who do not. The *o* has its long close sound, like the *oa* in *coast*, *toast*. Of words of this termination some are by the English pronounced in the manner I have just described; some with the short open *o*, as for example, *lost, cost, frost*. The bent of the Scotch pronounciation is to give both to the *o*, and *oa*, this last mentioned sound, in all cases. I believe the *oa* has constantly the long close sound in England whatever consonant follows. In *cloak, boar* &c as well as in *coast*. This general rule, and some few others in the course of this catalogue, I will venture to hazard, though I have already declared how dangerous I think general rules in every thing relative to English pronounciation. *Cost*,[271] *frost, lost* are the only words I now recollect terminating like *almost*, where the *o* is short, unless you reckon *crost, tost*, and participles of that sort. But they ought to be written *crosst, tosst*, or rather *cross'd, toss'd*. *Dost* the abbreviated participle of the verb *to do*, is pronounced like *dust*.

ALSO
The broad *a* as in *all* – So in *false*.[272]

ALTAR
The *a* has, in this word, and in *halt*, and *halter* its long broad sound, as in *all, hall*. The Scotch give it its short open sound.

ALTHOUGH
The *th* is soft, as in *thy*. The Scotch pronounce it as in *thought*.

AMOVE
Rhymes to *groove*.

AN
The Scotch, in general, pronounce this article as if written *een*, *Een angel*. The true sound of the *a* is the same as in *and*, or *Anne*. The

article *a* has commonly the same sound in England, and always in Scotland; but when the English mean to use it in an emphatical manner, they give it the long slender sound, which it has in *face*.[273]

ANGER, ANGRY

There are two ways of pronouncing *ng* in the middle of a word. viz.

1. Softly, so as that the simple[274] hard sound of the *g* is not heard at the beginning of the next syllable. Of this *hanger* and *singer* are examples; and these two words are sounded in the same manner by the Scotch, and English.

2. Strongly, so as that the[275] hard *g* is distinctly heard after the *n*, which in both cases, has always its second or more nasal sound. *Bangor*, and *clangor* are instances of this last pronunciation[276] both in the Scotch and pure dialects. All words that terminate in *ng* are pronounced in the first manner. I have heard some vulgar persons in England, from a sort of affectation, sound the hard *g* at the end of *sing*, *thing*, *king* &c and rest their voice upon it. But this is to be carefully avoided.

In almost all cases where *ng* is found in the middle of a word, the Scotch sound it as in *singer*. Thus they make *finger*, and *singer* a perfect rhyme, and *anger* and *hanger*. But in *anger*, *angry*, *finger*, *hungry*, and indeed, most generally, the *g* is to be pronounced in the same manner as in *Bangor*. *Bangor* and *anger* would therefore be much nearer a perfect double rhyme, than *hanger*, and *anger*. The rhyme in the following couplet is according to the true pronunciation not perfect.

> He sung Eliza, in gods *anger*
> Till all true Englishmen cry'd *hang her*[277]

According to the Scotch pronunciation it is. Pronounce the *ng* as in *Bangor* in these words. *Anger*, *angle* (verb and noun,) *angry*, *brangle*, *clanger*, *dangle*, *dingle*, *finger*, *hunger*, *hungry*, *jingle*, *linger*, *longer*, *mangle*, *new-fangled*, *singular*, *single*, *stronger*, *surcingle*, *wrangle*. And in all words compounded of *monger*. As *fishmonger*, *Ironmonger* &c.

In the following words *ng* is pronounced as in *singer*. *Bringer*,

> (Yet the first *bringer* of unwelcome news
> Hath but a losing office.)[278]

Hanger, *Ringer*, *Hanging* (noun and participle), *singing*, *bringing*, *hang'd*, *wing'd*, and all participles of this sort.

ANSWER

The *w* is mute as well in the pure dialect as in the Scotch, but many Scotchmen, aiming at propriety, pronounce it.

ANXIETY

The *x* in this word [279] has its soft sound composed of *g* and the sound of *s* in *wise*. The Scotch pronounce it in the same manner as in *extreme*. In *anxious*, which is pronounced properly in Scotland, the sound of the *x* may be resolved into *gsh*. It ought to be observed however that in both these words when we decompose the *x*, the *ng* has the soft sound as in *singer* not that which we have described as proper to *anger*, *Bangor* &c. In *luxury*, the Scotch fall into the opposite error, and pronounce the *x* soft when it should be pronounced like *ks*. In most of the compounds of *ex*, the Latin preposition, where a consonant follows, this last is the sound of the *x*, as *extreme*, *extirpate*. When a vowel follows, the *x* is resolvable into *gs*. As *example*, *exact*, *exigency*. Yet in *exercise* the *x* has its hard sound.

Pronounce also like *exercise*, *galaxy*, *Xerxes*, *axiom*, *luxury*. Pronounce as *anxiety*, *auxiliary*. It is observable that *g* not the hard *c* is the letter which is found in *angor* and *auger* from whence these two words *anxiety* and *auxiliary* are derived.

APOSTLE

The Scotch make the *o* long and close, as in *abode*. The English pronounce it short and open as in *cost*. The *t* is in a manner mute in both dialects.

APPLE

The *a* must be pronounced short and open as in *tap*, *rap*, *happen*. By the common Scotch pronounciation this word would rhyme to *Keppel*. According to the proper sound it rhymes to *grapple*.

APRIL

The Scotch in this word pronounce that *a* as it ought to be sounded in the foregoing; whereas, here it has its long slender sound, as in *ape*. See this word in Book 2.

APRON

Pronounce the *a* here too as in *ape*. The vulgar Scotch sound it long, and open, as in *father*; and others generally give it the Scotch sound of η. [280]

ARCHITECT

The *ch* has its soft sound; though[281] some English people pronounce it hard as in *arch-angel*.

ART, ARTIST

Pronounce the *a* short and open, as in *start*. The Scotch commonly give it its long slender sound. As in *fared*, *pared*. They commit the same error in most[282] other words of this[283] sort; as *cart, dart, hart, part, party, smart*. In avoiding this false pronounciation, care must be taken not to substitute the long open *a* as the inhabitants of the north of England particularly do, in the word *cart*.[284]

ASIA

The first *a* has its slender sound as in *ace, pace*; and the *si* is pronounced hard, [285]and like *ti* in *nation*, or *ci* in *Dacia*. *Asia* therefore and *Dacia*, notwithstanding the difference of orthography, form together a perfect rhyme. They are both, to the ear, disyllables. The Scotch make *si* in *Asia* soft, like the *s* in *pleasure*, or the French *j* in *ajouter*.

ASS

This word is not inserted on account of any provincial manner of pronouncing it, but to illustrate the pronounciation of another, which the English sound so very like this, as to give occasion to numerous ambiguities of a very coarse nature. I remember a popular ballad,[286] several years ago, which was in great vogue for some time in the streets of all the great towns of the kingdom, and which was not deficient in humour. The burthen of it was this word *Ass*. But it was only used for the sake of an indecent equivocation in the sense, by its similarity in point of sound to the other word to which I allude. In Scotland, where I then happened to be, the joke was scarcely understood, because in that country, the sounds of the two words differ nearly as much as those of *pass*, and *pairs*.

ASSIGNEE

In the English pronounciation of this word, and *consignee*, the *g* is not pronounced, & the *i* has its short close sound.[287]

AUNT

In the vernacular Scotch pronounciation of this word, the *au* is sounded like the open *a* but short. Nearly as the *a* in *ant*; but more open. Those who try to catch the English method sound it long and broad, like the *a* in *all*, or, as the English pronounce it in *haunt*. But in this word *aunt*, and several others, it has the long open sound of *a* – yet, less open, than in *father*. Indeed it appears to my ear, that not only this long open sound of the *au* differs[288] from that of the *a* in *father*; but that the short open *a*, as in *ant, scant, scar, cant, fast*, &c is not only, not the same in quantity, but also differs in quality, from the long open *a* in *father*. That it is, in short, a shade lying between that last-mentioned sound, and the slender *a*. This, I think, will be manifest to any one who will carefully attend to the English and

Scotch modes of pronouncing the word *ant*.[289] The difference between them will be very perceptible, and in the latter the sound of the *a*, seems exactly the same in quality, but shorter, than in *father*.

Pronounce the *au* as in *aunt*, in *haunch*, *launch*, *paunch*, *staunch*. All these words, make a perfect rhyme with *blanch*. In most other words as *paunch*, *haunt*, *daunt*, *sauce*, the *au* is sounded like the broad *a*, or like *aw*.

AY

When this word is synonimous to *ever*, or *always* (which sense is obsolete) it is pronounced like *bay*, *pay*, *stay*. In the familiar language of Scotland *ay* is almost always used instead of *yes*. That sense it also has in England; but it is now in a manner confined to parliamentary language, and then only used in[290] speaking of affirmative votes. On such occasions the *a* is sounded as in *father*, and protracted more than is usual, before the voice passes onto the *y*: so that *ay* makes a perfect rhyme to the Italian word *mai*. The Scotch pronounce it in this sense of *yes*, exactly like the pronoun *I*. And, in the former sense, as they do *ay* in most other cases; or like their sound of the diphthong *ei* in *Heister*; or *ey* in *Spey* (the name of a river).

BABEL, BABELMANDEL

In these words the *a* has its long slender sound, as in *babe*, *cane*, *face*.

BABYLON

Here, on the contrary, the *a* is short and open, as in *battle*, *baptist*.

BACON (pork cured in a particular manner; also a proper name)

The Scotch in this word utter both syllables in a manner almost equally distinct but, in the English pronounciation, the *o* is smothered, or rather totally suppressed, as it is both by the Scotch and English in the word *reckon*, or as the *e* in *taken*, *mistaken*, or in the French words *amener*, *Rabelais*. The following are perfect rhymes.

> Ah Madam cease to be *mistaken*
> Ten married fowl peck Dunmow *Bacon*.[291]

> He told him where they were *mistaken*
> And council'd him to save his *bacon*[292]

There are two very curious properties of the liquid consonants, *l*, *m*, *n* and *r*, which I do not recollect to have seen remarked,[293] although their influence in our language is very extensive. Perhaps the proper place to have explained them was in my observations on the alphabet. But that part of my work grew on me to a length much beyond what I intended, I therefore declined mentioning them there, as I thought they might be introduced with propriety when I should come to illustrate the pronounciation of the word now under consideration.

1. If any of the four liquids follow immediately a mute, at the end of a word; such liquid necessarily constitutes, to the ear, a separate (though obscure) syllable, without the intervention of a vowel. Let any one try to sound the words *bac'n*, *tak'n*, *sabre*, *able*, *apple*, *drachm* (pronouncing the *ch* like *k*) so as to form only one syllable, and he will find it impossible.[294] Hence all verses ending with such words, are of necessity of that sort in which there is a supernumerary syllable over the regular number;[295] although the poet perhaps may write *op'n*, *tak'n*, &c, that those words may appear as monosyllables to the eye. If indeed, a liquid preceded in this manner by a mute, is followed either in the same, or a contiguous, word, by a vowel, it has no longer this necessary effect. If followed in either case by a consonant of any sort, it has. You can easily pronounce *Bac'narose* so as to make but three syllables, like *acknowledge*.[296] So of *sabre* and *shield* like *Sabrina*, *Able artist*, like *ablative*.[297] In so doing however you must run the words together, in such a manner as to commence the first syllable of the contiguous word, with the liquid, just as the French do in every case where a word ending with a consonant is followed by one beginning with a vowel. If you have the smallest interval between the words *Bac'n* and *arose*, the first forms as necessarily two syllables as if you pronounce it singly, or at the end of a sentence.

Try now to pronounce a liquid preceded by a mute, and followed by another consonant, whether mute or liquid. First in the middle of a word. – Take, for instance, the French word *âpreté*. The *e* in the middle is feminine or silent. Yet it is impossible, by any effect of the voice, to make only two syllables of this word. Take the word *entremise* in the same language; suppress the *e* in the middle totally. Still you will find the *r* forms a syllable. In *âpreté* the liquid is followed by a mute; in *entremise* by another liquid. Try in like manner to sound the English compound word *apple-tree* so as to make it a disyllable, and you will find it equally impracticable.

I know a hasty reader will think, because in the orthography of such words a vowel is always used, that he in truth does and must pronounce such vowel. But upon consideration, he will find that in *apple-tree*, *âpreté*, *entremise*, the sounds which intervene between the *p*, and *t*, and the *t* and *m*, are nothing more than the simple sounds of *l* and *r*, as much, as in *calm*, *carmelite*.

The point is still clearer when the liquid is at the end of a word, and the next word commences with a consonant.

If parts allure thee, mark how *Bacon* shined[298]

167

In this line every English man pronounces *Bacon* in the manner I have described. Nor is it possible, by any means to pronounce *Bac'n*, in the position the Poet has here placed it in, so as to lose the measure of the verse. Now if you substitute a monosyllable the measure is immediately destroyed. The same experiment may be tried with the word *gentle* in the following line of Milton

What hard mishap hath doom'd this *gentle* swain[299]

and the result will be the same.

2. When a liquid intervenes between two vowels or diphthongs, the syllables on each side of the liquid may, in the measure of our verse, stand in the place of a single syllable of any other sort. Thus in the word *popular*, in the following line the two last syllables between which the *l* intervenes, supply the place of only one syllable in the fifth, or last foot of the verse.

This day the Phillistines a popular feast
Here celebrate in Gaza.[300]

The effect is the same if the liquid ends a word; provided the next begins with a vowel

With grave
Aspect he rose, and in his rising seemed
A pill*ar of state*. Deep on his front engraven
Deliberation sat, and public care.[301]

for in these lines the *r* at the end of the word *pillar* intervening between two vowels, the second foot consists of three syllables.

From the consideration of lines of this, and of another sort, which I shall presently mention, many of our later critics have treated it as a vulgar error to suppose that our regular heroic verse admits only of ten syllables; or, must necessarily be composed of disyllabic feet.[302] And this far they are right. But they go farther, and lay down the position *generally*[303] that a foot in such verse, may consist as well of three, as of two syllables. Now in this unqualified manner of putting it I conceive they are mistaken. It appears to me that it is only in two cases, that our ear will be satisfied with trisyllabic feet, or that the authority of classical writers justifies the use of them: One is where a liquid is placed, in the manner we have been just describing; and such instances are not only common in Milton, from whom the examples in proof of the general position have usually been cited; but also, in most of his predecessors. So common indeed are they, that it seems to have been formerly looked upon as the more regular way to compose the foot, on such occasions, of three syllables.[304] I could produce numberless passages from Chaucer, and Spenser, in support of this assertion.

A few from each will be sufficient to satisfy the curiosity of the reader.[305]

> Whan they have gon not fully half a mile
> Right as they wold han troden ove*r a stile*
> An olde man and a poure with hem mette[306]

> What Man art thou?
> Thou lokest as thou woldest find an hare
> For *ever upon* the ground I see the stare[307]

> He in the waste is sha-*pen as well* as I.[308]

> Hoste quod I, ne be not e-*vil apaid*[309]

> And let us dine as sone, as that ye may
> For by my Ka*lendar it* is prime of day[310]

> O happy earth
> Whereon *thy inno*cent feet do ever tread[311]

> His blessed body spoiled of lively breath
> Was afterward I know not how convey'd
> And from me hid, of whose most *innocent* death
> When tydings came &c[312]

> And Briton fields with *Sara-zin* blod be dyed[313]

> Thro' goodly tem*perance and* affections chanste[314]

> On th'other side they saw that *peri-lous* rock
> Threatening itself on them to ruinate.[315]

> That still it breathed forth, sweet spiri*t and* wholesome
> smell[316]

> That she to him dissembled wo-*manish guile*[317]

> With wo-*manish tears*, and with unwarlike smart[318]

> All change is pe-*rilous and* all chance unsound[319]

> As if in *Adamant rock* it had been pight[320]

> Hewn out of *adamant rock* with engines keen[321]

> As pilots well respect in *perilous wave*[322]

> But most of all *women are* thy debtors found[323]

> Envy pale,
> That all good things with *venimous tooth* devours[324]

As to Milton, every reader's memory will supply him with lines of this kind from all parts of his poetical works.[325] But it will be asked whether there are not instances where three syllables are thus crowded into one foot although the intervening consonant between two of them is not a liquid?[326] I answer that I do not know of any such instance either in Spensers Poems or Miltons *Paradise Lost*,[327] although I have turned them over very carefully with a view to this point.

The use of such feet has been sometimes considered as a beauty peculiar to Milton, who had studied, in that manner, as well as by other means, to diversify the measure of his verse. So great a master of poetical composition, was no doubt sensible of the advantage accruing from this variety; but it is evident that when he introduced those feet in his poetry he only adopted what he found already practised by the poets who had gone before him.

The only other case in which our regular heroic verse seems to admit of feet of three syllables, is where a word ending with a vowel is followed by another which begins with one. On such occasions, if the two vowels are considered as forming two syllables, it is necessary to consider the foot, to which they belong, as trisyllabic. Such verses also abound in Milton

> In adoration, at his feet I fell
> Submiss: he rear'd *me and* whom thou soughtst I am
> Said mildly[328]

> Others whose fruit burnish'd with golden rind
> Hung *amiable*; *Hesperian* fables true;
> If true, here only, *and* of delicious taste[329]

> No anger find in thee, but pity *and* ruth[330]

But neither are these peculiar to him. Of them, as of the other sort of trisyllabic feet he found patterns both in Chaucer, and Spenser.

> And many *a* grisly oth, than have they sworn.[331]

> Of many *a* lady and many *a* paramour[332]

It must however be owned that the proportion is much greater in Milton, than in either of these two poets, and I am inclined to think that he used this last sort of measure rather in imitation of the Italians. In their poetry, in all cases where a vowel ends a word, and the succeeding word commences with one, those two vowels count as but one syllable. Nay if a monosyllable consisting of a vowel intervene between them, all the three make but half a disyllabic foot. They are both, or all three pronounced, but the last of them most distinctly so that they form a diphthong[333] or triphthong in which the last vowel predominates, and it is not unlikely that Milton would have read his own verse of this sort in that manner

> [334]Spera *il* serin l'agricoltor che vede
> Dall' ondoso furer sommer*si i* campi;
> Calma *che al* fin al tempestar succede
> Spera *il* nocchier fra le procell*e e i* lampi:
> Spera talor del suo nemi*co al* piede
> L'atterrato guerrier ch'altri lo scampi:
> Ma non spera *il* tuo corcangiar mai tempre
> Perd*e'il* suo bene, e lo perde per sempre.[335]

What has contributed to establish the notion that both sorts of trisyllabic feet are peculiar to Milton is this, that they both fell into disuse with subsequent poets. There are few or no instances of either sort in Dryden or Pope. But of late years they begin to be revived. Most of the poets of our days would write *amorous* instead of *am'rous* in the following couplet.

> With tender billet-doux he lights the pyre
> And breathes three *am'rous* sighs to raise the fire[336]

and it has also become the fashion when the article *the* is followed by a vowel and the *e* is cut off in writing by the poet, which we find always done, even by Milton

> Whereto th'Almighty answer'd not displeas'd.[337]

to pronounce it in reading, in the same manner as is done by the Italians in reading their verse.

In a great many other words ending in *on*, and in *in*, which should be pronounced as *Bacon*, the Scotch sound the second syllable too distinctly. The following list contains most of those in which the last syllable is to be smother'd.

Advowson, Apron, Ashen, Aston, bacon, bason, beacon, beckon, blazon, Bolton, Boston, brazen, burden, or *burthen, button, capon, christen, cotton, cozen, crimson, damson, Deacon, deaden,* (and all other verbs and participles in *en*) *dozen, Drayton, drunken, Dryden, earthen, Eton, even, Falcon, Flaxen, garden, gladden, glutton, golden, Gordon, guerdon, haven, heathen, heaven, heron, hidden, Iron, kitten, lampron, leaven, lesson, Mason, Milton, mizzen, mutton, oaken, open, oven, oxen, Panton, pardon, parson, Penton, person, piston, poison, prison, raven, reason, reckon, saffron, season, seton, seven, silken, Stephen, sudden, Sulton, tendon, tuison, token, treason, vixen, Warden, weapon, whorson, wooden.*

Those of the two terminations, in which the second syllable is to be sounded more distinctly, are not so numerous.

Abandon, abdomen, amen,[338] *barren, basilicon,* (and all other words accented on the last syllable but two, both in *on* and *en*) *bracken, birchen, bitumen, brethren, canton, chicken, citron, colon, common, Demon, diapason, dragon,*[339] *Felon, Flagon, gammon, gorgon, Hymen, hyphen, jargon, Ichneumon, kitchen, lemon, linen,*[340] *mammon, matron, melon, myrmidon, omen, patron, patten, phaeton, salmon, sermon, siren, sullen, summon, talon, waggon, wanton, women, woollen.*

BALD

The *a* has its long broad sound, as in *call'd,* or like *au* in *maul'd, haul'd.* The Scotch give it the short open sound.

BASE[341]

Subst. and adj. (*Basis – Vilis*) and *base* in music (more commonly written *bass*). The *a* has its short slender sound, and the *s* its hard, as in *case,* or the *c* in *place.* – The following are perfect rhymes.

> A folio common-*place*
> Founds the whole pile – Of all his works the *base*[342]

> Their tops connected, but, at wider *space.*
> Fix'd on the center stands this solid *base.*[343]

Debase, rase, and *erase* (verbs) are to be pronounced in the same manner, so as to rhyme to *place.* Spenser and other old authors, sacrificing the etymology to the pronounciation (for we may fairly infer that their pronounciation was the same with that of the modern English) write *race* and *debase.*

> A rugged rout
> Of Fauns and Satyrs, hath our dwellings *raced.*[344]

> And Crete will boast the Labyrinth now *raced*[345]

> Ignorance, the enemy of grace
> That minds of men born heav'nly doth *debase*[346]

The Scotch pronounce *base* (in the two first senses) so as to rhyme to *graze.*[347, 348]

BEACON

Vide *bacon.* – The *ea* is pronounced as in *speak.*

BEAR (verb, and the name of a quadruped)

This word, to the ear, is, in both senses, exactly the same with *bare.* The Scotch generally pronounce it like *beer.* The English and Scotch pronounciation may be contrasted by the two following couplets.

> No pow'rs of body, or of soul to *share*,
> But what his nature, and his sex can *bear*.[349]

there the rhyme is perfect, according to the pure pronounciation.

> Now looking downwards just as grieved *appears*
> To want the strength of bulls, the fur of *bears*.

This rhyme is perfect according to the Scotch pronounciation, But according to the English, it is as little so, as *steers* and *mares* would be. Of these two sounds of the *ea*, the Irish, and the inhabitants of the west of England, use that in *bear*, in almost every word. I remember to have seen a book advertised in an Irish paper, wherein the Author, who was a [350] native and inhabitant of Dublin, undertook to prove that in this respect the Irish, was the true English pronounciation. I must question whether he made any prosylites to his opinion on this side of the water. The Scotch almost as generally use the other sound of the *ea*. Many who correct themselves in some words, retain the improper sound in others, and, as there is no rule to go by, they often in trying to shun their vernacular sound, where it is improper, introduce the other, in words in which (like *spear*) the English sound the *ea* in the Scotch manner. The following two lists will ascertain the proper pronounciation of all the words ending in *ear*.

Pronounce as *Bear*.[351] All the compounds of that word in both senses, as *bugbear*, *forbear*, *pear*, *swear*, *tear* (verb/*lacerare*), *wear*. Pronounce as *appear*. Arrear, *blear*, *dear*, *clear*, *drear*, *ear*, *fear*, *gear*, *hear*, *near*, *rear*, *sear* (*to burn*), *sear* (spelt also *sere*), *shear* (sometimes spelt *sheer*), *smear*, *spear*, *tear* (*lachryma*), *year*.

For the sound of *ea* in words ending with *st*, *t*, *ve*, *d*, *ch* &c see *Beast*, *Neat*, *Leave*, *dead*, *each*.

BEAST
The *ea* as in *appear*.[352]

BECAUSE
The Scotch pronounciation of this word is something between the Irish, and the English. Some of The Irish make the last syllable rhyme to *phrase*. The Scotch sound it short, so as to rhyme to *as*, *was*. It should be pronounced like *cause*, with the long broad sound of the *a* so as to rhyme to *pause*.

BEDIZEN
In this word, and its original (*dizen*) the Scotch pronounce the *i* short, and as in *phiz*, *mizzen*. In both it should have its long diphthongal sound, as in *wise*, *miser*.

BEHIND

The *I* has its diphthongal sound as in *Mind*.[353] The Scotch are apt to pronounce it as *rescind*. In the following stanza both rhymes are perfect.

> For who to dumb forgetfulness a prey
> This pleasing anxious being e'er resign'd
> Left the warm precincts of the cheerful day
> Nor cast one longing, ling'ring look behind.[354, 355]

Pronounce as *behind*: *Bind, blind, book-binder, find, gold finder, grind, hind, hind-er* adj, and its compound *hindermost, mankind, mind, rind, wind* (verb).

Pint (a liquid measure) is the only word ending in *int* in which the *i* has its diphthongal sound

Pronounce as *rescind, Abscind, wind* (subst). At least this last word is so pronounced in conversation. Some great speakers, in solemn discourse, or on the stage sound it as *mind*. So as to make the following a perfect rhyme.

> Lo the poor Indian whose untutor'd *mind*
> Sees God in clouds, or hears him in the *wind*.[356]

Lind (a proper name). *Ind*, for *India*.

BENEATH

The *ea* long and as in *fear*. The *th* soft as in *thou*. *Underneath* is pronounced in the same manner. They rhyme to *breathe* &c. The Scotch in both words pronounce the *eath* as in *breath*. Pronounce as *beneath, bequeath*. The following therefore is an imperfect rhyme.

> Those rites discharged, his sacred corpse *bequeath*
> To the soft arms of silent sleep, and death.[357]

sheath and *wreath* verbs. (more properly written *sheathe* and *wreathe*). Pronounce like *breath, death*.

There is still a third pronounciation of this sort of words where the *ea* has the same sound as in *beneath*, but is short and the *th* hard as in *thought, breath*. Such are *heath, wreath* and *sheath* subs, *eath*, (obsolete for *ease*).

BEWILDER[358]

The short obscure *i* as in *rescind*.

BIND

Vide *behind*.

BIRD

See Cap. 2.

BLYTH[359]

(Or *blithe*) the diphthongal sound of the *i*, but short, as in *bite*. & the *th* hard as in *bath*.

BOAST

In this and the following words, *coast*, *roast*, *toast* the Scotch give the *oa* the short and open sound of *o*, as in *lost*,[360] instead of the long close sound. I believe, except in the words *broad*, and *abroad*, the *oa* has uniformly this last mentioned sound, in the pure dialect, and the Scotch almost as uniformly sound it as in *lost*. In some few words as *foal*, they pronounce it properly.

BOATSWAIN

This word is pronounced as if written *Boason*. The *s* has its hard sound, and the *on* is sounded as in *bacon*.

To pronounce the two syllables in as distinct a manner, as when they form two separate words, would have (in conversation, at least) an air of utmost pedantry and affectation.

BOGLE

In this word, the *o* has its short open sound, as in *God*.[361] The Scotch are apt to give it the long close sound as in *brogue* – *Ogle* vide *Ogle*.

BOIL

There are great disputes among the English, about the proper method of pronouncing the *oi* in this, and many other words, *foil, oil, anoint, point, void*. The vulgar pronounciation makes the sound the same as that of the *i*, in *bile, file, pint*.[362] Those who are admirers of a full and solemn manner of speaking sound the *o* long, and very distinctly; and hurry over the *i*, as is always done in the word *noise*, or as the *oy* is pronounced in *boys, employs*. But this method is generally thought too stiff and formal. There is a middle way which is practised by some of the best speakers, in which the *o* in the diphthong is sufficiently uttered to be distinguishable from *a* but yet the two vowels are compressed together, if I may so speak, in the same manner as the sounds of *a* and *e* or *i* are in the diphthongal *i*. Vide *supra*.

BOLT

In this word, and in *colt, dolt, jolt*,[363] the *o* has its long close sound as in *pole*. The Scotch generally make it short. In *revolt* the *o* is short & open as in *God* – Vide *infra*.[364]

175

BOOK-BINDER

The i[365] long as in *mind*. Vide *behind*.

BOUGH

The *ou* has its true diphthongal sound, as in *vow*, *plough*, which is sometimes written *plow*. The *gh* is mute in both. The following is a perfect rhyme.

> Their wounded barks record some broken *vow*,
> And willow garlands hang on every *bough*[366]

I knew a schoolmaster in Scotland who was fond of general rules, and thought because *tough* was pronounced like *stuff*, *ruff*, *huff*, that *bough* should be so pronounced likewise. He taught his schoolchildren[367] to pronounce it in that manner. But this sounded so ridiculous, even in their ears, that they gave him the knick-name of *Buff*, which, if alive, he probably retains to this day.

BOUGHT

In this and similar words, as *sought*, *thought*, *fought*, *drought*.[368] The *ough* has the long open sound of the *o* in *corn*, or of *oa* in *broad*. This sound, if at all, is but just distinguishable from the long broad *a* in *all*, *malt* or *au* in *Paul*. Some writers on pronounciation consider them as entirely the same. They are generally made to rhyme with such words as *taught*, and *fraught*, but that is no proof that their sound is exactly the same.

> If e'er one vision touch'd thy infant *thought*
> Of all the nurse, and all the priest e'er *taught*.[369]

The Scotch, after they get rid of the more barbarous pronounciation in which the *gh* is pronounced as a strong guttural, generally fall into the mistake of using the long close sound of *o*, and making (for instance) *bought*, and *boat*, the same word to the ear. And this they do so generally that in endeavouring to mimic the Scotch pronounciation I have observed that the English are apt to hit upon this particular way of sounding this class of words. Yet this, in truth, is not part of the vernacular pronounciation of Scotland.

BOW (verb, and noun)

When applied to an inclination of the body expressive of respect, or to bending in general, is pronounced exactly like *bough*. And rhymes to *how*, *cow*, *sow*. When it means a weapon or instrument of offence (*arcus*) or is used as an epithet *bow-window*, or for a particular sort of knot, called a *bow-knot*, or *bow*, it is pronounced exactly as *beau*. The following are both perfect rhymes.

> Some Clergy too, she would *allow*
> Nor quarrell'd at their aukward *bow*.[370]

> When arm'd with rage we march against the *foe*
> We lift the battle-ax, and draw the *bow*.[371]

Scotchmen, who have acquired a good and ready pronounciation in other respects, often find themselves puzzled and confounded between the different pronounciations of this word.

It may be observed in general that the Scotch (when they do not pronounce the *ow* with the simple vocal sound of *oo* in *pool*, *u* in *pull* which is the true provincial manner) are inclined to prefer the diphthongal sound as in *how*, to that of the long open *o* as in *low* (adj).[372]

Pronounce as *how* or *now*. Allow, *avow*, *bow* (verb and noun, to stoop or bend, and the act of stooping or bending), *brow*, *cow*, *endow*, *enow*, *low* (as a cow), *mow* (of barley or corn of any sort), *now*, *plow*, *sow* (*sus*), *vow*.

Pronounce as *beau* or *foe*. Below, *bestow*, *blow*, *bow* (*arcus*), *crow* (verb and noun), *flow*, *glow*, *grow*, *know*, *low* (*humilis*), *mow* (verb), *prow*, *row* (*ordo*, *series*), to *row* (*remis impellere*), *show*, *slow*, *snow*, *sow* (both when it signifies *seminare* and *encire*), Stow, *Stowe*, *Strow*, *throw*, *tow* (verb and noun), *trow* (verb, *to imagine*, obsolete).

BOWL (a small bason)
Rhymes to *soul*, *foal*, *roll*. The Scotch generally give the *ow* here the diphthongal sound. The following is a perfect rhyme.

> In vain I trusted that the flowing *bowl*
> Would banish sorrow, and enlarge the *soul*.[373]

Bowl (verb and noun) *Bowling-green*, applied to a particular sort of game. Pronounced as *owl*. Tho' some pronounce this as the other word.[374] Pronounce in the first manner, *troul*, *soul*. Pronounce as *owl*, *cowl*, *fowl*, *foul*, *growl*, *howl*, *prowl*, *scowl*.

BREAD
The *ea* as in *bear*, but short. The Scotch pronounce it as *breed*. The following rhyme is perfect.

> Yet hence the poor are cloth'd, the hungry *fed*,
> Health to himself, and to his children *bread*
> The labourer bears[375]

Pronounce in the same manner, *dead*, *dread*, *head*, *instead*, *lead* (a metal), *read* (verb, perfect tense and participle), *spread*, *stead*, *thread*, *tread*.[376]

Pronounce as *breed*,[377] *bead, knead, lead* (verb), *mead*. (Yet the first syllable of *meadow* is pronounced as *bread*), *Plead*,[378] *read* (verb, present tense).

BREAST

The *ea* is sounded as in *bread*. The following is a perfect rhyme.

> When thou art in good humour *drest*
> When gentle reason rules thy *breast*.[379]

The Scotch pronounce it so as to rhyme to *priest*.[380] Which is the true pronounciation of all other words in *east*; as *beast, feast, least, Yeast*.

BROAD

In this word and in *groat*, the *oa* has the same long open sound approaching to the *a* in *all*, which we have described under the word *bought*. These two words are the only instances I believe where the *oa* has this sound. In *road, goad, toad, float* &c the *oa* has the long close sound as in *boat*.

If there is any simple vocal sound in the pure English dialect, not to be found in the Scotch, it is this long open *o*, or *oa*.

BUILD, BUILDING, BUILT[381]

These words according to the English pronounciation form perfect rhymes with *gild, gilding, gilt*.[382]

Many Scotch people sound the *ui* like the diphthongal *u* in *mule*, like the long first sound of *e*, or *ee*; so as to make *build* and *steel'd* or *wield* rhyme together. – Both these methods are erroneous.[383]

BULL

The *u* according to the pure pronounciation has its vocal sound like *oo* in *fool*. With this difference, that it is shorter in this, and other similar words; as *pull, full*, than the *oo* in *pool, fool*.

It is, in English, almost the constant effect of a double consonant, or of two combined consonants tho not the same, (as in *part, crept, slept*) to shorten the preceding vowel, so different is the genius of our language in that respect from the Greek, and Roman.[384, 385]

Pronounce as *bull, full*, (verb and noun) and *fuller* (comparative and subst.), *pull*. In all other words of this termination the *u* has the same sound as in *sun, gun*. And these, in Scotland and the north of England, are so pronounced.

BULLY

Vide *pully*.

BURIAL, BURY (a verb, and the name of a town)
These words are great stumbling blocks to many a Scotchman. The true provincial sound of the *u* in the southern counties, both in these and a great many others, is like the French *u*; And in the north of Scotland, they are pronounced *Beerial, beery*. Scotchmen soon discover that their vernacular pronounciation is wrong. But then they generally adopt the diphthongal *u*, and make *bury* and *fury*, *Burial* and *Escurial* rhyme together. This is equally wrong. When this is also discovered they recur to *beerial*, and *beery*. The true pronounciation is like the short *e* in *merry*; with which word *bury* forms a perfect rhyme. – Chaucer writes it *bery* or *berie*

> Now let us sit and drink and make us *mery*
> And afterward we wiln his body *bery*.[386]

Nor did he pronounce or write it so merely for the sake of the rhyme.

> Upon his bere ay lith this innocent
> Beforn the auter, while the masse last.
> And after that, the abbot with his convent
> Had sped him for to *berie* him ful fast.[387]

This circumstance affords a presumption that the pronounciation of these words, was the same in the reigns of Edward 3 and his son as now. Why the orthography came to be altered I cannot explain.

BUSINESS, BUSY
The *us* is sounded like the *izz* in *mizzen*, *dizzy*; or like *is* in *his*. The Scotch, in their vernacular pronounciation, sound it nearly in this manner; but they often when they aim at speaking well give the *u* the sound it has in *guzzle, puzzle*.
Chaucer writes *busy* also, with an *e*.

> In mirth all night a *besy* life they lede.[388]

The Scotch commonly make *business* (as it is written) a word of three syllables. But the English always suppress the *i*, not only in verse, but in prose, and in public speaking, as well as familiar conversation.[389]

CADIZ
This name of a town in Spain, is almost always pronounced as if written *Cales*. So as to rhyme to *Hales, Wails*.

CAIN
We have already had occasion to explain the pronounciation of this proper name (vide supra page). It is to the ear, exactly the same word with *cane*.

CALF

The *l* is mute in this word and in *half*. The *a* has the same sound as in *art*, but with this difference that a sort of obscure *i* or *y* is prefixed to it. It is only in that circumstance that the pure[390] English and the Scotch pronounciations of the word disagree. In general wherever the hard *c*, or *k*, or the hard *g* is followed either by the short open *a*, as in this word, or by the diphthongal sound of *i*, or *y*; as in *kind*, *sky*, the smothered sort of *y* just mentioned is introduced in the pure dialect of the English. It is so in *cart*, *carriage*, *casuist*, *garden*, *gadso*, &c. I call it smothered *y*, because the voice hastens over it to the *a*, or diphthongal *y*. Yet it is almost as much heard as the *i* in the Italian word *chiaro*, *chiedere*, *cuchiaio*. Indeed the *chiar*, in *chiaro*, has in every respect the same sound with our word *car*. To illustrate this matter still farther, this unwritten *y* before the *a* or *y*, is exactly the same with that, which makes the first part of the diphthongal sound of *u* in *use*, *abuse*.

It is a singular thing in Italian, that in almost all words taken from other languages, when in the original language the sound of a mute as of the hard *c*, or of *b*, *f*, *p* is followed by *l*, as in *clarus*, *clamo*, *clericus*, *claustrum*, *Blanc*, *blonde*, *flora*, *flabus*, *plenus*, *planus*, *templum*, *Exemplum*,[391] they almost always change that *l* into this obscure *i*. *Chiaro*, *chiarno*, *chierico*, *chiostro*, *bianco*, *biondo*, *fiora*, *fiato*, *pieno*, *piano*, *tempio*, *esempio*.[392] Whence arises this apparent dislike to the combination of a mute with the *l*; the consonant, which of all others is generally allowed to be the most grateful to the ear. The poets sometimes say *templo*, *esemplo* & *esemplare*; *esemplativo*, *contemplare* are used in prose, as well as verse, for *esempiare*, *contempiare*.[393]

In the pronounciation of the northern provinces of England, the unwritten *y* we have been describing is not used. And few natives of those provinces who leave them after their early youth, ever acquire that characteristic of the pure dialect.

CALF'S, WIFE'S, KNIFE'S[394]

The genetives of *calf*, *wife*,[395] *knife*, are pronounced by most English people[396] like the plurals of the same words, i.e. as if written, *Calves*, *wives*, *knives*. The Scotch, and some English people, retain in the genetive the same hard sound of the *f* as in the nominative. Some write these genetives with a *v*. The genetive of *life* is so written in the Catechism of the common prayer book 'and I pray unto God to give me his grace that I may continue in the same, to my lives end.' Yet, now, the *f* in the genetive of *life*, is generally pronounced as in the nominative.

CAME

Rhyme to *fame*. – In the Scotch pronounciation, to *ham*.

CAMEL

The true sound of this *a* is as in *calf*. *Trammel*, and *Camel* make a perfect rhyme. Many Scotch people aiming at the improvement of their pronounciation, sound the *a* as in *fame*.

CANAAN

Here the first *a* has the same sound as in *fame*, or *cane*, and the whole word is pronounced as a disyllable. The Scotch make two syllables of *naan*; and pronounce the first *a* as in *father*. Vide *infra*.

CAPON

The *a* as in *cane*. The *on* as in *bacon*.

CAR, CARRY,[397] CART

The *a* as in *calf*. Vide *supra*.

CATECHISM

The *ch* like a *k*, – The Scotch sound it as in *church*.

CAUSEWAY

The *au* as in *cause* or *Paul*, but short. The *s* is hard as the *ss* in *pass*. The *w* is pronounced. This is a strange orthography. The word is not a compound of *cause*, and *way*; but derived from the French *chausée*. It was formerly written *causey*. And so the Scotch pronounce it still. *Leghorn* (derived from *Livorno*) is another instance of a corrupted orthography giving to a foreign word the appearance of being compounded of two vernacular English ones.

CAUTION, CAUTIONARY

When used as a term of Scotch law, for bail or surety, is, by the Scotch, pronounced as if written *caition*, or like *patience*. The *au* of *caution*, in English is always pronounced as in *pause*, *cause*. *Cautionary* is not an English word.[398]

CHAIR

Rhymes to *fair*, *care*, *air*. In many parts of Scotland, and by some vulgar persons in England, it is pronounced *cheer*. The following rhyme is perfect.

> Whether thou choose Cervantes' serious *air*,
> Or laugh and shake in Rablais' easy *chair*.[399]

CHAMPAIGNE

The *ch* as in French or as in *Champerty* (a law term); *Chagrin*, *Chaise* – i.e. like the *sh* in *Sham*, *Shoulder*.

CHARIOT

The *a* as in *far, mar*. The Scotch sound it, as in *care, stare*. In familiar conversation in England, the *i* in *chariot* is seldom sounded. It is pronounced as if written *charet*, which was the old orthography.

> Mounted in Phoebus *charet* fiery bright.[400]

> And mounted straight upon a *charet* high.[401]

According to this colloquial pronounciation, the following are a perfect rhyme.

> From drawing-rooms, from colleges, from *garrets*
> On horse, on foot, in hacks, and gilded *chariots*.[402]

CHARLOTTE

Pronounce the *Ch* as *Champaigne*. Vide *supra*.[403]

CHART

The *ch* as in *charter, church*.

CHASM

The *ch* like *k*

CHEARFUL, OR CHEERFUL, CHEARFULLY

In conversation, the first syllable is in England most generally pronounced like the first syllable in *cherry, merry*. Yet the primitive, to *chear*, or to *cheer*, is always pronounced like *appear*. Dr Johnson adopts the latter way of spelling these words; but the other is the most usual. He writes *cheer*, in the following couplet.

> Hark, a glad voice the lonely desart *cheers*,
> Prepare the way, a God, a God *appears*.[404]

but in all the editions of Pope, it is written *chear*.

CHERUB

The *ch* as in *church*. Many Scotch people pronounce it like *k*.

CHICANE

The *ch* like *sh*.

CHIMNEY

This word by many vulgar people both Scotch and English[405] is pronounced (very unaccountably) as if written *chimley*.

CHIROGRAPH, CHIROGRAPHER (terms in the law of England)
The *ch* in these two words, is by English lawyers sounded like *s*, and the *i* has its diphthongal sound. I know of no other instance where the *ch* is so pronounced.

CHOCOLATE
Often pronounced in Scotland as if written *Jocolate*. The *ch* in the pure dialect has the same sound as in *church*.

CHRISTMAS
The Scotch improperly pronounce this word as if written *christenmas*, or rather *chrissnmas*. The *t* is mute in the English pronounciation both in this word and in *christen*, *christening*, and *Christendom*.

CICELY (a proper name)
The *i* has the diphthongal sound, as in *nicely*. These two words make a perfect rhyme; for *Cicely* (which is a surname still in use among the lower classes of people in some parts of England) is a disyllable although it is made a word of three syllables in the old lines cited by Pope

> And for her bucket in went *Cicely*.

CIRCUIT
The *u* is not sounded in the most usual[406] pronounciation, any more than in *biscuit*; it only serves to show that the *c* is *hard*.

CLARET
The *a* short, and as in *far*, *mar*. The Scotch sound it long, and as in *Clare*. *Claret* rhymes exactly to *Garret*.

CLEMENCY, CLEMENT, INCLEMENT
The *e* is short, and as in *pen*, *hen*, *Pembroke*. The Scotch pronounce it long, and like their sound to the Greek ε; or like the English pronounciation of *ay* in *pay*, *say*, *a* in *phrase*, and *eigh* in *weigh*. In *delicate*, *delicacy*, *indelicacy* &c there is the same difference between the Scotch and English pronounciations of the *e*. This particularity, like the Scotch manner of pronouncing *bought*, *sought* &c, is among the things which are most striking to an English ear, and are generally laid hold of in 'taking off the Scotch dialect,' as the phrase is.

CLERGY, CLERGYMAN
The short close *e* as in *berry*, *merry*. The Scotch pronounce it long and like their sound of the Greek η or the *a* in *bare*. The proper sound

approaches near that of the *i* in *fir, stir*, but is not the same. It is a shade between that sound, and the *e* in *pen*. The Scotch in *merry, ever, never, every*, sound it exactly as the *i* in *fir*.

CLOTH, OR CLOATH (a substantive)

The *o*, or *oa* has its short open sound, and the *th* is hard as in *broth*. But the plural of this word is differently pronounced, according to the difference in signification. When it means *panni* it is pronounced as the singular. When it signifies *vestimenta* the *o*, or *oa* is long and close, and the *th* soft as in the verb to *clothe* or to *cloathe*.

CLERK

The *e* like the *a* in *far*. *Clerk*, and *lark, park, remark* rhyme together. In all other words of this termination as *jerk, perk*, & also in *Berks, Berkshire* it is pronounced as in *fern*.

CLEVER

Pronounce the *e* as in *clergy*. The Scotch make *clever* rhyme to *liver*.

CLIMB

The Scotch pronounce the *i* short, and as in *trim, limb*. But the *i* has its diphthongal sound, and the *b* being mute, this word to the ear, is exactly the same with *clime*. The following are perfect rhymes.

> Mov'd in the orb, pleas'd with the *chimes*,
> The foolish creature thinks he *climbs* [407]

> Virtue again to its bright mansion *climb*
> And beauty fear no enemy but *time*. [408]

indeed Spenser writes it clime. [409]

CLOSE (adj. & subst. meaning field or enclosure)

The *o* is short, and close, the *s* hard. [410] *Dose* (verb & subst. – a certain quantity of any medicine, or to give a dose of medicine) is I believe the only other word of the sort in the language which is so pronounced. Or which will form a perfect rhyme with *close* used in the above senses. The Scotch pronounce both words wrong. For they make *close* rhyme to *toss, moss, loss, gloss*; making the *o* short and open [411] and *dose, to close* (verb & subst. – *to shut* or *terminate* and *a termination*, or *ending*) so as to form the sound with the verb *dose* when it signifies *dormitare*. To slumber.

CLOVER

The *o* long, and close as in *Jove*. The Scotch often make this word rhyme to *lover*.

COAST, COAT, COAX

The *oa* as in *boat*. Not long ago, a Scotch Gentleman, in a debate in the House of Commons upon the Affairs of America, began a speech, in which he proposed to examine whether it would be more advisable to adopt compulsive, or soothing measures towards the colonies. Unfortunately instead of *soothe*, *coax* was the word that had presented itself to his mind. And he pronounced it as if written *cox*. This, added to several other peculiarities of manner and dialect, tickled the House extremely, and produced a general laugh. The Gentleman was unconscious of the false pronounciation into which he had fallen. His speech had been premeditated, and *coax* was, it seems, a sort of cue, or catch word. Every time therefore that the silence of his hearers permitted him to resume his harangue, he began by repeating this unlucky word. But every fresh repetition of it occasioning a louder burst of laughter, he was obliged at last fairly to give the matter up. And break off his oration in the middle.

COFFER

The English[412] make the *o* long & open as in *Corn*, *fork*. The Scotch always pronounce it short, so as to make *coffer*, and *offer* rhyme together.

COGNIZANCE

The *g* is mute. The Scotch pronounce it. In English law books this word is often written *conusance*. Vide *infra* B.2.C.12.

COMBAT, COMFORT, COMPASS

The *o* is pronounced as in *come*, *some*, or like *u* in *Cumberland*. The Scotch pronounce it as in *conduit*, *compact*.

CONDUIT[413]

This is a disyl. according to the English pronounciation & the *u* is sounded as *w*. The Scotch are apt to make it a word of three syllables: *con-du-it*.

CONSIGNEE

The *g* is silent. Vide *assignee*

CORN

The long open *o* as in *broad*. So in *horn*, *scorn*, *forlorn*, *love-lorn*, and all other words of this termination.

COVET

The *o* short, and as in *love*, *shove*. The Scotch make it long as in *cove*, *jove*, *rove*.

COUGH

The *o* long and open as in *corn*. The *gh* like *f*.

CRADLE

The Scotch (endeavouring to speak properly) are apt to pronounce the *a* short & as in *bad, addle, paddle*. But it should be pronounced as in *shade, glade*. Or as *ladle*. The following rhyme is perfect.

> And to the Coffin from the *cradle*
> 'Tis all a wish, and all a *ladle*.[414]

CREAM

The *ea* as in *appear*. So all other words in *eam* are pronounced. The Scotch sometimes pronounce *cream*, like *fame*.

CRIMSON

The *s* soft as in *praise*; The Scotch make it hard as in *past*.

CUCKOO

The *u* has the long vocal sound, exactly as *oo* in the second syllable. (Can there be a more striking example of the capriciousness of our orthography?) The Scotch sound the *u* as in *duck, cuckold*.

CUCUMBER

The *u* in the first syllable is uniformly by the English pronounced with the diphthongal sound of *ou*, or *ow*; the first syllable being the same with the word *cow*. This I believe is the only example of the kind. Hence Scotch people find it very difficult to reconcile themselves to this pronounciation.

DAMSEL

The first syllable as *dam*. The *s* is soft.

DANIEL

Pronounce the *a* short as in *fan*, and in the same manner in *spaniel*. In both words, the Scotch, when they try to catch the right pronounciation, sound the *a* long, as in *fane, Danish*.

DATIVE

Here the *a* is sounded as in *fane*, or *fate*. The Scotch sound it as in *father*.

DAVID

The *a* as in the foregoing word.

DEAD
The *ea* short, and like the *e* in *fed*, *bed*, *shed*.[415] Vide *bread*.

DEAL (verb and noun)
The *ea* as in *appear*. Or like *ee* in *wheel*. Pronounce in the same manner all other monosyllables of this termination, and all polysyllabes like *conceal*, *reveal* &c where the *eal* makes but one syllable, and has the accent upon it. Many Scotch people pronounce all & most some of these words as *breast* is sounded in the pure dialect.[416]

DEATH
As *breath*. They are the only two words in *eath* where the *ea* is not pronounced as in *appear*. So that you cannot form a perfect rhyme, with one of them, and any other word. *S'death* is only an abbreviation of *his death*.

> Yet tell one frighted reason! What is *death*?
> Blood only stop'd, and interrupted *breath*.[417]

DEITY
The *e* like *ea* in *appear* – The Scotch generally pronounce this word as if written *Dei-ity* giving the first syllable a diphthongal sound.[418]

DELICATE
The *e* short, and as in *Belvidera*. Vide *clemency*. *Memory* is another word in which the *e* has this sound, and is pronounced as the *a* in *phrase* by the Scotch.

DESIGN
The *s* hard like the double *s* in *assign*. In *resign* it is soft as in *phrase*. The Scotch reverse the English pronounciation of these two words, making the *s* hard in *resign*, and soft in *design*.

DEMOSTHENES
The *th* is sounded like *t*.

DIALOGUE
The diphthongal sound of the *i* as in *dire*, *Dier*.[419]

DINNER
Rhymes to *sinner*, in Scotland it is often pronounced as if written *denner*.

DIRECT, DIRECTION

In solemn reading, or speaking, many English people give the *i* its diphthongal sound, as in *five*.

DIZEN

The diphthongal *i*, as in *bedizen*. The Scotch make *dizen*, and *risen* rhyme together.

DOOR

The *oo* is sounded like the long close *o* as in *score*, *lore*, *more*. The Scotch, and some few English persons aiming at peculiar propriety, sound the *oo* as in *poor*, *moor*.

In the following passage this word, which is spelt *dore*, forms a perfect rhyme with *lore* and *sore*.

> Most noble virgin, that by fatal lore
> Hast learn'd to love, let no whit thee dismay
> The hard begin', that meets the in the *dore*
> And with sharp fits thy tender heart oppresseth *sore*.[420]

So in Pope's *Epistle on Taste*

> Shall call the winds thro' long arcades to *roar*,
> Proud to catch cold at a Venetian *door*.

DOSE

See *close*.

DOTAGE, DOTARD

The long close *o* like *oa* in *doat*, or *dote*, the verb from whence it is derived. The Scotch pronounce the *o* as in *dot*, so as to make *dotage* rhyme to *pottage*.

DOVE

Rhyme to *love*. The following rhymes are perfect.

> The Queen of Beauty stop't her bridled *doves*
> Approv'd the little labours of the *loves*.[421]

> Not Hermia but Helena, I *love*
> Who will not change a raven for a *dove*?[422]

The Scotch make it rhyme to *rove*, *Jove*.

DOUGH

To the ear the same word with *doe*. Two words can hardly be more unlike, especially to the ear, than this is to *Teig* the corresponding word in German. Yet nobody who knows the history and analogy of the two languages will hesitate in considering them as being only deviations from the same word in the old Gothic or Teutonic original.

DRAGON
The *a* as in *drag, brag, waggon.* The Scotch, when they aim at propriety of pronounciation are apt to sound it as in *plague.*

DRAMA
The *a* short and as in *manna.* The Scotch, in aiming at propriety, are apt to pronounce it as in *same.*[423]

DRAYTON
See *bacon.*

DREADFUL
Pronounce as *dread.*

DROUGHT
Formerly perhaps this word was pronounced in English as in Scotland, with the diphthongal sound of the *ou,* and as if written *Drouth.* Milton writes it so. It is now pronounced as *sought, bought, thought.*[424] Vide *bought.*

DRYDEN
See *bacon.*

EACH
Rhymes to *speech.* Pronounce in the same manner all other words of this termination.

EAR
Rhymes to *appear.* See *bear.*

> More tuneable than lark to Shepherds *ear*
> When wheat is green, when hawthorn buds *appear.*[425]

This is a perfect rhyme.

EARL, EARLY
The *ea* as in *earth.* Vide *earth.*

EARN
Rhymes to *fern.* Vide *infra.*

EARTH

The *ea* like the short *e* in *clergy*. Pronounce in the same manner *hearth* and *dearth*.[426]

EASE, EASY[427]

The *ea* as in *appear* the *s* soft as in *please*.

> Correct with spirit, eloquent with *ease*,
> Intent to reason, or polite to *please*.
> Essay on Man

pronounce in the same manner, *appease, disease, please, tease, lease* verb synonymous to *glean*. In the following words the *ea* has the same sound but shortened and the *s* is hard: *cease, decease, surcease, lease* verb and noun (to let to farm, a letting to farm), *release, crease*, noun and verb (a fold, a plait). (The Scotch pronounce this often *cress*.) *Decrease* noun and verb, *increase* noun and verb, *grease* noun and verb. (The Scotch pronounce this as *please*.)

EAT

The *ea* as in *appear*. – The following rhyme is perfect.

> A man first builds a country *seat*
> Then finds the walls not good to *eat*.[428]

Pronounce in the same manner *beat, bleat, cheat, defeat, entreat, feat, heat, ascheat, meat, neat, peat, retreat, repeat, seat, treat, wheat*. Pronounce as *breast, threat* (n & v), *sweat* (noun and verb), *teat*. In *great* (which is properly pronounced in Scotland) the *ea* has a thinner and somewhat longer sound like the thin slender *a* in *pate, state*.[429] *Eat*, the perfect tense (sometimes written *ate*) is pronounced like *pet*, yet *beat* the perfect tense of the verb *to beat* is pronounced like the present.

ECHO

The *e* short and exactly as in *beckon*, or *beck*. The Scotch pronounce it as they do in *clemency, delicate*.

EDGE

The *e* short, as in *bed*. The Scotch pronounce it as they do in the foregoing word, or like *a* in *page*; so as to make *edge* and *age* the same word to the ear. *Hedge* is to be pronounced like *edge*.

EDICT

The *e* like *ee* in *deed*.

EDINBURGH

The inhabitants of this city pronounce its name as if written *Ainbro*. The English as if written *Edinborough* which is a more familiar termination of the name of a city with them, as *Peterborough*, *Knaresborough*, *Scarborough*. In like manner the English pronounce *Hamburgh*, as if written *Hamborough*. 'A *Hamborough merchant*'. But *Petersburg* is pronounced as it is written. (Vide *burgh* infra Book.)

E'ER (abbreviated from *ever*)
Pronounce exactly as *air*, or *ere*. The Scotch sound it as *ear*.[430]

EGOTISM, EGOTIST
The *e* is to be sounded as[431] in *here* or as *ee* in *eager*, *dear*.[432]

EIGHT
Rhymes exactly to *pate*, *weight*. The Scotch affecting the English pronounciation, are apt to make it rhyme to *bite*.[433]

EITHER
There are two ways of pronouncing the *ei* in this word, and in *neither*. 1. with the diphthongal sound of *i* or *y*. As in *blithe*, *Scythe*. 2. as *ay* in *pay*, *day*, *lay*, or *ei* in *weigh*, that is with the Scotch sound of ε. This last pronounciation is, I believe, the most approved. The common vernacular pronounciation of Scotland differs from it only in making the first syllable short. But in endeavouring to catch the true English sound most Scotch people (who do not adopt the first method) pronounce the *ei* like *ee* in *Steel*, or like the *e* in *ether*.

ELOISA
The English pronounciation of the *i* is with its first vocal sound, or that of *ee*. So it is now also sounded in *Clementine* and *Louisa*. This is the vernacular Scotch method; but most Scotchmen exchange that, for the diphthongal, sound as in *Eliza*.

ENTICE
Rhymes to *ice*, *nice*. The Scotch make it rhyme to *wise*, *prize*.

EPILOGUE
The *e* short, and as in *step*, *delicate*, *memory*. The Scotch pronounce it as the *a* in *ape*, *tape*, or as their sound of the ε.

E'ER (BEFORE)
This word as well as *ere* is, to the ear, the same with *air*, and rhymes to *there*. The Scotch pronounce it (as they do *e'er*) like *ear*. Pronounce

as *there* (besides this word) only *where*. *Were* is short, and the *e* pronounced something between its sound in this word & in *clergy*.[434] Pronounce like *ear*, *adhere*, *affear* (often written *affere*), *atmosphere*, *austere*, *cere*, *cohere*, *here*, *interfere*, *mere*, *persevere*, *sere*, *revere*, *sincere*, *sphere*.

ET*E*RNAL

The *e* as in *clergy*. The Scotch pronounce it longer and more open like *a* in *bare*. Pronounce as *eternal*, *external*, *internal*, *infernal*, and all other words of this termination.

*E*THER

The *e* has its first, or long sound, like *ee* in *steel*.

ETON (sometimes spelt Eaton)

The *e* as in the foregoing word.[435] The *on* as in bacon.

EVER, EVERY

The *e* short, and as in *bed*. The Scotch pronounce it like the short close *i* in *liver*, *livery*. In familiar conversation most English people make it a shade nearer this close *i*, than the *e* in *bed*; Yet not the same. But it requires great attention, and an ear practised in these niceties of articulate sound, to perceive the distinction.

EXAGGERATE

Some English people pronounce the *gg* hard, as in *waggon*, but the most general pronounciation is like *dg* in *badger*.

EXCUSE[436] (noun)

The *u* has its diphthongal sound, but is short, and the *s* hard. So that this word rhymes to *use* a noun, or *Bruce*, *spruce*, *truce*. The Scotch pronounce it in the same manner, as the verb to *excuse*, which they sound as the English do. *Profuse*, and *recluse*, are pronounced likewise as *spruce*, *Bruce*.

EXHORT

The *x* as in *anxiety*. The *h* mute. The *or* as in *corn*.

EXPATIATE, EXPATRIATE

The *a* as in *patience*.

EXTOLL

The *o* is short, and open. As in *loll*. The Scotch are apt to pronounce it long and close; so as to make *extoll* rhyme to *coal*, *foal*, *hole*. Vide *poll*.

EXTREMITY

The second *e* as in *delicate*, *memory*. So in *supremacy*. Yet in *extreme*, and *supreme* and the adverbs *extremely* and *supremely* the *e* has the same sound as in *ether*. Vide *supra*. Which misleads many Scotch people in the pronounciation of the two derivatives *extremity*, and *supremacy*.

FAMINE

The Scotch pronounce the *a* long, and as in *fame*, *game*, *tame*. The true pronounciation of it is, as in *ham*, *swam*, *ram*.

FATHER

The *a* as in the foregoing word but longer. Some Scotchmen pronounce it here likewise as in *fame*.

FERN

The *e* as in *clergy*, *eternal*. Pronounce in the same manner *stern*, and all other monosyllables having the same termination, and words of more than one syllable also, where the accent is on the last. As *discern*, *concern*. The Scotch pronounce the *e* in these words as they do in *eternal*.

FILL

I have already endeavoured to explain the true English sound of the short *i*. Perhaps some further illustration may be necessary. In *is*, which the Scotch pronounce in the same manner with the English, the sound seems to be somewhat different from what it is in the English pronounciation of *fit*, *wit*, *fin*, something nearer the *i* in *caprice*. But this I believe is owing to a property common to all the softer semivowels and mutes (viz. this soft *s*, the *v*, the soft *th*, the *b* the *d* and the[437] *g*) by which they reflect back as it were, a sort of hollowness on a preceding obscure and short vowel. What I mean will be manifest by attending[438] successively to the sound of the obscure *u* first in *luck*, *skull*, *bur*, *but*, *buss*, *sup*, *scum*, *bun*; and then in *tug*, *bud*, *tub*, *buzz*. Of the short open *a* first in *pass*, *pack*, *pap*, *pat*, *path*; and then in *as*, *bag*, *babble*, *pad*, *father*. Of the obscure *i* first in *kick*, *kill*, *kin*, *kit*, *ship*, *skim*, *pith*, *Liffy*; and then in *big*, *bid*, *crib*, *smithy*, *live*. This sort of hollow sound is very perceptible in the following lines

> And Kettle-drum, whose sullen dub
> Sounds like the hooping of a tub.[439]

As there is only a slight shade, or gradation, between the Scotch method of sounding the *i*, in *fill*, *fit*, *wit* &c and the English, the difference generally escapes the attention of Scotchmen who are endeavouring to mend their pronounciation. It is however so sensible to the English, that when they mean to ridicule the Scotch dialect they frequently lay hold of this circumstance, at the same time with the provincial sound of the *ou* in *bought* and *sought*, and of the *e* in *clemency, memory, echo* &c. Indeed as caricature [440] adds to the ridicule in all sorts of mimicry the English in their imitation exaggerate the Scotch pronounciation of the short *i*, and turn it into the obscure *u* or *a*. '*Whats your wull?*' '*You have a great deal of wat*'.

FIND
Vide *bind*.

FIR[441]
The *i* is sounded nearly like the short obscure *u* in *burst, fur*. But not exactly so. Vide *supra*.

FIRE
This word is pronounced properly by the Scotch. I have inserted it here for the sake of the following observation. viz, that in this word and others of the same termination as *squire, desire*, the *ire*, (or *ier* according to the old orthography) is not infrequently made two syllables by several classical poets from Chaucer downwards to very late times.

> He lulleth *hire* he kisseth hir full soft
> With thicke bristles of his beard unsoft;
> He is a gallant *squier* by my trouthe[442]

> Then stept a gallant *squire* forth[443]

> The purple drops from Tanereas sides down rail'd
> But from the Pagan ran whole streams of blood;
> Wherewith his force grew weake, his courage quail'd
> As *fiers* do, which fuel want, or food.[444]

> O! who can hold a *fire* in his hand
> By thinking of the frosty Caucasus;
> Or wallow naked in December snow
> By mere remembrance of the summers heat.[445]

> Rumble thy belly-full, spit fire, spout rain.
> Nor rain, wind, thunder, *fire* are my daughters[446]

in the first of these lines it is a monosyllable, in the second a disyllable.

> Of a heav'nlier influence
> Than that which mountbanks dispense
> Tho by Promethean fire made[447]

194

> Fierce desires will prevail
> You are fair, and I am frail.[448]

> Boastful and rough, your first son is a squire
> The next a tradesman meek, and much a Lyar[449]

In the first couplet indeed we might suppose that Pope meant to abbreviate *Lyar*, by syndiosis, but[450] in all the other instances the verse absolutely requires the two syllables.[451]

Shakespear in like manner makes *hour* a disyllable in the following passages.

> So many hours must I tend my flock;
> So many hours must I take my rest;
> So many hours must I contemplate;
> So many hours must I sport myself.[452]

Power and *flower*, which in prose, and conversation are always pronounced as monosyllables, are often disyllables in verse. But this is authorized by the orthography.

FIRST

as *fir*. Vide *supra*.

FLAUNT

Here the proper pronounciation is the broad open sound. Vide *Aunt*.

FLOOR

verb and noun. As *door*.

FORBES

By the English this name is always made a monosyllable. So is *Fiddes*. This by analogy to *Hobbes*, *Greaves* &c. The Scotch make *Forbes* & *Fiddes* disyllables. Thomson has done so in his encomium on the Lord President Forbes, in his Seasons,

> Thee Forbes! too, whom every worth attends,
> As truth sincere, as weeping friendship kind.[453]

It is natural enough, on the first view of the matter, to think that proper names, whether of places or persons, should be pronounced, as in the country where such places are situated, and such names of Persons prevail. I have known some Scotchmen of excellent taste, who, though in other respects they approved of the endeavour of their countrymen to attain the English pronunciation, have been scandalized when any one of their acquaintance has adopted (even in London) the English way of pronouncing his own name. But if it sounds no less uncouth to the ears of those who speak English well, to hear Douglas (for instance) pronounced as if it were *Dooglas*, than to hear a *cow*, called a *coo*, there seems to me as much reason for laying aside the provincial pronounciation of the one word, as of the other. There are many who think it a ridiculous circumstance belonging to the French language, that, in it, almost all foreign names are metamorphosed or curtailed. That *London* is changed to *Londres*; *Titus Livius* to *Tite Live*; *St Desiderius*, to *St Didier*;[454] *Stephen* to *Etienne*, *Dyonisious* to *Denis*. In truth however something of the same kind happens in all other languages. What a corruption of *Livorno* is *Leghorn*! Yet a person who should talk in England of the town of *Livorno* would be accused of unpardonable affectation. In many Latin names, the English, like the French, reject the terminating syllable. They say *Virgil*, *Horace*, *Ovid*, *Lucan*, *Mark Anthony*. The Scotch use the same sort of abbreviation of many ancient names not allowed by the English: For they say *Sueton*, *Thucidyde*, *Herodote*. The Romans had the like custom of altering Greek names; *Ulysses* for Οδυσσευς, *Proserpina* for περσεφονη, &c. And all the names of the barbarous nations; *Caractacus*, *Arviragus*, *Arminius*, must have been greatly changed before they could acquire so classical an air, as we find they have in the writings of the Roman historians.

FORCE (noun and verb)
The *o* has its long close sound. The Scotch make it short, and open. By their pronounciation this word rhymes to *indorse*, or to the French word *ecorce*. According to the true pronounciation it rhymes to *coarse* or *course*, (which to the ear, are the same). The following rhyme is perfect.

> Nor widow tears not tender orphans cries
> Can stop th'invaders *force*
> Nor swelling seas nor threat'ning skies
> Prevent the pirates *course*[455]

FORK
The long open *o* as in *corn*. *Cork* is pronounced in the same manner. The Scotch make the *o* short in both.[456]

FORM (noun and verb)
This word in the ordinary acceptation and its compounds, are pronounced with the long open *o*, as *fork*,[457] *corn*. When it signifies a class in a school, or a bench, the *o* has its long close sound. To acquire a clear idea of the distinction between these two sounds of the *o*, I cannot recommend a better method, than to get an English man who

speaks well, to pronounce *form*, first, as used in the one sense, and then, as in the other.

There are but three monosyllables in the language, *form*, *storm*, and *worm*, of this termination; And in each the *o* has a different sound. In *storm* it differs from its sound in *form*, when used in the last mentioned sense; and in *worm* it is pronounced like *u* in *cud*.

FOOT

The Scotch, Irish, and Northern English, pronounce the *oo* like the *u* in *shut*, *hut*, *cut*. It should be pronounced as in *fool*, and so the *oo* is to be sounded in all other words of this termination. Some few English people who speak well pronounce it in *soot* as the *u* in *shut*.

FORT

The long close *o* as in *ford*, or like the *ou* in *court*. Pronounce in the same manner *port*, *sport*. Pronounce with the long open *o*, *escort*, *short*, *exhort*, *extort*, *retort*, *snort*, *sort*, *tort*, *contort* &c. *Wort* rhymes to *hurt*, which indeed is also the Scotch pronounciation.

FORTH (extra)

The Scotch pronounce this *o* like the short close *u*, or as it is sounded in *wort*. Indeed till lately, they used to write this word with an *u*, *Furth*. The true pronounciation is with the long[458] close *o* as in *fort*.

FREQUENT (noun and verb), FREQUENCY, UNFREQUENT &c

The *e* has its first vocal sound, like *ee* in *feet*.

FROTH, FROTHY

The short open *o* and the *th* hard. *Froth* and *broth* form a perfect rhyme. The Scotch use the long close sound of the *o*, and the soft *th*. So as to make *froth* and *loathe* (verb, *to have an aversion to*) rhyme together. In *oath* the *oa* sounded as the *oa*, in *loathe*, but the *th* is hard as in *froth*. The Scotch make it soft in *both*.[459]

FRIDAY

The diphthongal *i* as in *bride*, *ride*. The Scotch pronounce the first syllable like *bed*.

FRIEND

Pronounce the *ie* as *e* in *mend*. In the vernacular Scotch pronounciation it rhymes to *feend*. The following is a perfect rhyme

> See some strange comfort ev'ry state attend
> And pride bestow'd on all, a common friend[460]

FROWN

The *ow* has its diphthongal sound as in *cow*, *vow*. Vide *bow*. The Scotch are apt to make it rhyme to *shown*. Pronounce as *frown*, *down*, *gown*, *clown*, *renown*, *brown*, *crown*, *drown*, *town*. Pronounce as *shown*: *own* (verb and adjective), *blown*, and all similar participles.

FULL

The *u* has its distinct vocal sound like *oo* in *foot*, *fool*[461] but shorter.[462] In Scotland and in the North of England it is pronounced as in *dull*. The rhymes in the following celebrated couplet of Durham is not perfect.

> Tho' deep yet clear, tho' gentle, yet not *dull*
> Strong without rage, without o'erflowing, *full*.

Vide *bull*.

GARDEN

The *a* as in *calf*. In Scotland it is pronounced as in *cave*.

GARTER

The *a* as in *calf*.

GEOGRAPHY

The Scotch make this a word of four syllables, *Ge-o-gra-phy*. This may be more agreeable to the etymology, the *e* being long in the original language. But its only effect in the true English pronounciation of this word, as in *George*, *Georgics*, is to show that the *g* has its hard sound. The *i* has the same effect in *Giorgio*, *giusto*, in Italian. *Geography* therefore is a trisyllable.

GHOST

The Scotch make the *o* short, and open, as in *lost*. In the pure dialect it is long and close, like the *oa* in *boast*. Pronounce as *Ghost*: *host*, *most*, *post*. Pronounce as *lost*: *cost*, *accost*, *frost*, *pentecost*, *tost*.

GLOUCESTER

The Scotch following the spelling, make this word, *Worcester*, *Leicester* and *medicine*, trisyllables, the English pronounce them as two, suppressing the middle *e*. Shakespear writes *Gloster*; and indeed that manner of writing *Gloster*, and *Worcester* was frequent, long after his times. I have known some few English people pronounce *medicine* as a trisyllable. But they were not good speakers. The *ou* in *Gloucester* has the sound of the short open *o*; In *Worcester* it has that of *oo* in *boot*, *shoot*, *foot*.

GOD

The short open *o*, as in *Noll, Moll.* This is the only word of this termination in which the *o* has that sound. In *rod, nod* &c, it has the short close sound. Vide *supra*.

GONE

The short[463] open *o*[464] as in *Don.* The Scotch are apt to make it long, when they endeavour to pronounce well. The following is a perfect rhyme.

> As well his Grace reply'd, Like you Sir *John*!
> That I can do, when all I have is *gone*.[465]

Pronounce in the same manner *shone.* In *none* the *o* is short but close. *Done* is properly pronounced in Scotland, being, to the ear, the same word with *dun.* Very few Scotchmen acquire the true pronounciation of *one.* The English fanaticks of the last age used to sound it like *bone*, and that method has remained with some people in Scotland when they read. Most Scotch people when they try to adopt the common pronounciation of England say *wan.* It should be sounded short, and like the first syllable of *wonder*.[466] All other words of this sort, are pronounced so as to rhyme to *bone*, or *moan.* As *stone, prone* &c.

GOSLING

The short close *o*. The soft *s*. The Scotch use the long close *o*, but pronounce the *s* properly.

GREASE (verb and substantive)

The *s*, in the substantive, has its hard sound. It is, to the ear, the same word with *greese.* The Scotch make it rhyme to *ease.* Which the verb to *grease* does, in the pure dialect. The *s* is soft also in the adjective *greasy.*

GROSS, ENGROSS

The *o* has its long close sound as in *fort, port.* The Scotch give it the short open sound. In all other words ending in *oss*, it has that last mentioned, but these two rhyme to *dose* (a term of medicine, Vide *supra*). The rhyme is therefore imperfect in the two following distichs.

> A clerk foredoom'd his fathers soul to cross
> Who pens a stanza when he should engross.[467]

> But all our praises why should Lords engross
> Rise, honest muse! and sing the man of Ross.[468]

GROVELING

The first syllable as in *Love*. The Scotch generally pronounce it as in *grove, Jove*.[469]

GUARDIAN

Some Scotch people pronounce the *u* in the same manner as the Italians do in *guardiano*; i.e. so as to form the same diphthong with the *a*, that *w* does, in *ward, wander*. But the *u* is of no use in the true pronounciation, the first syllable being the same, to the ear, with the first of *garden*, or with the primitive word *guard*.

HALF

The short open *a* as in *part, pan, hat*. The Scotch vernacular pronounciation makes it long as in *father*. The *l* is mute here as in *calf, walk, stalk, talk, salmon, psalm*. It is generally sounded in *scalp, calm, balm, psalmody*. In *walk, stalk*, and *talk*, the *a* is broad, and open as in *all*. In *scalp, psalm, psalmody* and *balm*, it is pronounced as in *half*. In *calm* as in *calf*, being preceded by a hard *c*. Vide *supra*.

HALT, HALTER

Vide *altar*.

HANDKERCHIEF

The *d* (in familiar speech at least) is mute, and the first syllable pronounced as in *hanker*. The *ei* in the last syllable, like the short *i* in *if*.

HARRY (a proper name)

The short open *a*, as in *parry, tarry*. The Scotch generally pronounce it in all these words with the slender *a* as in *pare*, but shorter.[470]

HARVEST

The same observations apply to the pronounciation of the *a* in this word.

HAUNCH, HAUNT

Vide *aunt*.

HAVE, HAVING

The *a* has its short open sound as in *hat, hard*. The ill educated among the Londoners, and many of the Scotch, make it long and slender as in *save*. This is to be avoided. But all other words like these (even *behave*, which seems to be formed from *have*) rhyme to *save*.

HEAD

See *bread*. In their vernacular pronounciation, the Scotch make this, to the ear the same word with *heed*. The following is a perfect rhyme.

> Not ev'n the chief by whom our hosts are *led*,
> The king of kings, shall touch that sacred *head*[471]

HEARD

The *ea* as in *earth*. To the ear this word is the same with *herd*.[472]

HEARTH

The *ea* as the *a* in *art, part, start*.[473]

HEATHEN

The *ea* as in *appear*. The *th* soft, as in *breathe*. The *en* as *on*, in *bacon*. The Scotch pronounce the *ea* with the slender sound of *a*, as in *wave*, or of *ei* in *weigh*, but shorter; and they make the *th* hard.

HEAVY

Rhymes to *bevy*. The *ea* being sounded as in *head*. The Scotch pronounce it with the short obscure sound of *i* as in *living*.

HELEN

The *e* short, and as in *bell, pen, bed*. The *h* is pronounced. The Scotch do not sound the *h*. And are apt, when they mean to speak correctly to sound the *e* as they do in *clemency*.

HERB

The *e* as in *eternal*. The *h* mute.

HERON

The *h* is pronounced, and the *e* sounded in the same manner as in the foregoing word. The *o* is mute. So that, to the ear, *Heron* is a monosyllable.[474] And so it probably [475] was in Spenser's time.

> And when Jove's harness-bearing bird from high,
> Stoops at a flying Heron, with proud disdain.[476]

A Note

(In this passage *harness* means armour, as *arnese* does in Italian). Modern writers generally omit the *o* in the orthography.

> Loud shrieks the soaring hern.[477]

HIDEOUS

The Scotch make this word, and *odious*, trisyllables.[478] But in

English,[479] *ious*, forms a diphthong and expresses nearly the same sound as *yes*. In the following lines to make odious a trisyllable would destroy Popes measure.[480]

> Odious! in woollen! 't would a saint provoke.[481]

HIS

At Edinburgh, and in the adjoining counties, this pronoun, instead of being made to rhyme to *is*; is pronounced, as if written *hees*. *She* instead of being rhyming to *he*, *me*, *bee*, *pea*, is there pronounced with the sound of the french *eu*, in *peur*, *coeur*. I have known few persons educated in that part of Scotland, who have ever got rid of these two peculiarities.

HOARSE

The *oa* is pronounced with the long close sound of *o*. *Hoarse* rhymes exactly to *force*, *course*, and *coarse* (which two last words are, the same). The Scotch are apt to pronounce *hoarse*, in the same manner with *horse*.

HORACE

The *o* is short and open, as in *Porsenna*. The Scotch make it long and close as in *Boreas*.

HOST

The *o* long and close as in *ghost*, or like *oa* in *boast*. vide *Ghost*. The first of the two following couplets is a perfect rhyme. The other not.

> The sacred rulers lead. The following *host*,
> Pour'd forth by thousands, darkens all the *coast*.[482]

> Now shameful flight alone can save the host
> Our blood, our treasure, and our glory lost[483]

HOUSES (the plural of *house*)

The Scotch, and some provincials of England, pronounce the *s* hard in the plural, as it is in the singular; but it ought to be soft as in the verb to *house*; and in the singular and plural both, of *spouse*, *spouses*.

HOVER

The Scotch make the *o* long and close as in *rover*. But according to the true pronounciation *hover*, and *lover* form a perfect rhyme. Pronounce like *hover*, *cover* (the vulgar English say *kiver*), *lover*, *glover*, *plover*. As *rover*: *over*, *drover*, *trover* (a law term). In *approver*, and *disprover*, the *o* has the same sound as in *approve*.

HUMBLE, HUMBLY

The *h* is mute, and the *u* as in *tumble, stumble, rumble*. The *b* is to be pronounced in all this class of words. In the vernacular pronounciation of Scotland it is silent. Many Scotch people sound the *h* in *humble*, and *humbly*.

HUMILITY

Here the *h* is to be pronounced, and the *u* has its diphthongal sound as in *Hume, humane*.

HUNDRED

Pronounced (in conversation at least) as if written, *hunder'd*. In *Birmingham* the *r* is transposed in quite the opposite manner. For that word is always pronounced *Briminjam*, or rather *Brimijam*.[484]

HUNGER, HUNGRY[485]

The hard *g* to be sounded distinctly. See this explained under *anger*.

IDEA

The *i* has its diphthongal sound, as in *tide, wide*. The Scotch often give it its long vocal sound as in *caprice*,[486] *magazine*. The *e* has that sound in the true pronounciation, & by the Scotch is pronounced as in *pen*.[487]

IDES

The *i* as in the foregoing word.

IMPLACABLE

The first *a* has its long slender sound, as in *rake*; the Scotch pronounce it as in *black*.

INCOME

The *n* has its more nasal sound as in *ink, anger*. The Scotch pronounce it, as it would be, if *in* and *come* were two distinct words. *In*-come.

JEALOUS, JEALOUSY

The *ea* as in *death, breath*. The Scotch pronounce it as they often do in *death* and as they sound the *e* in *clemency*.

JACQUES (the name of a Character in Shakespear)

A monosyllable and pronounced so as to rhyme to *stakes, lakes*.[488]

JORDAN

The long open *o* as in *corn*.

JOB (proper name)

The long close *o* as in *robe*. The Scotch sound it as in *bob*, *rob*, *mob*, *knob*. They make this the same word with *job*. (A low, lucrative piece of business). This last word is sometimes written *jobb*. The difference will be rendered very palpable by attending to the two following couplets. The rhyme is perfect in each.

> This Man of Uz, script of his Hebrew *robe*,
> Is just the proverb, and as poor as *Job*.[489]

> No cheek is known to blush, nor heart to *throb*
> Save when they lose a question, or a *job*.[490]

KEPT

The *e* as in *step*, *stept*. *Kept*, and *stept* form a perfect rhyme. *Slept* is to be pronounced in the same manner. In Scotland they are frequently sounded as if written *keept*, *sleept*.

KNOWLEDGE

The general pronounciation in England, as in Scotland, is to give the *ow*, in this word, and in *acknowledge*, and *acknowledgement*, the sound of the short open *o* as in *solitary*. Some English people affect to give it the long close sound, as in *flow*, *know*.

LANGUAGE

The *g* has its distinct sound as in *anger*; and the *u* is sounded before the second *a*; as it is before the *i*, in *languish*. The Scotch pronounce the *ng* as in *singer*, and suppress the *u*, sounding the *a* like the short *i*, as if it were written *langige*.

LARGE, LARGESS

The *a* as in *far*, *bard*. The Scotch sound it as in *clare*, *ware*, *stare*. *Barge*, and *large*, form a perfect rhyme.

LATHER

The *a* short. In other respects as, in *father*. The Scotch are apt to make it long.

LATIN

The Scotch pronounce the first syllable *late*. But the *a* is to be sounded as in *fat*, *latch*.

LAUNCH

See *Aunt*. The Scotch pronounce this word as if written *lench*. So as to rhyme to *stench*.

LAVISH (adj. and verb)
The *a* short and open as in *lather*. The Scotch sound it as *slavish*, *knavish*.

LEAD (noun, a metal)
The *ea* as in *bread*. The following is a perfect rhyme.

> Here pleas'd behold her mighty wings out-*spread*
> To hatch a new Saturnean age of *lead*.[491]

LEARN, LEARNED
The *ea* like the *e* in *fern*, *hern*.[492] The English contrary to their practice in most other words of this kind, almost always pronounce the *ed* in *Learn'd* when used as an adjective. The Scotch generally suppress the *e*.[493] Even in poetry it is seldom abbreviated by the English. Pope himself, who was not one of those who were 'for restoring *ed*', yet preserves it, in this word, although in the very same line he abbreviates its compound, *Unlearned*.[494]

> Such labour'd nothings, in so grave a style
> Amaze th'unlearn'd, And make the learned smile.

I do not believe there is another instance of the termination *ed*, forming a distinct syllable, throughout his works. When a participle, *learned*, like other participles, is pronounced as if written *learn'd*, and is so written in verse.

> Against the poets, their own arms they turn'd
> Sure to hate most, the men from whom they learn'd.[495]

LEIZURE, LEIZURELY
The Scotch who aim at the proper sound, either pronounce these words as if written *leezure*, *leezurely*, or so as to rhyme to *pleasure*, *measure*. But the *ei* ought to be sounded as *ay* in *say*, *day*, *pay*; or *eigh* in *weigh*. The first syllable is long. The first in *pleasure*, and *measure* is short. The *sure* is pronounced exactly as in *pleasure*.

LEGHORN
The Scotch pronounce the *h*. But in the pure dialect it is suppressed.[496]

LENGTH, LENGTHEN[497]
Pronounce the *ng* as in *singer*, *hanger*. So *strength*, *strengthen*. The Scotch, and inaccurate speakers among the English, sound both words, as if written *lenth*, *strenth* – I believe few people will agree with

205

Dr Foster that the 1st syllable of *strengthen* has a quick and easy pronounciation as that of the word *oozy*.[498]

LEICESTER
A disyllable. Vide *Gloucester*.

LEONARD
A disyllable. Pronounce as if written *Lennard*.

LEOPARD
This word is made a trisyllable in Scotland, *Le-o-pard*. In the true pronounciation it is a disyllable, and the *eo* sounded as *e* in *step*, *lend*, *shepherd*. Spenser, and Milton write *libbard*.

LIBERTY, LIBERAL
The *i* short, and as in *live*. The Scotch are apt to give it the long vocal sound of *e*, or *ee* as in *leer*, *leave*. *Liberal* is pronounced as a disyllable, *Lib'ral*.

LIMB
The *b* is[499] silent. The Scotch vernacular pronounciation of this word is almost the same with the English. It rhymes to *him*, *swim*, *whim*.

LINGER
The *g* is to be pronounced forcibly as in *anger*. Not as in *singer*.

LODGE, LODGING, DISLODGE
The *o* has in these words, its[500] short open sound as in *God*. The Scotch give it that of *u* in *budge*, *trudge*. *Dodge* is pronounced in the same manner with *lodge*. The following is a perfect rhyme.

> With fate's lean tipstaff none can *dodge*.
> He'll find you out where'er you *lodge*.[501]

LONDON
The formal way of pronouncing this word, is to sound the *d*. The more usual and familiar method is to suppress it. Both are countenanced by the example of good, and unaffected speakers.

LOSE (verb)
The *o* is long, and has the second sound of *u*, as in *pull*, or of *oo*, as in *choose*. The *s* is soft as in *choose*. These two words therefore form a perfect rhyme. This is the only word, of the sort, where the *o* has that

sound. In *loose*, verb and noun, & *unloose*.[502] The *s* has its hard sound, as in *goose* and *noose*.

LONGER

The *g* is to be pronounced forcibly as in *anger*. Vide *anger*. The Scotch pronounce this word as *singer*.

LOVAT

The English always pronounce the first syllable of this name short. And as *love*. The Scotch make it long, as in *grove*.

LUSTRE

This word rhymes exactly to *muster*. Many Scotch people pronounce it as if written *lusture*.

LUXURY

The *x* has its hard sound composed of *k* and *s* as in *axiom*. The Scotch pronounce it like *gs* as in *example*. Vide *anxiety*. The second *u* has not the diphthongal sound which some Scotch people give it; but the same short, close vocal sound, as the first, or as it has in the words *stuck*, *luck*, but more obscure.[503]

MARCH

The *a*, in Scotland, is commonly pronounced as in *have*. But it ought to be pronounced exactly as in *art*, *part*.[504] *Starch*, and *March* form a perfect rhyme. The Scotch pronounce the latter word also improperly, sounding it as they do *March* but shorter.

MARE

Rhymes exactly to *pare*, *stair*, *fair*. The Scotch make it, to the ear, the same word with *mere*. And to rhyme to *here*, *deer*, *fear*.

MARS

The *a* as in *March*. So the Scotch also pronounce it; but they make the *s* hard, so as to form a perfect rhyme between *Mars* and *farce*. But the English give the *s* its soft sound, so as to make this, to the ear, the same word with *mars* part of the verb to *mar*. The following is a perfect rhyme.

> 'Tis yours, my fair one, then to end these *jars*.
> Love you like Venus, and I'll fight like *Mars*.

In reading Latin, all other words of this termination are so pronounced by the English, as *ars*, *pars*.

MASTER, MASTERY

The *a* as in *mast*. The following rhyme is perfect.

> Unlucky Welsted! thy unfeeling *master*
> The more thou ticklest, gripes his fist the *faster*.

The Scotch pronounce the first syllable like *mess*. Perhaps this was the old English pronounciation, since Chaucer and Spenser both write maistery.

> Love wol not be constrained by maistrie
> When maistrie cometh, the God of Love anon
> Beteth his winges, and farewell, he is gon.
> Love is a thing, as any Spirit free.[505]

> Ne may love be compell'd by maistery
> For soon as maistry comes sweet love anon
> Taketh his nimble wings, and soon away is gone.[506]

The reader will not be displeased to observe, that the foregoing beautiful passage of the father of our poetry, has been in a manner transcribed by Spenser, in the lines last cited, and closely imitated by Pope in the following.

> Love, free as air, at sight of human ties
> Spreads his light wings, and in a moment flies.[507]

Plaister is still often spelt with an *i*, when it signifies *emplâtre*, but in the modern English pronounciation it rhymes to *Master*.

MATERNAL

The *e* as in *eternal*.

MAY

Vide *ay*.

MEDICINE

This word is constantly made a disyllable by the generality of the English, both in speaking and reading, whether prose or verse. There are some low people from vulgarity, and some few persons of learning from affectation, who sound the middle *i*. The old Poets make *medicine* a trisyllable in some instances. As 'seeking *medicine*, whence she was stung.'[508] See also a passage in Ben Johnson's *Every Man in his Humour*. 2. *Venison* is in like manner generally made a disyllable in pronounciation, though there are many English people who pronounce the *i*. The *s* in venison has its soft sound.

MEMORY

The *e* is to be pronounced short, and as in *men*, *clemency*. The Scotch pronounce it like the English sound of *ay* in *pay*, *may*, &c. Vide *clemency*, *delicate*.

MERCHANT[509]

The *e* as in *Berks*, *Berkshire*. The first syllable is the same with *March*. Some English people pronounce the *e* as in *eternal*.

MERCURY, MERGE, MERRY

The short close *e* as in *Eternal*. See *eternal*. The Scotch pronounce the *e* in the three first words, as they do the *a* in *March*, or like their sound of η. And in *merry* like the short obscure *i* in *mist*.[510]

MICHAEL

This is a disyllable. The *i* has its diphthongal sound as in *mine*. The *ch* is pronounced like *k*, and the *ael* like *el* in *Babel*. The Scotch make *Michael* a trisyllable.

MOROSE[511]

The *s* hard as in *case*, *base*. The second *o* short and close. *Morose* and *close* form a perfect rhyme. The Scotch pronounce the last syllable as *rose*.

MORN, MORNING

The long open *o* as in *born*, *scorn*, *broad*. When the Scotch have got rid of their vernacular pronounciation of *mourn*, and *mourning*, they are apt to confound those two words with these.

MORTGAGE

The English suppress the *t*, pronouncing the word as if written *morgage*. The Scotch are apt to sound the *t*, and to lay too great a stress on the first syllable.

MOST

The *o* is long and close like *oa* in *boast*, and *o* in *host*. The Scotch sound it as in *lost*. Of the following rhymes the first is perfect the other not.[512]

> Sure if they catch to spoil the toy at most
> To covet flying, and regret when *lost*.[513]

209

MOTE
Here the *o* has its long close sound. *Mote* makes a perfect rhyme to *boat*. The Scotch [514] make it rhyme to *spot*.

MOTLEY
Here the *o* ought to be sounded as in *spot*, and some Scotch people are apt to pronounce it as they should in *mote*. *Motley* and *hotely*[515] rhyme exactly together.

MOURN, MOURNING
The *ou* has the sound of the long close *o*. As in *bore*. The Scotch vernacular pronounciation, gives the *ou* the sound of the short close *u* as in *return*. According to this pronounciation, the following would be a perfect rhyme which it is not.

> The trembling Priest, along the shore return'd
> And in the anguish of a father, mourn'd.[516]

MOVE
This word rhymes to *groove*. The Scotch are apt to pronounce it as *love*. Vide *above*.

MOUTHS (plural of mouth)
The *th* has the soft sound as in the verb to *mouthe*. The Scotch sound it hard as in the singular.

MOW
Vide *bow*.

NAPKIN
The *a* short and open as in *nap*, *rap*, *sap*. The Scotch[517] make the first syllable of this word and of *Neptune* the same.

NEAT
The *ea* as in *appear*. The Scotch generally pronounce it as in *bear*. Vide *eat*.

NEPHEW[518]
The *ph* in the pure dialect is pronounced as *v*. In Scotland & the North of England it has its usual sound of *f*.

NE'ER (abbreviated from *never*)
Pronounce so as to rhyme to *e'er*, *bear*, *stare*. The Scotch often[519] make it, to the ear, the same with *near*.

210

NEITHER
As *either* supra.

NEVER
As *ever* supra.

NEWTON
The *on* as in *bacon*, supra.

NONE
The *o* is short, as in *gone*, *shone*, but close instead of open.

NOTICE
The long close[520] *o* as in *note*. The Scotch pronounce it as in *not*.

NOUGHT
The *ou* has the long open sound of the *o* – as in *sought*, *bought*, *ought*.

NUSANCE
The *s* is hard, as in *use*.[521] The Scotch make it soft. The *u* is diphthongal.[522]

OATH
The *oa* has the long close sound of *o* as in *boast*. In this, as in most other words the Scotch give the *ou* the short open sound of *o* as in *moth*. This may have been the ancient English pronounciation. Chaucer writes this and several other words, of the same sort, without an *a*

> And many a grisly *oth*, than have they sworn.[523]

> Now Sires, quod he, if it be you so lefe
> To findeth deth, tourne up this croked way
> For in that Grove, I left him, by my fay
> Under a tree, and there he wol abide
> Ne for your *bost* he will him nothing hide.[524]

OAT-MEAL
In this (I believe single) instance, the English pronounce the *oa*, like the short open *o*, in *not*, insomuch that to make it long & close[525] (altho in the primitive word *oat*, the *oa* is sounded as in *oath*) would appear pedantic, and affected.

OBLIGE[526]
There are two ways of pronouncing this word, and both practised by

good speakers. Viz. Either to give the *i* its diphthongal sound, as in *hide*, or its long vocal sound as *Eloisa*. The latter pronounciation is, I believe, considered as the most elegant.[527] The following is, according to that pronounciation, a perfect rhyme.

> Dreading ev'n fools. By flatterers besieged
> And so obliging, that he ne'er obliged.[528]

ODIOUS, Vide *hideous*
The following is another passage in Pope, where *his* measure would be destroyed, if *odious* were made a trisyllable.

> A park is purchased, but the fair he sees
> All bath'd in tears, – Oh *odious, odious* trees.[529]

OF, OFF, OAF
These three words afford examples, of three, out of the four sounds of *o*. In the first it is short, and close; in the second short, and open; and in the third, the *oa*, has, as in other cases, the long close sound of the *o*.

OGLE
The *o* is long, and close; the Scotch make it short and close. And the same difference is to be observed, between the proper pronounciation and theirs of the proper names, *Ogleby* and *Ogilvie*.

OIL
Vide *Boil*.[530]

OLIVE
The *o* is short, and open, the Scotch pronounce it long and close.

ONE
Vide *supra*.[531]

ONLY (formerly written *onely*)
The *o* is long and close. The Scotch make it short and open. *Only* makes a perfect rhyme to *lonely*.

OPAQUE
The *a* as in *snake, take, make*, with which words this forms a perfect rhyme. The Scotch pronounce it so as to rhyme to *hawk, walk*.

OPEN
The long close *o*, as in *token*. The *en* in both words, as *on* in *bacon*.

OUGHT
The long open sound of *o* as in *bought*.

OVEN
The *o* has exactly the same sound as in *love*. The Scotch pronounce it as in *over*; where it has the same sound as in *Jove*. The *en* is pronounced like the *on* in *bacon*. *Sloven* rhymes to *oven*. Vide *sloven*.

OVID
The *o* here, is short and open. The Scotch make it long and close as in *over*.

OWN
The *ow* has the sound of the long close *o*, or *oa*; as in *moan*.

PAGEANT
The *a* short and open as in *Madge*, *fadge*. The Scotch pronounce it as in *page*.

PATERNAL
The *e* as in *eternal*, *fern*.

PATENT
The *a* is to be pronounced short and open as in *pat*. The Scotch often sound it as in *pate*. In *latent* that last is the true pronounciation, the first syllable of that word being the same with the word *late*.

PATHOS
The *a* as in *late*, *pate*, *latent*.

PATRICK
The *a* long and open as in *father*.[532]

PAUNCH
Vide *aunt*.

PEAR (a fruit)
Pronounced as *bear*, *care*. The Scotch sound the *ea* as in *appear*. But, according to the true pronounciation, this is, to the ear, the same word with *pare*.

PEASANT
The *ea* as in *bread*. The Scotch sound it as in *pease*.

213

PEDANT

The *e* is to be sounded exactly as in *bed*, *sped*, *edge*. The Scotch make it long, and pronounce it as they do in *clemency*, *memory* &c.

PENCIL

The Scotch generally pronounce this word as if written *Pincil*. But this is improper. The *e*, in the pure dialect, has nearly the same sound as in *pen*, only not so open.

PERFECT[533]

In all words ending with *ct*, except this one, the vernacular Scotch pronounciation rejects the *t*. But in this single word the *c* is suppressed by the Scotch; and the *t* only pronounced. So that they sound *perfect*, as if written *perfet*. The *c*, and *t*, should both be pronounced.

PHEASANT

The *ea* as in *head*, *bread*, or as *e* in *bed*. The Scotch sound it as in *appear*.

PHILOSOPHER, PHILOSOPHY

The *s* hard as in *case*, *morose* or as the *ss* in *moss*. The Scotch make it soft as in *Rose*.[534]

PIAZZA

The first *a* is long and slender, as in *blaze*. And the two *zz* have the same sound as the one in that word, or in *amaze*.

PIRACY, PIRATE

The *i* has its diphthongal sound as in *pride*. The Scotch give it its short close sound.

PISTACCIO[535]

The *a* is pronounced as in *station*; and the *cci* like *ti* in that word. The Scotch are apt to make the *a* short, and as in *thatch*, *attach*, and the *cci* like *tch* and *ch*, in these two words.

PLAID

The stuff of which the highland dress is made. The Scotch pronounce this word long, like *playd*, the participle of the verb to *play*. In England it is pronounced so as to rhyme exactly to *lad*, *glad*, *mad*.

POKE

This word (which signifies a little bag) is now hardly ever used in England, except in the proverbial expression of 'buying a pig in a poke.' The word is still in general use in Scotland, but it is there pronounced short, as if written *pock*, so as to rhyme to *lock*. Whereas, by the true pronounciation it rhymes to *joke*. – Chaucer writes it *poke*.

> Were it *gold*,
> Or, in a poke, nobles *untold*
> Thou shuldest it have.[536]

POLAND, POLISH (belonging to Poland)
The *o* long & close as in *Pole*.[537]

POLICY
The *o* is short and open as in *politicks*. The Scotch are apt to make it long and close.

POLISH (v. & subst.)
The *o* is pronounced in the same manner as in the preceding word. The Scotch commonly sound it as in *pole*.

POLL
When this word signifies the crown of the head, or a certain mode of election (which is a figurative derivation from the other sense) or is a verb signifying to vote at such election, the *o* is long, and close, as in *toll*; And this to the ear, is the same word with *pole*. When it is used as a cant name for a parrot, or is an abbreviation of the name of *Polly*, the *o* is short and open, as in *extoll*. Pronounce in the first manner *knoll* (in which the *k* is mute) *clodpoll*, *catchpoll*, *roll* (verb, and noun), *scroll*, *droll*, *troll*, *toll* (verb, and noun) *stoll*, *comptroll*. Pronounce as *extoll*, *loll*, *doll* (a girl's puppet), *Noll* (a cant name for Oliver Cromwell). The two following passages illustrate the different pronounciations of the word *Poll*. The rhyme is perfect in both.

> His beard as white as snow
> All flaxen was his *poll*
> He is gone, he is gone, and we cast away mourn
> Gramercy, on his *soul*.[538]

> Fondly, let me *loll*
> Pretty, pretty *Poll*.[539, 540]

PORK
The *o* long and[541] close as in *pore*. The Scotch[542] pronounce it as in *fork*, *cork*; *Work* rhymes to *lurk*. All other words of this sort rhyme to *fork*.

215

POSSESS, POSSESSION[543]

The first *ss*, in these words, has the sound of the soft *s* as in *praise*, or of *z* in *lazy*, *crazy*. The Scotch give them the hard sound, or that of the *c* in *recess*.

POST

The *o* here has its long close sound as in *host*, *most*. Vide *supra*.

POSTSCRIPT[544]

PRECEDE, PRECEDING, PRECEDENT (adj)

The *e* has its[545] long sound as in *these*, or like the *ea* in *appear*, and *ee* in *freeze*. In *Precedent* (subst.) the *e* is short & as in *preside*. Vide *infra*.[546]

PRECISE

The *i* has its diphthongal sound, but is short, and the *s* is hard as in *loose* (adj.), or like the *i* in *ice*, *nice*, *vice*. With these words *precise* forms a perfect rhyme. The Scotch make it rhyme to *wise*.

PRESIDE, PRESIDENT

The *s* has the soft sound in these words as in *presence*. The Scotch make it hard, and exactly like the *c* in *Precedent*.[547]

PRIVATEER

The *i* has its long diphthongal sound as in *private*, *alive*, *arrive*.

PRIVY (subs. and adj.)

The *i* has its short close sound as in *river*, *prithee*. The Scotch are apt to give it its diphthongal sound, as in *private*, especially in the expression *Privy-Counsellor*. This arises from an idea that such is the true (for it is not their vernacular) pronounciation. Yet nothing appears more uncouth to an English ear.

PROFIT, PROPHECY, PROPHET

[548]The *o* is short and open in all these words. Hence *profit*, and *prophet* are, to the ear, almost the same; for the unaccented *i*, and *e*, can hardly be distinguished.[549] The Scotch commonly make the *o* long, and close, in *prophet* and *prophecy*.

PROFUSE

The *s* has its hard sound, as in *use* (noun), *excuse* (noun) or like *c* in *produce*. The Scotch pronounce it soft as in *use*, and *excuse*[550] (verbs). The following is a perfect rhyme.

> You show us Rome was glorious, not *profuse*,
> And pompous buildings once were things of *use*[551]

PROGRESS
The *o* is short and open, the Scotch[552] make it long and close.

PRONOUNCIATION
The Scotch sound the *ou*, like the *u* in *Nuncio*. And the *ci*, like the hard *s*. As if the word were written *pronunsation*. But the *ou* has the proper diphthongal sound, as in *renounce, flounce* (in which words likewise, the vernacular Scotch method is, to sound it like the *u* in *Nuncio*) and the *ci* is either sounded, as in other cases, like *sh*, or often, to avoid the close repetition of that same sound twice in the same word, with the distinct sounds of the hard *s*, and the short *i* making it a separate syllable thus *pro-noun-ci-a-tion*.

PROJECT
The short open *o*, as in *progress*.

PROPHET
Vide *profit*.

PULL[553]
The *u* as in *full, bull* (vide *supra*). The *u* in *pull* and *full* has the same sound in quality with that of the *oo*, in *pool*, and *fool*, and they are all four long syllables. Yet every body perceives, that *fool* and *full*, and *pool* and *pull*, are not, to the ear, the same words. They differ in two respects. First, the vocal part in *pull*, and *full*, is short; in *pool*, and *fool*, long. Secondly, *pull* and *full* are long syllables by means of a protracted stress of the voice on the *ll*; which does not take place in the pronounciation of *pool*, and *fool*.

PULLY (one of the mechanical powers)
Here the *u* is to be sounded both in quality, and quantity as in *pull*, *full*. But this word does not rhyme exactly to *fully*. In *fully* the same stress is laid on the *ll*, as in *full*, and accordingly the first syllable is long; in *pully* there is no such stress laid on the double liquid.[554] The voice hurries over the *ll* and the first syllable is short. *Bully* rhymes exactly to *pully*.

217

PULPIT

The *u* is to be pronounced as *oo* in *foot* or as it is sounded in *pull*, and in the first syllable of *cuckoo*.[555] The Scotch sound it as in *pulp*, *gulph*.

PUT

Here too, the sound of the *u*, is, as in *pull*. *Put*, and *boot*, however do not form a perfect rhyme, the quantity of *boot* being longer.[556] The Scotch make *put*, and *but*, rhyme together. In the pure dialect every word in *ut* except *put*, is to be pronounced as *but*.

QUESTION

In the southern counties of Scotland the *e* in this word is commonly pronounced very broad, like the sound of *a* in *bare*, or the Scotch sound of the η. This peculiarity has been often remarked in the House of Commons when the gentlemen of Scotland have happen'd to unite in calling for the *question*.

RACHEL

The *a* as in *race*, the *ch* as in *Chester*, *church*. Many Scotch people substitute, in this word, for their vernacular and guttural sound of the *ch*, that of *k*.

RALPH

The same long slender *a* as in *race*. The *l* is not pronounced.

RAPHAEL

The same sound of *a* as in the two foregoing words. The Scotch are apt to pronounce it, as in *rap*. The *ael* as in *Michael*.

RASE (verb)

The *s* hard, as I have described under *base*. This, to the ear, is the same sound with *race* and Spenser, consulting the sound more than the etymology, writes it *race*. The Scotch make it the same word to the ear, with *raise*.

RATHER

The *a* as in *lather*. The Scotch either sound it like the *ea* in *feather*, *leather*, so as to form a perfect rhyme with those words; and this is the vernacular pronounciation; or they make it like *a* in *rate*. The following rhyme is perfect according to the proper sound of the *a*,

218

but not as to its quantity. The *a* being longer in *father*, than in this word.[557]

> You urged me as a judge, but I had *rather*
> You would have bid me argue like a *father*.
> > Rich. 3. Vol. 5. p.153

RAVISH

The short open *a*, as in *rap, radical*. The Scotch often pronounce it as in *rape, rave*.

RECENT

The *e* has its first long vocal sound, as in *decent,* or like that of *ee* in *Greece*, but longer. The Scotch pronounce it like *a* in *race*.

REMAINDER

The Scotch, in this word, pronounce the *ai*, like the short smothered *i* in *Minden, wind*. It should be pronounced exactly as in *remain*. But the great fault of the Scotch pronunciation of this word, consists in a wrong position of the accent. Vide B.2.c.II.

REMEMBER

The second *e* is to be pronounced nearly as in *member*, though perhaps not quite so distinctly and fully. The Scotch sound it, as they do the short obscure *i* in *limber, window*.

REPRIEVE

The *ie* here, as in *field, mien*, &c has the long vocal sound of *e*, or *ee*, or the second sound of *i*, or that of *ea* in *appear*; which are all one and the same. The Scotch in this word give it the diphthongal sound of *i*, so as to make *reprieve*, and *thrive* form a perfect rhyme.

RESIDE, RESIDENCE, RESIDENT

The *s* has its soft sound as in *praise*, or that of *z* in *graze, razor*. The Scotch in these words as in *preside, president*, &c make it hard, like the *c* in *precede, recede*.

RESIGN

Here too the *s* is soft, and is pronounced hard by the Scotch. Vide *design*.

219

RESORT

The *s* soft. The long open *o* as in *corn*, not as in *sport*, *fort* where the *o* is close.[558]

RETREAT

The *ea* as in *appear*. The Scotch are apt to pronounce it as in *bear*. The following is a perfect rhyme.

> Thy forests, Windsor! and thy green *retreats*,
> At once the Monarch's and the Muses' *seats*.

REVOLT

The short open *o* as in *God*.[559]

ROAST

The *oa* has, as in other words, the long close sound of *o*. The Scotch very generally give it the short open sound. The four following words exemplify the four different sounds of *o*. *Rod*, *rot*, *rote*, and *wrought*. In the first you have the short close sound. In the second the short open sound. In the third the long close sound, and in the fourth the long open sound.

ROUGH

This word is, to the ear, the same with *ruff*, and rhymes exactly with *stuff*, *muff*, *tough*. Perhaps it was formerly pronounced as *bough*. The following lines of Spenser seem to authorize this conjecture.

> Sweet is the Juniper, but sharp his bough
> Sweet is the fir-bloom, but his branches *rough*.[560]

It would be difficult to imagine a worse rhyme, if we supposed Spenser pronounced the word *rough*, as we do. Some striking instances occur in the French poets, where words are made to rhyme together whose pronounciation now differs as widely as that of *bough* and *rough*; but they were written at a time when the words composing those rhymes had not entirely ceased to resemble in sound, as well as in orthography. Boileau, though so correct a writer, makes *françois* the adjective rhyme to *loise*, and *decroit*, to *disparoit*.

> Durant les premiers ans du Parnasse françois
> Le caprice tout seul, faisoit toutes les loise.[561]

> Sous leurs pas diligens le chemin disparoit
> Et le Pilier loin d'eux deja baisse et decroit.[562]

According to the modern pronounciation of French these rhymes are as imperfect, as *buy*, and *say* would be in English. And indeed so they were according to the colloquial mode of speech in Boileau's own time. The *oi* in all cases was formerly pronounced as in *bois*, *poids*; but in the days of Catherine of Medici the Italian courtiers changed the sound in many words, especially in the tenses of verbs, to that of *ai*; and that sound came particularly into use in the pronounciation of *françois*, which was thereby distinguished from *François* the name of a man, that word still retaining the old diphthongal sound of *oi*. However many persons of letters continued advocates for the ancient pronounciation. Henry Stephen speaks with great indignation concerning this piece of innovation, and it is not unlikely that when Boileau wrote, there was a sufficient number of people, who still affected the former mode of speaking, to justify and render not offensive the rhymes I have cited.

ROW[563]
The Scotch generally make this word rhyme to *vow*; but, both as a verb and a substantive, it is, to the ear, exactly the same with *roe*.

SAID
The *ai* short & like the *e* in *bed* or the *ea* in *dead*, frequently in this manner. It has been already mentioned that *again* is sometimes written *agen* at the end of a verse by very modern authors.[564]

SAFFRON
The short open *a*, as in *baffle*. The Scotch often pronounce it, as in *share*, *wafer*, *paper*.

SAMUEL
The English, in this proper name, give the *u* the diphthongal sound, so as to make the word as trisyllable. The Scotch pronounce the *u* like *w* in *well*; as if the word were written *Samwell*.

SATURDAY
The *a* short and open as in *Sardinia*. The Scotch pronounce it as in *state*, *share*.

SATURN
The *a* as in the foregoing word.

SCALP
The *l* is pronounced.

SPORT[565]
The long close *o* as in *fort*.

221

SCÆVOLA
As *Sceptre*, Vide *infra*.[566]

SCEPTIC, SCEPTICISM
The *c* has its hard sound or that of *k*. The Scotch in these and all other words where *sc* are followed by *i*, or *e*, pronounce them as the Italians do; or like *sh* in English. Dr Johnson writes *skeptick*, and *skepticism*.[567]

SCEPTRE
The *c* is silent in the true pronounciation. The word being pronounced as if written *septre*.

SCHISM, SCHISMATIC
Here the *ch* is not to be pronounced. The Scotch pronounce these words, as if written *shism*, *shismatic*.

SCIPIO
The *c* mute. The word to be sounded as if written *Sipio*.

SCITE
The *c* mute. The diphthongal *i*.

SCIMITAR
The *c* mute. The *i* as in *Scipio*.

SCROLL
The *o* long and close. This word makes a perfect rhyme to *soul*.

SCYTHIA, SCYTHIAN
The first syllable as the first in *Scipio*.[568]

SEAL
The *ea* as in *appear*. Vide *deal*.

SEIVE
This word rhymes to *give*. This is the vernacular Scotch pronounciation; but many people make it rhyme to *receive*.

SEWER (a conduit, or subterraneous kennel, generally coupled with the epithet *common*)
This word is by most English people[569] pronounced as if written *shore*.

SHE
Vide *His*.

SHEW (verb)

This word by the English (except in the Northern provinces) is pronounced as if written *show*. Of the following rhymes the first is imperfect, the other two perfect.

> Full hearty was his love, and I can shew
> The tokens on my ribs, in black and blue.[570]

> Here to her chosen all her words she *shews*
> Prose swell'd to verse, verse loit'ring into *prose*.[571]

> Life is a jest; and all things *shew it*,
> I thought so once; but now I *know it*.[572]

SHIRE

In this word (and in this word alone) of this termination, the *i* has its long vocal sound as in *Eloisa*. To the ear *shire*, and *sheer*, are the same. The Scotch, and some English provincials make *shire* rhyme to *fire*, *hire*. The following, is, according to the true pronounciation, a perfect rhyme.

> The next, we heard it in a neighbouring *shire*
> That day, to church he led a blushing bride
> A nymph, whose snowy vest, and maiden *fear*
> Improved her beauty, while the knot was tied.[573]

SHORT-LIVED

The *i* has its long diphthongal sound. The Scotch sound it short as in the verb to *live*, and its participle *lived*.

SHOULDER

The *ou* has the sound of the long close *o*, as in *bold*, or as *ou* in *soul*. The Scotch are apt (when they aim at propriety) to give it the diphthongal sound as in *foul*. The following is a perfect rhyme.

> With that, all laugh'd, and clap'd him on the *shoulder*
> Making the bold wag, with their praises *bolder*.[574]

SICK

The *i* has its short obscure sound as in *thick*. The Scotch make this the same word, to the ear, with *seek*.

SLEPT

The *e* as in *kept*. The Scotch are apt to pronounce it as *ee* in *sleep*.

SLOTH

The long close *o*. This word rhymes to *oath*; the Scotch make it rhyme to *broth*.[575]

SLOVEN

The *o* to be pronounced as in *love*. The Scotch pronounce it as in *woven*, *Jove*.

SOUGHT

This word rhymes to *bought*, the *ou* having the long open sound of *o*. Vide *bought*.

SOURCE, RESOURCE

Some English people pronounce the *ou* in these words as in *course*, or like the *o* in *force*. But it seems to me that the more usual practise of approved speakers, is to sound it like *oo* in *soon*.

SOW

When it signifies either *semer*, or *coudre* is to the ear the same with *so*, but longer. The Scotch vernacular pronounciation, when it has the latter sense, makes it the same word with *shoe*. But Scotch people often pronounce it with the diphthongal sound so as to rhyme to *how*, *cow*. This is the proper pronounciation when it signifies a certain domestick animal. In the Two Gentlemen of Verona *sow* (*coudre*) is written *sew*, and yet we must suppose it was pronounced then as it is at present, otherwise the play upon the word would be lost.

> Speed. – Ihsu she can *sew*.
> Launce. – That's as much as to say can she *so*.

SPANIEL

This word rhymes to *Daniel*. Vide *supra*.

SPEAR

The *ea* as in *appear*. The Scotch often sound it as in *bear*. Tho' the other is their vernacular pronounciation.

SPHERE[576]

Rhymes to *clear*, *near*, *mere*. Of the following the first is a perfect rhyme, the second, not.

> Yet you, the murderer, look as bright, as *clear*
> As yonder Venus, in her glimmering *sphere*
> > Midsr. Nts Dr.

Some thought it mounted to the lunar sphere
Since all things lost on earth, are treasured there
R. Lock

SPORT
The long close *o*. The following rhyme is perfect.

From the loud camp retired, & noisy *court*
In honourable ease, & rural *sport*
H. and Emma

STALK (verb and noun)
The *a*, as in *all*, *walk*. And the *l* mute as in *walk*.

STAPLE, STAPLETON
The *a* long and slender, as in *rape*. The Scotch are apt to pronounce
it, as the *e* in *step*.

STATUE, STATURE, STATUTE
The short open *a* as in *hat*. The Scotch sound it long, and as in *state*.

STAUNCH
Vide *aunt*.

STOMACH
The *o* short, and almost as in *comfort*. Vide *comfort*.

STORK
The long open *o* as in *fork*.

STRENGTH
To be pronounced[577] as *length*. Vide *length*.

SUBLIME
The *u* as in *subject*, *subdue*. The Scotch, when they mean to speak
well, give[578] it the diphthongal sound, as in *sure*.

SUDDEN
Vide *bacon*.

SUGGEST, SUGGESTION
The first *g* has its hard sound, as in *shrug*, *dug*. The second is soft like
the *j* in *just*. *Sug-gest*. In the same manner as in *ac-cent*; the first *c* is

hard and the second soft. The Scotch only use the soft sound of the *g* as the Italians in *suggerire*. The French sound the first *g* hard in *suggerer*.

SUNDAY

The Scotch in this word, pronounce the *ay*, like an obscure *a*; but it should be sounded here, and in the other names of the days of the week, as in *day*, *say*.

SUPREMACY

The *u* as in *sublime*. The Scotch aiming at the English pronounciation, sound the *e* as in *decent*. It should be pronounced as in *pen*, *stem*. In supreme it ought to be sounded as in *decent*.[579]

SWEAR

As *bear*, vide *bear*. The following rhyme is perfect.

> As waggish boys themselves in game *forswear*
> So the boy Love, is perjured every *where*.[580]

SWORD

The Scotch pronounce the *w*, and sound the *o*, so as to make *sword* and *word*, a perfect rhyme. But according to the proper pronounciation, *sword* and *soar'd* are, to the ear, the same.

TALENT

The *a* short and open, as in *palate*. The Scotch often pronounce it as in *tale*.

TALK[581]

The *l* mute. The *a* broad as in *all*. The following is a perfect rhyme.

> A faulc'ner Henry is when Emma *hawks*,
> With her of tarsels & of lures he *talks*
> H & Emma

TEA

In the North of Scotland, they pronounce the *ea* as the English do the *ay*, in *day*, *Tay*, the *ey* in *obey*, or the *a* in *tale*. That is, with the second, or thin sound of the slender *a*. According to the English pronounciation of *obey* and the Scotch pronounciation of *tea*, the following is a perfect rhyme.

> Here thou, great Anna! whom three realms *obey*
> Dost sometimes counsel take, and sometimes *tea*.[582]

But the English now (whatever may have been the case when the *Rape of the Lock* was written) pronounce *tea* as *appear*.

TEAR (verb)
As *bear*.

TEAR (noun)
As *appear*.

TEAT
The *ea* as in[583] *threat*. Vide *eat*.

TECHNICAL
I have known some Scotchmen, I know not upon what authority, pronounce the *ch* in this word, which in England has the sound of *k*, as if written *th*. They are perhaps led into this singularity from some supposed resemblance between the Scotch guttural sound of *ch*, and the English sound of *th*. I presume that it is upon this idea that the translator of Ossian's poems has altered the name of one of his heroes, from *Cuchullin*, as it stood in the first edition, to *Cuthullin*. But surely the sound of *k* is much more like the Scotch *ch*, than that of *th* is.

TENURE
The *e* as in *these*, or as *ee*.

TESTER (an old word for a sixpence,[584] still in use in certain colloquial expressions, and also the usual word for the roof of a bed)
The first *e* as in *these*.[585]

TERENCE
Here the same observation is to be made on the first *e*, as in *supremacy*.

THAMES
The *th* has the sound of *t*. The Scotch, following the analogy of other words spelt in this manner, as *lame*, *same*, *blames*, pronounce the *a* long and slender. They make *Thames*, and *tames*, (*Mansue facit*) the same word, to the ear. But in England the *a* is short, and has the same sound with *e* in *ten*, *hem*, *pen*. In the following passage *Thames*, and *hems*, and *gems*, form a perfect rhyme.

> When I, when sullen care,
> Through discontent of my long fruitless stay
> In princes' courts, and expectation vain
> Of idle hopes, which still do fly away,

> Like empty shadows did afflict my brain,
> Walk'd forth to ease my pain
> Along the shoar of silver-streaming *Thames*
> Whose rushy bank, the which his river *hems*
> Was painted all with variable flow'rs,
> And all the meads adorned with dainty *gems*,
> Fit to deck maidens' bowres,
> And crown their paramours.[586]

Yet *Thame*, the name of the river before it unites with the Isis, is pronounced exactly as *tame*.[587]

THANET (the name of an Island in the county of Kent)
Most Scotch people would pronounce the first syllable as *Thane*. But the English always sound it exactly as *ten*. This pronounciation is probably what prevailed in very ancient times. In Asser's life of King Alfred, the word is written *Tenet 'Insula quo dixitur Saxonicâ lingua Tenet, Britannico autem sermone, Ruim.'* In *Apothecary*, *Chatham*, *Thomas*, *Thyme*, the *th* is sounded as *t*.

THEME
The *e* as in *these*.

THEN
The vernacular Scotch pronounciation is *than*, and so Chaucer writes it

> And many a grisly oth; than have they sworn.[588]

but it should be pronounced as *men*, *pen*.

THENCE
The *th* has its soft sound as in *thou*, *then*. The Scotch make it hard, as in *thought*, *thin*.

THESE
Rhymes to *please*.[589]

THITHER
Here too the Scotch at the beginning of the word substitute the hard sound of the *th*, for the soft, which is the true pronounciation.

THREAT, THREATEN
The *ea* as in *bear*, but shorter. The *en* as *on* in *bacon*.

TOAST
The *oa* as in *boast*.

TOMB, HECATOMB
The *o* has the second, or long vocal, sound of *u*, or that of *oo*, and the *b* is silent.[590] So that these two words rhyme to *bloom*, or *room*. The following are perfect rhymes.

> Left me to see neglected genius *bloom*,
> Neglected die, and tell it on his *Tomb*[591]

> Is this a dinner, this a genial *room*!
> No 'tis a temple, and a *hecatomb*.[592]

TOUCH
The Scotch, in general, pronounce this word properly, so as to rhyme to *such*, *much*. But I know a Scotchman who[593] from the rule of analogy had persuaded himself that it should be pronounced so as to rhyme to *crouch*, *pouch* &c; and constantly did pronounce it in that manner. The reader will judge of the ridicule this necessarily brought upon him.

TREACLE
This word, by the true pronounciation is a disyllable; and the *ea* has the same sound as in *appear*, *seat*. The vulgar Scotch pronounciation is to make it a trisyllable thus *tré-a-cle*; and to pronounce the first syllable like the first of *trial*.

TREMBLE
The Scotch are apt to suppress the *b* in this, and other words ending in *ble*; and they sound the *e* like a short *i* as in *thimble*. But the *e* is to be pronounced as in *member*. And the *b* to be sounded, both in this, and all other words of the same kind.

TRAJAN
The *a* short and open, as in *Tragedy*.

TROJAN
The *o* short and open as in *Roger*. The Scotch in both words make it long and close as in *Moses*.

TROUGH
This word rhymes to *off*, *cough*.

TRUMPS

The Scotch pronounce this word as if written *trumphs*. Perhaps this was formerly the English pronounciation, for the word is derived from *triomphe*, the term formerly used by the French, for which they have substituted *A-tout*.

TWICE, THRICE

Pronounce so as to rhyme to *ice, nice*. The Scotch make these words rhyme to *wise, dies*.

TWILIGHT

The first *i*, (as the second,) has the diphthongal sound. The Scotch pronounce the first, as *ee* in *tweezer*.

TYRANNY

In this word the *y* is, by the most correct speakers, pronounced with the [594] vocal sound of *i*, as in *shire, caprice*. But in

TYRANT AND TYRANICAL

It has the diphthongal sound as in *twilight*.

UNDERNEATH

The *ea* as in *appear*. The *th* soft as in *breathe*. The following is a perfect rhyme.

> So down he fell, and forth his Life did *breathe*,
> That vanish'd into smoke, and cloudes swift:
> So down he fell, that in th'earth him under*neath*
> Did groan as feeble so great load to lift.[595]

VENICE

The *e* as in *vendible*. The Scotch pronounce it like the short obscure *i* as in *fin, winning*.

VENISON

The *i* is silent (in conversation at least) and the *s* soft. Vide *medicine*.

VICAR

The short obscure *i* as in *victory*. The Scotch, when they aim at the English pronounciation, are apt to give it the diphthongal sound as in *vice*.

VOYAGE

A disyllable, to be pronounced as if written *vo-age*. The Scotch make it a monosyllable, sounding the three vowels between the *v* and *g* like the long close *o*.

WADE (verb)

To be pronounced as *blade, glade, shade*. The vulgar Scotch pronunciation makes it to the ear, the same word with *wide*.

WALK

The *l* is always silent. The *a* long, and broad as in *all*.

WANT

The broad *a* as in *all*, but not quite so long.[596]

WATER

The long broad *a*, as in *walk*.[597] The Scotch use the short open *a* in pronouncing this word, as is also done in the North of England.

WAX

The Scotch pronounce the *a too* open. It should be sounded something between the *a* in *wafer*, and that in *father*.

WEAPON

The *ea* to be sounded as in *threat*, or like the *e* in *pen*. Chaucer wrote *wepen*.

> Sampson, this noble and mighty champion
> Withouten wepen but his handes twey.[598]

WEAR

The *ea* as in *bear*. Vide *bear*. The following rhyme is perfect.

> A wreath of darkness round his head he *wears*,
> Where curling mists supply the want of *hairs*.[599]

WEATHER

The *ea* as in *weapon*. The Scotch pronounce it like the short *i* so as to make this word, to the ear, the same with *wither*.

WEIGH

The vernacular Scotch pronounciation makes this word rhyme to *eye*, *try*, *high*. Those who endeavour to speak with more propriety make it rhyme to *see*, *pea*. But the true pronounciation is with the thin slender sound of *a* or *ay*, in *pay*. Or as the second sound of *ne*, or *nae*, in the vulgar Scotch dialect, when used instead of *no*. Both the following rhymes are perfect.

> One self-applausing hour, whole years *outweighs*
> Of stupid starers, and of loud *huzzas*.[600]

> Where in nice balance, truth with gold she *weighs*
> And solid pudding against empty *praise*.

WHEAT
As *eat*. Vide *eat*.

WHETHER
The Scotch besides their vicious guttural method of sounding the *wh* (vide *supra*) pronounce the *e* like the short *i*. Making this, the same word, to the ear, with *whither*.

WHIM
In this word and in *swim*, the Scotch give the *i* its long vocal sound like the *ee* in *seem*. But it should be pronounced short as in *him*. The following is a perfect rhyme.

> Alas! how changed from *him*
> That life of pleasure, and that soul of *whim*[601]

WHOLE, WHOLLY
The *w* is generally silent in these words as it is in *whore*. And the *o* in *both* has its long close sound. Chaucer writes *hole* & *holly*.

> It shall not be
> That ever in word, or werke I shall repent
> That I you gave my heart in *hole* intent.[602]

WICK
Pronounce like *lick*. The Scotch make this, to the ear, the same word with *week*.

WIDTH
The short obscure *i*.[603]

WIFE's (the genitive of *wife*)
Pronounce as if written *wives*.

WIND (noun)
The *i*, in conversation, is always pronounced as in *sin*, *fin*. Vide *Bind*.[604]

WIND (verb)[605]
Rhymes to *mind*.

WOLF
The *o* has the long vocal sound of *u*, or *oo*, as in *tomb*.

WOMB
The *o* has the sound of the long vocal *u*, or *oo*, and the *b* is mute[606] as in *tomb*.

WORCESTER[607]
Here too the *o* has the sound of *oo*. The *ce* is silent; so that this word (like *Gloucester*, and *Leicester*) is always, in England, pronounced as a disyllable.

WORSTED
The *o*, as in the three foregoing words.

WORK
Rhymes to *lurk*. Not to *cork*;[608] as the Scotch often pronounce it.

WORLD
The *o* here has the sound of the short *u*. The following is a perfect rhyme.

> Both in one instant from the Chariot *hurl'd*,
> Sunk in one instant to the nether *world*.[609]

WOUND
There are two ways of pronouncing this word in England. First, by giving *ou* the diphthongal sound as in *found*, *hound*. Second, by making wound rhyme to *swoon'd*.

WRITHE[610]
Pronounce exactly as *wreath*. The *th* soft.

WROUGHT
As *brought*, *sought*, &c.

YARD
Rhymes to *hard*, *bard*. The Scotch make it rhyme to *air'd*, *spared*, *dared*.

YEAST

The *y* mute, the *ea* as in *please*. To the ear, this is the same word with *East*.[611]

ZEAL

The *ea* as in *sea*, *seal*, *appear*.

ZEALOT, ZEALOUS

Here, the *ea* is sounded as in *head*, *weather*, *weapon*, or like the *e* in *pen*.

ZEPHIR

The *e* as the *ea* in the foregoing words, or like the *e* in *reptile*. Some Scotch people, aiming at the right pronounciation, give the *e* its first sound, as in *precede*, *decent*.

NOTES TO THE *TREATISE*

1 in the Isle of France and] in A
2 is situated in the Isle of France] in A
3 only] erased in S
4 crowns] erased in S
5 considered] erased in A
6 entirely] erased in A
7 before] erased in A
8 Ronsard, in the infancy of the French language, attempted, both by precept and example, to recommend a mixture of the different provincial dialects, in French composition. Tu scauras (says he) dextrement choisir et approprier a ton oeuvre, les mots significantifs plus des dialectes de nôtre France, et ne se faut soucier si les vocables sont Gascons, Poiterins, Normans, Manceaux, Lyonnois, ou d'autres pays, que tu veux dire, sans affecter par trop, le parler de la cour, lequel est quelque fois res mauvais pour être le langage des Demoiselles, et jeunes gentilhommes qui sont plus de profession de bien combattre que de parler. Abregé de l'art poétique de François. Spenser's Shepherd's Calendar may be regarded as a similar attempt in English] footnote to ff.4–5
9 as well as several others] erased in A
10 Whoever has travelled into Italy, or is acquainted with the Italian comedies of Goldoni, or those which are daily represented at Paris, know that Pantaloon, Harlequin, and the Dottore, characters constantly introduced in those plays, speak the several dialects of Venice, Bergamo, and Bologna, of which places they are respectively supposed to be natives. Tartaglio is a Neapolitan character lately added to the others, by a living actor, who possesses great talents for that burlesque species of humour peculiar to his country] footnote to ff.5–6 in S
11 Bologna] in A
12 A few real or supposed barbarisms in the *Gierusalemme Liberata* were considered as such blemishes by the rigid critics of the *Academia della Crusca*, that it is not

yet many years since this great and eloquent poet was first admitted into their list of writers of classical authority. 'L'Academia della Crusca,' says a modern author 'non ostante i piu gran contrasti, e le piu severe critiche fatte al Tasso clovette porre *finalmente* trai *citabile* un poeta che é tradotto in ogni lingua forastiera, in ogni dialetto d'Italia; un poeta letto e reletto, e cantato della moltitudine.' Algarotti Pensieri Divini.] added as footnote in D's hand in S; not in A

13 distant] erased in S
14 widely distant from each other] added to S in D's hand
15 different] erased in S
16 in any respect] added in D's hand to S
17 several instances] erased in S
18 examples] erased in S
19 forcible] erased in A
20 Ecorcher la langue] footnote to f.9 in S
21 eloquence] erased in S
22 observed] erased in S
23 meddle with] erased in S
24 certainly] erased in S
25 words] erased in A
26 distinguishing] erased in S
27 some] erased in S
28 There is just as little relation] erased in A
29 The Jesuitical doctrine of equivocation would never have excited the spleen of the satyrist, and the indignation of all honest men] erased in A
30 when they use the word] erased in A
31 and accurate] erased in A
32 road] in A
33 liquids and] erased in A
34 effort] erased in S
35 feathered tribe] erased in A
36 give virtue scandal, innocence a fear,
    Or from the soft-eyed virgin, steal a tear] erased in A
37 and semivowel] erased in A
38 in these words] erased in S; Or, in other words] in A
39 I believe this rule is adhered to in all European languages but our own] deleted from the main text in f.23 in S and entered as a footnote
40 language] erased in S; written language] erased in A
41 Latins] erased in A
42 that language] erased in A
43 Bug] erased in A
44 the first syllable of the word *Unity*] inserted in S in D's hand
45 sound] erased in S
46 in the first syllable of *Unity*] inserted in S in D's hand; in the first syllable of *Duty*] erased in A
47 sound] erased in S
48 characters] erased in A
49 written] erased in S
50 & there is no question] erased in A
51 adopt into] erased in A
52 Grammar prefixed to Dr Johnson's Dictionary] footnote to f.27
53 This parenthesis to be put in a Note] on page facing f.28 in S in D's hand

54   trusting no doubt] erased in A
55   was so different that] erased in A
56   Quor. In Sueton] footnote to f.29 in S
57   Note. Trissino however was successful in some improvements of this sort. He first employed, in Italian, separate characters for the consonantal I and V, & they have been since universally adopted. He also began the practice, now become general, of writing zi for ti in words like notizia, accusazione &c. Mattei Pref. alle Opera di Trissino] on page facing f.29 in S
58   clearly] erased in A
59   same] erased in S
60   Or to mention . . . by *ee* or *ea*.] on facing page in A
61   language] erased in S
62   your] erased in A
63   erroneous conclusion] erased in S
64   (though this is likewise a semivowel)] erased in A
65   pronounciation of] erased in A
66   Chommoda . . . Dicere] inserted in S in D's hand
67   the language of] erased in A
68   present book] erased in A
69   If the last proposition were not true] erased in A
70   The only objection which can be made to such a plan] erased in A
71   the word past] erased in A
72   repeatedly] erased in A
73   more than one] in A
74   of one particularly whose name were I to mention it would stamp a value on this humble performance which it never can deserve from that of its author] erased from S
75   he is told by] erased in A
76   London's dialect] in A
77   pronounciation] erased in A
78   branches of science] erased in A
79   have produced ten false for [every single:erased] one just pronounciation] in A
80   greatest] erased in A
81   English] erased in A
82   the last mentioned has been called the broad] erased in A
83   *malt*] erased in A
84   He may also consult the appendix to Mr Prior's *Art of Reading*] erased in a footnote to f.42 in S
85   dist calls them ā1, ā2 &] erased in A
86   slender] erased in A
87   open] erased in A
88   *base*] erased in A
89   The open being however . . . more commonly long] inserted in D's hand in S
90   slender *a*] inserted in S in D's hand
91   sorts] inserted in S in D's hand; sounds] deleted in S
92   2. The long close strong slender *a* in *pare*. 3. The thinner slender *a* in *waste* (The sound of the stronger when short is in English always represented by *e* as in *better*, *rest*, &c) is also either long as in *glaze* or short as in *race*, *bass* &c. The open in *father* or short as in *Hat* & 4 the broad *a* which is always long as in *all*] erased in A (ff.100–102)
93   and the open] erased in A
94   broad] erased in A

95   are not only to be considered as shades or gradations of the same sound like to the lighter and darker shades of the same colour] erased in A

96   green] erased in A

97   despair] erased in A

98   French as well as English] erased in A

99   Triphthongs] on leaf facing f.107 in A

100   position] erased in A

101   greater number of those in the Greek alphabet. For many of those which] erased in A

102   B is mute in *debt, subtle, limb* – & a few other words] on leaf facing f.116 in A

103   The Anglo Saxons used the third letter of their alphabet C, in all words where we use K or the hard C] erased on leaf facing f.119 in A

104   It is not my ambition to be classed with those Aristarchi of the Dunciad who made it the object of their most serious disquisitions whether they 'To give up Cicero to *C* or *K*'] erased by D in S

105   Dunciad, Book 6, v. 222] footnote to f.51 in S

106   chiefly derived] erased in A

107   In *Chiromancie* the French pronounce the *ch* as *k*. We have the best authority for this in the preface to the Dictionary of the Academy 'Nous avertissons qu'on prononce *Ki romancie*, quoiqu' on ecrire Chiromancie' Ed. 1765] footnote to f.51 in S

108   combination of *c* and *h*] erased in A

109   as between *sh* & *s*, *th* as *thought* and *t*, *z* in *azure* & *s* in *as*] erased in A

110   but shortened] erased in A

111   I perceive indeed by the Port Royal Grammar that [was written:erased] there] erased in A

112   If we can venture to assume it was probable that where several nations agree in the pronounciation of certain Latin words, such pronounciation has come down by tradition from the Romans themselves & is what they used. I would propose a new observation in favour of the Scotch method of sounding the η. It is this. The English, Scotch, French and Italians, & I believe all the other European nations agree in pronouncing [sounding:erased] the *e* in *Septus, Festus* and other Latin names of that sort according to the Scotch sound of the η. Now we must suppose that the Greeks expressed those names [when:erased] by letters in their alphabet corresponding as nearly as possible to the living Roman pronounciation, & in Plutarch, Dionysius, Halecarnasseus, Dio Cassius, and other Greek Historians they are written φηστος &c. So much for controversy! which bears no small resemblance to that between the big-endians and the little-endians in the Kingdom of Lilliput both in the frivolity of the matter of dispute, the pigmy size of the greater part of those engaged on the different sides considered as members of the republic of letters, & the zeal & warmth with which they [carried on the dispute:erased] contested the lists a specimen of which is to be seen in the very book I have cited.] erased in A; ff.129–133

113   or whoever he was who] erased in A

114   3. The third sound of *e* is what [corresponds exactly to: erased] we have called the thin slender sound of *a* & is found in th*e*n, c*e*lebrate, p*e*d*e*stal. It is what the French call the *e* fermé or close *e*: as in port*e*r, aimé] erased in A, f.135

115   the Scotch in p*e*rceive] erased in A

116   in w*o*men erased in A

117   I am acquainted with a *single* vocal+++] in A; facing f.139 is: +++ To be inserted as a note under the words '*single vocal character*'. A vocal character joined with another expresses no separate sound in the instances we have so

often had occasion to mention where such a combination represents only a simple not a diphthongal sound as in *bear, main* etc.] in A

118 happy imitation by the same author of the last speech of Othello will serve to show] version in A

119 *Encor* is always written in prose *encore*. But by a poetical licence, they can write it *encor* in poetry, in order to make it a disyllable. By a similar licence, *avec* may be written *avecque* in Poetry to make it a trisyllable] footnote to f.59

120 Grotius wrote many verses in his own language. Vondel and Dudaan are names of high estimation in Holland. The general treatment of the Dutch as incapable of taste, or genius of any sort, by some of our most celebrated writers, is a proof of local prejudice and illiberality which our Swifts, Addisons and Popes should have disdained. There can be no physical impossibility for wit or genius to grow in that soil which produced an Erasmus. Writers of universal talents should write for universal fame, and strive not to [affront: erased] revolt their readers of whatever nation or country.] footnote to f.61 in S

121 termination] erased in A

122 Didactic] erased in A

123 For the [satisfaction: erased] sake of the reader who does not understand German I have subjoined the following feeble imitation of the last two foregoing passages] erased in A, with ff.150–1 left blank

124 in both languages] erased in A

125 vowel] erased in A

126 As we sometimes] erased in A

127 In most instances] erased in A

128 It is however pretty universal among the lower ranks of people in Staffordshire, and some of the adjoining counties] footnote to f.68 in S

129 Atrophy] in A

130 example has not occurred to me] erased in A

131 an attentive] erased in A

132 In none I believe that have been completely naturalized or that are of a Teutonic origin] erased in S

133 and some other names of that sort] erased in A

134 Johnson's Grammar] in the margin of A

135 In the word *women*, *o* has this sound] footnote to f.71

136 before] erased in S; also when it follows] added in S in D's hand

137 K is a letter adopted] erased in A

138 *nom*] added to S in D's hand

139 semi[liquids:erased] vowels] in A

140 as well as in quantity each of which is long in some words, and short in others] erased in A

141 micron] erased in A

142 Mr Sheridan and other] erased in A

143 manifest] erased in A

144 and *o* and *i*] erased in A

145 at the end of a word] erased in A

146 *Windore* for window is a common barbarism among the vulgar English, but perhaps that was the original pronounciation, as etymologists have considered this word as a compound of *wind* and *door*. Butler used *windore*

> Knowing they were of doubtful gender
> And that they came in at a windore
> Hud. P.1. Cant. 2.213

Love is a burglarer, a felon,
That at a windore eye does steal in
                    Id. P.2. Cant. 1.415

] footnote to f.86 in S

147 in certain cases] erased in A

148 They also often prefix l' to the pronoun *on* when preceded by a vowel as, 'Si l'on vous a dit cela' &c and they use the old adjective bel for beau, when the ensuing word begins with a vowel. Bel homme. Bel arrangement.] footnote to f.87 in S

149 in narration] erased in A

150 Virg. 3 Ecl.] footnote to f.88 in S

151 Tasso G.L. C.4] footnote to f.88 in S

152 Milton's Lycidas] footnote to f.89 in S

153 Pope's Imitation of Horace] footnote to f.89 in S

154 or before a consonant as] erased in A

155 slippery] erased in A

156 hard] erased in A

157 best older] erased in A

158 [Milt: erased] P.L. Book II, v. 234] footnote to f.91 in S

159 F.Q. B. 3.1.6. st. 35] footnote to f.91 in S

160 of the sh] erased in A

161 semivowel] erased in A

162 in writing] in A

163 foreigners] in A

164 English] erased in A

165 A Diphthongal sound composed] erased in A

166 and *blood*] added in S

167 the second sound is also sometimes expressed by a single *o* as in *glove, love, dove, sloven*. A single *o* also sometimes represents the first shade as in *some, come*. Sometimes *ou* has that sound as in *couplet*. Sometimes *o* has the first sound of the *u* as in *move, prove, tomb*.] in A

168 rue] in A

169 and of *t* the hard *th*] in A

170 Of the use of rhyme considered as a means of contributing to the pronunciation of words] in A

171 To be inserted as note to folio 109. where *sum* is employed in the same manner.] in A

Note. On the other hand, some modern languages decline their nouns, as the German, & in the Genitive case, the English. In all of them some tenses of verbs are expressed by a change of termination not by the auxiliaries.

The reader will give me leave to transcribe a short passage from the miscellaneous thoughts of the Count Alyavolti relative to this matter Gli Articoli, ed.] erased in A

Note 'Gli articoli, e i verbi ausiliari che formano un elemento della nostra favella non sono altrimente, come si tiene longue oltramontane con la Latina, donde sia poi derivata L'Italiana. Degli articoli ne trapari scono essempi anche negli antichi autori latini; e gli stessi autori Latini del meglior tempo dissero "*Satis jam dictum habeo*", "*Habere cognitum scouolam*", "*Cognitum habeo insulas*". Il greco vulgare, dove tramontane, a anch'esso i verbi ausiliari, e, per il futoro, si serve del "θελα" come del "*Will*" si servono gli Inglesi. Talche un celebre scrittore a tenuto l'uso degli ausiliari essere originariamente Latino.' Alg. *Pensiari Diversi.*] on leaf facing f.109 in S, in D's hand

172 perfect] erased in A

173 *Vide* Du Cange *Vers. Polit.*] footnote to f.109 in S

174 Dr Foster, indeed, questions the received opinion that the *Versus Politici* were scanned by accent – Ess. p. 204, 2nd Ed. – But he has not explained his reasons – Vide infra] on leaf facing f.109 in S in D's hand

175 The example of rhyming verses in the best antient poets are much more numerous than is generally supposed. Without looking in purpose for them. The following lines accidentally occurred to me in the course of my reading since I began this work.] erased in S. Ff.111–114 have been left blank by the scribe of S; he clearly meant to fill them at a later date with the contents of ff.237–243 in A, which contain many quotations from Greek and Latin classical literary sources, notably the *Iliad*, *Aeneid*, Horace's *Satires*, and Ovid's *Georgics*.

176 sufficient] erased in S; *seem*] added in S in D's hand

177 there is not an instance of false quantity in the whole of his Iliad] erased in S

178 This is not inconsistent with what is afterwards advanced in favour of rhyme. Though this innovation [rhyme: erased] should be thought an acquisition and embellishment to modern verse, it may be justly said that it could only be a tame and finical taste that could give it the preference [could prefer such an innovation: erased] to the genuine magic inventions of true poetry. A new measure in Lyric Poetry may have been an improvement among the antients, but it must be a barbarous age that would prefer such a discovery to the sublime flights of Pindar, or the graceful elegance of Horace.] footnote to f.115 in S

179 a whole poem composed of] erased in A

180 Musat De Rythm. veterum Poese Antiq. Med. Ovi Fort. Bib. Dissert. 40. Med. ætat. *v* Fortunatus apud Tyroli Cantab. Inies] footnote to f.115 in D's hand

181 A very accurate and learned Critic to whose work I am obliged for the historical part of what I have advanced in this subject informs me] erased in A

182 'That is . . . Maledictionem'] added in D's hand to S

183 That barbarous nations and more barbarous time
   Debased the Majesty of verse with rhyme] erased in A

184 everything but his plays] erased in A

185 dictated by] erased in S; the result of temporary impressions] inserted in S in D's hand

186 Spectator No. 285] footnote to f.117 in S

187 Critics] in A: In his notes to the translation of *The First Canto of Ricciardetto* (1822:172), Douglas observes: 'Before the great Revolution produced in their versification by Klopstock, the most general heroic verse in German was on a like model with the French Alexandrines, having the constant pause in the middle, that is, at the end of the sixth syllable, or of the first hemistich, and the alternation of masculine with something corresponding to the French feminine rhymes.'

188 Note: And perhaps their inventor. A contemporary writer calls him so in a dedication addressed to himself 'Voi forte il primo, che questo modo di scrivere in versi materni, liberi dalle rime, poneste in luce.' Palla Mucellai nella dedicazione delle Api di Gior. Muccellai] on leaf facing f.121 inserted in D's hand.

189 Note: In one of the [most striking: erased] finest Scenes of Voltaire's Semiramis there is a passage where the rhyme has always appeared to me to [prod have: erased] produce a very bad effect on the stage. After many delays Semiramis, who had poisoned her former husband, finds herself under a necessity of making choice of another – Assur – her minister confident & accomplice

[aspired: erased] aspires to that rank. But the Queen has fixed her mind on Arvaces a young General, who had achieved great conquests, but was born, as was supposed, in [great: erased] obscurity. He [was: erased] is the beloved Lover of Azema a Princess of the Royal family. At a solemn Assembly [being:erased] of all the Grandees of the State the Queen in an eloquent [speech: erased] harangue proceeds to declare the object of her choice Assur, Azema, Arsace are present, & all for different reasons equally anxious for the event! The speech [is: erased] concludes as follows – (Vide the play)

> Adorez le heros que va ragner sur vous
> Voyez..en..les Princes de ma race
> Ce heros, cet epouse, ce vainqueur est – Arsace.

Now [does not: erased] the rhyme [in this case: erased] seem completely to announce to all the audience before the last line is finished [uttered: erased; & the name: erased] that Arsace is the person on whom the choice is to fall – Yet both [Assur, Azema & Arsace himself: erased] all continue to listen without any [expressions: erased] symptoms either of scruple or disappointment till [the word Arsace: erased] his name is pronounced. When Azema & Assur immediately ... [express themselves with all the : erased; discover burst forth: erased] discover marks of astonishment and rage. What made this [observation: erased] more [obvious: erased] striking was that Mlle Dumesnil in most respects the greatest actress I ever saw though when I first saw her I believe she was past fifty used to make a considerable pause before she pronounced the name] on leaf facing f.123 in D's hand

190 By the regular structure of our verse, of whatever number of syl. the last syllable of each line is accented. This which I shall take occasion to explain in another place, I will now take for granted and consider such monosyllables as *fruit* and *taste*, *thing* and *things* which conclude the first lines of the Essay on Man as having on account as much as the last syllable of the word *supply* at the end of the third line of the same poem.] erased in A

191 If both of them begin with one or more consonant. The consonant which is next to the] in A

192 next two lines scored through in S

193 Rape of the Lock C.2.47] footnote to f.126 in S

194 last in the passage] erased in S

195 C.9.10] footnote to f.127 in S

196 Windsor Forrest] footnote to f.127 in S

197 P.L. C.2.55,6] footnote to f.128 in S

198 C.3 131,2] footnote to f.128 in S

199 C.3.97,8] footnote to f.128 in S

200 P.L. C.2,1,2] footnote to f.129 in S

201 C.2 7,8] footnote to f.129 in S

202 C.2.13,4] footnote to f.129 in S

203 Pope's Il. Lib. 18] footnote to f.129 in S

204 Dryd. Cym. & Iphi] footnote to f.130 in S

205 Essay on Man. Lib. 2] footnote to f.130 in S

206 Ess. on Cr. 285] footnote to f.130 in S

207 Il. Lib. 1] in A

208 P.L. C.2. 133] footnote to f.130 in S

209 Prior's Soln B.2] footnote f.130 in S

210 Dryd. Cym. & Iphig.] footnote to f.131 in S

211 P.L. C.2.5,6] footnote to f.131 in S

212 no reference in A or S
213 Shakes.] footnote to f.131 in S
214 Different] erased in S; different in quality] added in D's hand to S
215 Pope's [H.Lit:erased] Il. Lib 18] footnote to f.132 in S
216 no reference in A or S
217 and Swift] erased in A
218 F.Q. B.2. C.4. st.30] footnote f.133 in S
219 Dunc. 2. 357–8] footnote to f.134 in S
220 offensive] erased in A
221 The Italians admit of a word rhyming to itself whether it is used in different senses in the two corresponding lines or in the same sense] erased in A
222 G.Lib. C.1. St.56] footnote to f.135 in S
223 So is *volto* in the two following lines.

> Sono ambo stretti al palo stesso, e volto
> E il tergo al tergo, e'l volto ascoso al volto

Indeed in this instance the sound of the middle *o* in *volto* the adjective differs somewhat from that in *volto* 'countenance'. However this rhyme would not be permitted in English, since it sins against the first of the rules we have explained] erased in S

224 G.L. Cant. 3. st 29] footnote to f.136 in S
225 Ib. st. 31] footnote to f.136 in S
226 Though the instances I have already cited from the most correct of all the Italian poets are sufficient to prove that rhymes of this sort however contrary to our notions concerning English verse are allowable in Italian, yet perhaps the following stanza will afford the reader more satisfactory evidence. If the repetition of the same word to form a rhyme were in the least exceptionable in Italian verse, Tasso would never have suffered it to deform so beautiful and laboured a passage.] erased in S

227 G.L. C.4. st.32] footnote to f.137 in S
228 Paradiso C.19] footnote to f.138 in S
229 I have given this short account to render more intelligible the arrangement of the rhymes in the 3 different passages in Dante where he has made the word *Cristo* the rhyming word in the three corresponding lines of those passages as follows] f.296 in A

230 Charlot. Comide Volt.] footnote to f.138 in S
231 La Font. Conte de la Clochette] footnote to f.138 in S
232 Chauc. Merchts tale] footnote to f.139 in S
233 Chauc. Pardoneres tale. Note to be printed at the bottom. This term *blake-beried* is one of Mr Tyrwhit's list of words not understood] footnote to f.139 in S
234 Merchts. tale] footnote to f.139 in S
235 F.Q. B.1 C.2.43] footnote to f.139 in S
236 F.Q. B.3 C.3 st.1] footnote to f.130 in S
237 Milt. Sonn.9] footnote to f.140 in S
238 P.S. B.2] footnote to f.141 in S
239 Which made my grand-dame always stuff her ears,
       Both right and left as fellow sufferers.
            D. Swift to Dr Debarry] footnote to f.141 in S

240 R.L. C.3. 153,4] footnote to f.141 in S
241 Essay on Man] footnote to f.141 in S
242 Pope's *Wife of Bath's Tale*] footnote to f.142 in S
243 Prior's *Alma* Canto 1st] footnote to f.142 in S

244 Pope's Epistle to a Lady] footnote to f.142 in S
245 Essay on Man] footnote f.142 in S
246 Prior's Paul's Purganti] footnote to f.142 in S
247 Thence to the right and moving through there] illegible in S and partly in A
248 Prior's Epis. H. Sheppard] footnote to f.143 in S
249 A Table of Words] in A
250 Abhorrence] erased in A
251 are apt to] inserted with a caret in A
252 Hudi. p.1 C.1] footnote f.144 in S
253 the pronounciation of this word] erased in A
254 Note, the word *perfect* is I believe the only exception, vide *perfect*] footnote to f.145 in S
255 derived from different words] erased in A
256 *o*] erased in A
257 Those which the Scotch pronounce improperly are printed in Roman characters] erased in S
258 To each is subjoined a set of words in wh] erased in A
259 2 *Move* (pronounced by the Scotch like *Love*) *Amove, remove, behoove, prove, reprove, improve, approve, disapprove, disprove.* All often pronounced by the Scotch like *Love*
3 *Jove, Cove, Alcove, Hove, Clove* (verb and noun), *Rove, Drove* noun and verb, *Grove, Throve, Stove* noun and verb, *Wove.* The following is a perfect rhyme

> The . . . of motion from above
> Hung down on earth the golden chain of Love
> Dryden, *Knights Tale*

] erased in A
260 Abstract, see Abject] erased in A
261 Prior's *Solomon*] footnote to f.147 in S
262 those whose termination is *ct*] erased in A
263 which is universal] erased in A
264 G.L. C.6. st.8] footnote to f.148 in S
265 or the French] erased in A
266 Detrudant *naves scopula* – Æn. 1. 149] erased in S
267 Lycidas. 39th Epis.] footnote to f.149 in S
268 Both the *Acorn* and *Acquaint* entries are inserted in D's hand on leaf facing f.149 in S; the *Acquaint* entry is in A
269 This entry not in A; added to S in D's hand
270 The *a* here too has its long] in A
271 *Tost*] erased in A
272 This entry not in A; entered in S in D's hand
273 No] on leaf facing f.151 in S
274 strong] erased in A
275 strong] erased in A
276 of the ng] erased in A
277 Swift] footnote to f.152 in S
278 Shakespeare] footnote to f.153 in S
279 represents the hard *g* and the soft *s*] erased in A
280 stronger sound of the] erased in A
281 I believe] erased in A
282 many [most:erased]] in A
283 termination] erased in A

284 Vide *cart*] footnote f.155 in S
285 like *shi* in *Fashion*] erased in A
286 song] in A
287 & the *i* has its short close sound] not in A
288 a little] in A
289 Aunt] erased in A
290 taking the votes] erased in A
291 Prior: Turtle and Sparrow] footnote to f.159 in S
292 Ib. Conversation or tale] footnote to f.159 in S
293 & which I did not take notice of before because I was unwilling to pr] erased in A
294 Although it is usual at the end of a verse to write *op'n*, *tak'n* etc] erased in A
295 Vide supra page] footnote to f.159 in S
296 As *hackney* has but two] erased in A
297 In the following couplet

> Or why so long (if life so long can be)
> Lent Heav'n a parent to the poor and me?
> Ess. on Man 4, 109.10

Heavn is but one syllable, or more properly *Heav'n a*, are but two. But in this other of the same author

> Soft the slumbers of a saint forgiv'n
> Mild as op'ning gleams of promised heav'n

Heav'n to the ear is, a disyllable.] on leaf facing f.345 in A; all erased
298 Es. on Man] footnote to f.161 in S
299 Lycidas] footnote to f.161 in S
300 Sams. Agon. 434] footnote to f.162 in S
301 P.L. Book 2. 300] footnote to f.162 in S
302 you said just now *this* had not been observed] erased by D in leaf facing f.353 in A
303 Trr. C.T. V.4 p.92. Foster on Accent p.509] inserted on leaf facing f.163 in D's hand
304 Note. In Sydney's verse *evil*, *ever*, *over* & words of that sort always reckon as one syllable] inserted on leaf facing f.163 in D's hand in S
305 What deintee shuld a man have in his lif
   For to go love another manne's wif] erased in A
306 Ch. Pardoneres Taale] footnote to f.163 in S
307 Pr to Sir Thop – Those words are addressed by the host in the Canterbury tales, to Chaucer himself] footnote to f.164 in S
308 Ibid] footnote to f.164 in S
309 Ibid] footnote to f.164 in S
310 Shipman's Prol] footnote to f.164 in S
311 F.Q. 1.10] footnote to f.164 in S
312 1.2.24] footnote to f.164 in S
313 1.11.17] footnote to f.164 in S
314 no reference given to footnote mark in text
315 F.Q. B.2. C.12.7] footnote to f.165 in S
316 Q.12.51. This is an alexandrine] footnote to f.165 in S
317 3.3.2] footnote to f.165 in S
318 3.11.44] footnote to f.165 in S
319 5.2.36] footnote to f.165 in S
320 1.11.25] footnote to f.165 in S

321 1.7.33] footnote to f.165 in S
322 2.7.1] footnote to f.165 in S
323 Col Clouts come home again] footnote to f.165 in S
324 Menopotmos] footnote to f.165 in S
325 The poets after Milton began to write such words with an apostrophe. Thus per'lous, am'rous, iv'ry and that being in most of them consonant to familiar pronounciation] erased on leaf facing f.357 in A
326 although the intervening consonant between two of them is not a liquid. In answer to this I [will: erased] would almost venture to assert that there is no such instance in all the numerous verses of Spenser, except in the case of the words innocent] erased in A
327 mention the Paradise Lost as the work in which versification is most to be admired. In his other poems we find many lines (some indeed even in it) which are too anomalous to be explained by any rules.] footnote to f.166 in S
328 P.L. 8.315] footnote to f.167 in S
329 Ib. 4. 349. As for the instances (which are but few) where two vowels meet in the middle of a word, and would in prose form two syllables, it seems the natural way to consider them as united *synoresis* into one. Such is the word *amiable* in the passage above cited, and *Diet* in one of the [words: erased] lines referred to by Mr Tyrwhit in his notes upon Chaucer:

> No inconven*ient diet* nor too light fare
> 5.49.5

this makes the line consist only of ten syllables, for *ient*, like *ion*, never makes two syllables, even in prose.] footnote to f.167 in S: Note facing f.361 in A
330 Added to S in D's hand; Milton Sonn. 9] footnote to f.167 in S
331 Chaucer Pardonner's tale] footnote to f.168 in S
332 F.Q. 2.12.75] footnote to f.168 in S
333 I have in general used the word Diphthong for a combination not only of two, but also more, vowels into one syllable] footnote to f.168 in S
334 In this passage don't mark the Scores or Divisions.] in D's hand on leaf facing f.363 in A. [A has foot divisions marked as: Spe*ra il*|seren|l'agri|coltor|che vede:CJ] You should have quoted an older Poet, one that Milton had read too.] on leaf facing f.363 in A in D's hand (?) but different ink
335 Metastasio's *I Voti Publici*] footnote to f.169 in S
336 R.L.2.41] footnote to f.169 in S
337 P.L.3.397] footnote to f.169 in S; displeas'd] in A
338 ashen] erased in A
339 Dryden] erased in A
340 London] in A
341 Banker] erased on leaf facing f.171 in S
342 Dunc. 1.15.9] footnote to f.171 in S
343 Pope's Il. 23.326] footnote to f.171 in S
344 Tears of the Muses] footnote to f.171 in S
345 Ruins of Rome] footnote to f.171 in S
346 Tears of the Muses] footnote to f.172 in S
347 *Base* in musick (more commonly written *Bass*) has the same sound with *bass* signifying foundation. But *base* the synonim to mean or vile is properly pronounced in Scotland. The *s* has the same sound as in the other word, but the *a* has its long slender sound.] erased in A
348 And Crete will boast the labyrinth, now *raced*. Id. Ruins of Rome. [In other words: erased]] in A to face f.371

349   Essay on Man 1] footnote to f.172 in S
350   schoolmaster at] erased in A
351   Pronounced as *Appear*
        Ear, Hear, Gear, Shear (sometimes [generally: erased] spelt *sheer*) *Blear,
        Clear, Smear, Near, Appear, Spear, Rear, Drear, Arrear, Sear* (Dry (spelt also
        sere)), *Sear, to burn, Tear* (*lacryma*), *Year*] erased in A
352   added in D's hand to leaf facing f.173 in S
353   kind] erased in S; mind] added in D's hand to S
354   Gray's Elegy in a churchyard] footnote to f.174 in S
355   In citing such passages as this, I find it requires considerable effort to confine
        one's observations to the meer mechanical propriety of the rhymes] erased in
        S; Pronounce as *Behind, Kind, Find, Goldfinder,* [*Bo*:erased] *Bind, Bookbinder,
        Grind, Mind, Rind, Hind* (s and adj), *Hinder* [*for*:erased] (adj and its compound),
        Hindermost, Mankind, Blind, Rind, Wind, verb, *Pint* (a liquid measure).] erased
        in A
356   Essay on Man. 1.99. Pope's Il. 16.317] footnote to f.175 in S
357   viz infra] footnote to f.175 in S
358   *Bewilder*
        The *i* has its diphthongal sound as in *wild*. The Scotch often pronounce it as
        in *children*.] on leaf to face f.381 in A
359   this entry inserted in S in D's hand, not in A; *bible*] erased in S
360   abode] erased in A
361   S reads: In the word [and in *ogle*: erased] the *o* has its [long close: erased] short
        open [added in D's hand] sound, [as in Brogue, disembogue. The Scotch, in
        both, make it short, as in *bog, dog*:erased] as in *god* [inserted in D's hand]. The
        Scotch are apt to give it the long close sound as in *brogue* – *Ogle* vide *Ogle*
362   According to this method the following is a perfect rhyme] erased in A
363   *Revolt*] in A
364   In *revolt* . . . Vide *infra*] inserted in D's hand in S
365   short as in *Cinder*] erased in A
366   Garth's Dispensary] footnote to f.177 in S
367   scholars] in A
368   Drought] inserted in D's hand in S
369   R.L.1.29] footnote to f.178 in S
370   Swift] footnote to f.179 in S
371   Prior's Hen. & Em.] footnote to f.179 in S
372   Pronounce as *How,* or *Now: Bow* (v & noun) (*To stoop* or *bend*) & the act of
        stooping and bending), *Cow, Endow, Allow, Plow, Now, Enow, Brow, Sow* (*Sus*),
        Vow, Avow, Low (as a Cow), *Mow* (of Barley or Corn of any sort). Pronounce as
        Beau or *foe: Bow* (Arcus), *Show, Low* (*Humilis*), *Blow, Below, Flow, Glow, Stow,
        Show* (verb), *Know, Snow, Row* (*ordo, series*), *To row* (*remis impellere*), *Crow* (n &
        v), *Grow, Throw, Prow, Trow* (v *to imagine,* obsolete), *Strow* (verb, both when it
        signifies *seminare* & *encire*), *Tow* (v & n), *Stow, Bestow, Stowe*] erased on leaf to
        face ff.389–90 in A
373   Prior's Solomon. B.2] footnote to f.180 in S
374   According to them the following is a perfect rhyme:

        O thou of bus'ness the directing soul!
        To this our head, like biass to the *bowl.*
        Dunc. I.169

        ] inserted in D's hand on leaf to face f.180 in S
375   Pope's Epist. on the use of Riches] footnote to f.181 in S

376 Pronounce in the same manner *Dead, Head, Lead* (a metal), *Read* (perfect tense & participle), *Bread, Thread, Spread, Tread, Stead, Instead*] erased on leaf to face f.391 in A

377 breed] inserted in D's hand in S

378 knead] erased in A

379 Prior's Ladys looking glass] footnote to f.181 in S

380 beast] erased in A

381 built] added in D's hand in S

382 gilt] added in D's hand in S

383 The following rhyme is perfect

> Not that which antique Cadmus whylome built
> In Thebes, which Alexander did confound;
> Nor that proud towre of Troy, though richly gilt,
> From which young Hector's blood by cruel Greeks was spilt
> F.Q. B.2 C.9.45

] entered in D's hand on leaf to face f.182 in S

384 Vide Johnson's Grammar prefaced to his Dictionary. Vide also infra p.] in A

385 [The:erased] In Scotland & the North of England, *Bull* & all other words of that termination are pronounced with the short obscure sound of *u* as *Skull, Sun*] erased in A

386 Pardoner's tale] footnote to f.183 in S

387 Prioresse's tale] footnote to f.184 in S

388 The Shipman's tale] footnote to f.184 in S

389 In the following passage it was probably a poetical license, even in Shakespeare's time, to make business a trisyllable

> I must employ you in some business
> Against our nuptial
> Midsummer Night's Dream

] Inserted in D's hand on leaf to face f.184 in S

390 true] erased in A

391 Blanc . . . Exemplum] inserted in D's hand in S

392 bianco . . . esempio] inserted in D's hand in S

393 Here is a problem whose solution would puzzle the most astute Etymologists] erased in S; The poets sometimes say *templo, esemplo* & *esemplare*] inserted in D's hand in S

394 life's] in A

395 Life &] in A

396 by most English people] missing from A

397 Car, Carry] inserted in D's hand in S

398 Vide Infra Book] in A

399 Dunc. 1.21.2] footnote to f.188 in S

400 F.Q. 3.3.19] footnote to f.188 in S

401 Ib. 5.8.28] footnote to f.188 in S

402 Dunc. 2.23.4] footnote to f.189 in S

403 *French*, or like *sh* in *shoulder, sham*] erased in S; *Champaigne, Vide supra*] inserted in D's hand in S

404 Messiah] footnote to f.189 in S

405 both Scotch and English] inserted in D's hand in S

406 English] in A

407 Prior's simile] footnote to f.192 in S

408 Garth's Epis. to Cato] footnote to f.192 in S
409 Wake now my love, awake, for it is time,
     The rosie morn long since left Tithon's bed,
     All ready to her silver coach to clime,
     & Phoebus gins to shew his glorious head
                    Spens. Epithal.

     ] inserted in D's hand on leaf to face f.192 in S
410 The Scotch pronounce it like *Toss*, *Moss*. This is the only English word so
     pronounced so that there is not in the language a perfect rhyme of which this is
     one of the corresponding words. The Scotch pronounce] erased from f.417 in A
411 making the *o* short and open] inserted in D's hand in S
412 The English [most commonly:erased] make the *o* long [& open:inserted in D's
     hand in S] [as in *Jove*, *rove*:erased in S] [as in *Corn*, *fork*: inserted in D's hand
     in S]
413 This entry inserted in D's hand in S
414 Prior] footnote to f.195 in S
415 The Scotch vernacular pronoun] erased in A
416 [The:erased] Many [inserted in D's hand] Scotch people [inserted in D's hand]
     often [erased in S] pronouce *all* [& most:inserted in D's hand] [or:erased] some
     of these words] in S
417 Prior's Solomon. B.3] footnote to f.197 in S
418 This entry inserted in D's hand in S
419 This entry inserted in D's hand in S
420 F.Q. 3.3.21] footnote to f.198 in S
421 Prior's Hen. and M] footnote to f.199 in S
422 Mids. N. Dream] footnote to f.199 in S; this quotation inserted in D's hand in S
423 This form of the *Drama* entry not in A, which has instead: The *a* short and as in
     Drama. The Scotch in endeavouring at propriety, pronounce it as in *same*] on
     leaf to face f.429 in A
424 It rhymes to *sought*, I think] in A in what might be D's hand; It is now [made to
     rhyme to *wrote*:erased in S] pronounced as [inserted in D's hand] [*boat*. Not
     to:erased in S] *sought*] in S
425 Midsummer's Nights Dream] footnote to f.200 in S
426 The *ea* . . . and *dearth*] inserted in D's hand in S
427 This entry erased by D in S
428 Prior's Alma C.1] footnote to f.201 in S
429 In *great* . . . *pate*, *state*] inserted in D's hand in S
430 or *Ere* (before)] erased in A
431 *ee*:] erased in S
432 This entry is inserted in D's hand on leaf to face f.202 in S
433 This entry is inserted in D's hand in S
434 *Were* is short and the *e* as in *Clergy*] in A
435 *ee* in *fleet*] erased in S; in the foregoing word] inserted in D's hand in S
436 V &] erased in A
437 *hard*] erased in S
438 to the successive to the sound of *but* [slack but short:erased] and *buzz*, *above*,
     [*mother*:erased] *bud*, *dub*, *smug*. Of *at*, *Path*, *Tup*, *pack*, *tap*, *ass* and *as*, *father*,
     halves (the *l* mute) *drab*, *drag*, *pad*. Of *fit*, *fill*, *fin*, *thin*, *sip* & *in*, *crib*, *live*, *lid*.
     What is sensible is that you may to a certain degree produce this hollow sound,
     before the hard mutes *p*, *t*, *k* & the hard semivowels *s*, *th*, or the liquids *l*, *m*, *n*
     & *r*. In Staffordshire and other parts of the North of England they sound *Skull*,
     Hull as *Bud* & *Dub*. But it is almost impossible by any effort of the voice to

sound the short vowels in that clear sharp manner before the *b*, *d*, *v*, *th* & *m* in which they are pronounced in *but*, *pat*, &c.] erased in f.438 of A

439 Hudibras Part I: Canto 2. 589.90] footnote to f.207 in S
440 & Exaggeration] erased in A
441 *Fir* & [*First*: erased] as *Thirst* [vide As *First* supra as *Thirst*: erased]] in A
442 Merchants tale] footnote to f.208 in S
443 Chevy Chase] footnote to f.208 in S
444 Fairfax's Tasso C.19. st.20] footnote to f.208 in S
445 Pray look out this passage in Shakespeare & cite the play] on leaf to face f.442 in A, in D's hand; Shak. Ric.2. Act 1. Scene 3] footnote to f.208 in S
446 King Lear] footnote to f.208 in S
447 Hudibras B.1. C.2. 229] footnote to f.209 in S
448 Prior] footnote to f.209 in S
449 Ethic Epis. 151.2] footnote to f.209 in S
450 in that case he would probably have written *ly'r* or *lir* all] erased in A
451 This sort of figure (if it may be so called) is still extremely common with all the tribe of the occasional & newspaper poets. I believe the Scotchman in writing verse would never fall into it.] erased in A
452 Shakespear] footnote to f.209 in S in D's hand
453 Autumn] footnote to f.210 in S
454 Egidius to Giles] in A
455 Nor widow tears nor tender orphans cries
Can stop th'invaders force
Nor swelling seas nor threat'ning skies
Prevent [th'Invaders:erased] the pirates course
                    Congreve

] on leaf to face f.447 in A
456 Ford & Afford
The long close *o* as the *oa* in *board*. The Scotch sound these words as if written *foord*, *afoord*] on leaf to face f.448 in A
457 horn] erased in A
458 open] erased in A
459 Is not the *th* hard in both] in margin in A
460 Essay on Man, 2.271.2] footnote to f.214 in S
461 Then *full* and *fool* would be the same word which [they are:erased] it is not. *Full* rhymes to *bull*] erased in leaf to face f.452 in A
462 but shorter] inserted in D's hand in S
463 close] erased in A
464 Vide Johnson's Dictionary, Letter *o*] footnote to f.216 in S
465 9 Ethic Epis. 317.18] footnote to f.216 in S
466 Note: 'We, in English have the sound of the *w* where we use no character at all. The word *one* we pronounce as if it were *wone*' Foster *Essay* p.124, 2nd Edn. He should have said 'as if it were *won*', for a stranger reading this passage would suppose that *one* rhymes to *bone*.] inserted in D's hand on leaf to face f.216 in S
467 Pope Prol. to satires] footnote to f.217 in S
468 Eth. Ep.] footnote to f.217 in S
469 This entry inserted in D's hand on leaf to face f.217 in S
470 short] erased in A
471 Pope's Il. 1.175.16] footnote to f.217 in S
472 This entry inserted in D's hand in S
473 though some English people make it rhyme to *earth*. See *Earth*] erased in S; A's version of this entry reads: Rhymes to *Earth* – No – See *Earth*] f.460

474 vide Bacon] footnote to f.220 in S
475 seems to have been] erased in A
476 F.Q. B.2] footnote to f.220 in S
477 Thoms. Winter] footnote to f.220 in S
478 *hi-de-ous, o-di-ous*] in A
479 Scotland] erased in A
480 Note: I say Pope's measure, because he never uses trisyllabic feet] on leaf to face f.463 in A
481 Ethic. Epis. 1.246] footnote to f.221 in S
482 Pope's Il. 2.109] footnote to f.221 in S
483 Pope's Il. 2.146.6] footnote f.222 in S
484 or rather *Brimijam*] not in A
485 This item in A, f.467
486 position] erased in A
487 & by the Scotch is pronounced as *pen*] inserted in D's hand in S
488 This entry inserted in D's hand in S
489 Prolog. Dryden] footnote to f.224 in S
490 Pope] footnote to f.224 in S
491 Dunc. 1.27.8] footnote to f.226 in S
492 Heron] in A
493 according to the English practice in most other words of this kind] erased in S
494 although in the very same line he abbreviates its compound *Unlearned*] added to S in D's hand
495 Essay on Cri.] footnote to f.226 in S
496 Vide Infra Book] in A
497 Lengthen] added in D's hand in S
498 I believe few people . . . the word *oozy*] added to S in D's hand; with a footnote to f.227 in D's hand in S: Ess. on Acc. & Qu.9.2 Ed. p.40
499 mute] erased in A
500 broad] erased in A
501 Prior] footnote to f.228 in S
502 & *unloose*] added in D's hand to S
503 but more obscure] added in D's hand to S
504 *start*] in A
505 Chauc. Franklin's tale] footnote to f.230 in S
506 F.Q. 3.1.25] footnote to f.231 in S
507 Eloisa to Abelard] footnote to f.231 in S
508 F.Q. 2.12.93] footnote to f.231 in S
509 This entry is added in D's hand in S; The first syllable . . . *e*ternal] on leaf to face f.232 in S
510 No] in A at end of entry; might be D's hand
511 This entry on leaf to face f.232 in S; in A on leaf to face f.488
512 No first rhyme example in either S or A
513 Ethic. Ep. 2.233] footnote to f.233 in D's hand
514 are apt to] erased in A
515 Hotly] in A
516 Pope Il. 1.47.3] footnote to f.234 in S
517 pronounce it as in *nape, cape, rape* but long] erased in S] but short] in A
518 This item added in D's hand in S; not in A
519 often] inserted in D's hand in S
520 open] erased in A
521 (noun)] in A

522 The *u* is diphthongal] added in D's hand to S
523 Pardoneres Tale] footnote to f.235 in S
524 Pardoneres Tale] footnote to f.236 in S
525 & close] inserted in D's hand in S
526 Vide Lord Chesterfield's Letters] on leaf to face f.236 in S; in D's hand
527 But Vide Lord Chesterfield] footnote to f.236 in S
528 Pope's Prologue to the Satires] footnote to f.236 in S
529 Eth. Epis. 2.39.40] footnote to f.237 in S
530 Inserted in D's hand in S; not in A
531 Not in A
532 *pate, fate, patent*] erased in S; *pat, fat*] in A
533 *People*] in D's hand on leaf to face f.239 in S
534 This entry added to S in D's hand; not in A
535 This entry erased in S
536 Miller's tale] footnote to f.241 in S
537 This entry inserted in D's hand in S; A reads: Polish (belonging to Poland). Here the *o* is to be pronounced as in *Pole*: f.504
538 Hamlet] footnote to f.242 in S
539 Beggars Opera] footnote to f.242 in S
540 Poor] erased in D's hand in S. A reads Poor (to be inserted here)
541 open] erased in A
542 (improperly)] erased in A
543 Poor, Pour] inserted here in A
544 Postscript] added to S in D's hand
545 first] in A
546 In *Precedent* . . . Vide infra] inserted in D's hand in S
547 *precise*] in A
548 *Profit*] erased in S
549 Vide supra] footnote to f.244 in S
550 soft . . . and excuse . . . (verbs)] inserted in D's hand in S
551 Pope 4. Ethic. Epis.] footnote to f.244 in S
552 are apt to] erased in A
553 Prunes. Vide Shakespeare] in A
554 *ll*] erased in D's hand in S; double liquid] inserted in D's hand in S
555 the first syllable of *cuckoo*] inserted in D's hand in S
556 however do not] inserted in D's hand in S] the quantity of *boot* being longer] inserted in D's hand in S; *Put* and *boot* form a perfect rhyme. no] in A
557 The following . . .] inserted in D's hand in S in leaf to face f.247
558 This entry added to S in D's hand
559 This entry not in A
560 Sonnet 26] footnote to f.249 in S
561 Hot. Poet. Ch 1. 113,4] footnote to f.249 in S
562 Lutr. Ch. 5 90,2] footnote to f.249 in S
563 V] in A; and n] erased in A
564 This item inserted in D's hand in S; frequently . . . modern authors] inserted in D's hand on leaf to face f.251
565 This item erased in S; not in A
566 This item inserted in D's hand in S
567 *these* overwrites *this* in S in D's hand
568 This entry inserted in D's hand in S
569 always] erased in S; by most English people] inserted in S in D's hand
570 Pope's Wife of Bath's tale] footnote to f.253 in S

571   Dunc. B.1. [127:erased] 173,4] footnote to f.253 in S

572   Gray's Epitaph: Contemplation in a Colledge] footnote to f.253 in S

573   On evening] footnote to f.253 in S; An evening contemplation in a College – A Parody of the Elegy in a country church yard. Published by Dodsley, 1753] in A

574   Shakespear, Loves Labour Lost] footnote to f.254 in S

575   This item inserted in D's hand in S

576   *Sphere* item inserted in D's hand on leaf to face f.255 in S; *Sport* item here in A only

577   mostly] erased in S; exactly] in A

578   are apt to] erased in A

579   The *u* as in *sublime*] added in D's hand to S; In *supreme* . . . in *decent*] added in D's hand to S

580   Mids. N. Dream] footnote to f.257 in S in D's hand

581   This entry inserted in D's hand in S; The following . . .] inserted in leaf to face f.257 in D's hand

582   Rape of the Lock] footnote to f.258 in S

583   *Eat*] erased in A

584   Shilling] in A

585   *Theme* rhymes to *dream*, *stream*. The following is a perfect rhyme. *These*. The *e* as in the foregoing word. The following rhyme is perfect: Yet those were pedants whom compared to these –] in A

586   [Supra:erased] Spenser's Pro[la:erased]thalum] footnote to f.260 in S

587   Sic voluit usus] erased in S by D

588   Supra] footnote to f.260 in S

589   This entry inserted in S in D's hand; The following is a perfect rhyme;

> O could I flow like thee, & [Could I:erased] make thy stream
> My great example . . . illeg . . . as it is my theme.
>   ?Danb. – Cooper's Hill

> But [Yet:erased] those were Pedants when compared to these
> Who know not only to construct but please
>   Essay on Crit
>   Dryden & D. of Buclu. Ess. on Lat. Verse 5

] inserted in D's hand on leaf to face f.260 in S

590   mute] erased in A

591   Epis. to Arbuthnot] footnote to f.261 in S

592   4 Ethic Epistle] footnote to f.261 in S

593   though he had long resided in London, but having] erased in A

594   long] erased in A

595   F.Q. 1.11.54] footnote to f.263 in S

596   but not quite so long] inserted in D's hand in S; not in A

597   the former words] erased in S; *walk*] added in D's hand in S

598   Monk's tale] footnote to f.265 in S

599   Congreve] footnote to f.265 in S

600   Essay on Man 4] footnote to f.265 in S

601   3 Ethic Epis.] footnote to f.266 in S

602   Clerke's tale] footnote to f.266 in S

603   This entry inserted in D's hand in S

604   This entry inserted in D's hand in S

605   noun] erased in S

606   mute] erased in A; silent] in A

607   This is not to be inserted, it is only a memorandum – Agurondesham –
       Leominster] on leaf to face f.550 in A
608   *fork*] in A
609   Pope's Iliad, 20] footnote to f.267 in S
610   Entered on leaf to face f.288 in S in D's hand
611   This entry inserted in D's hand in f.268 in S

Bibliography

Abercrombie, D. 'Steele, Monboddo and Garrick', *Studies in Phonetics and Linguistics*, pp.35–43, Oxford University Press, London, 1965.

Abercrombie, D. 'Forgotten Phoneticians', *Studies in Phonetics and Linguistics*, pp.44–53, Oxford University Press, London, 1965.

Adams, J. *The Pronunciation of the English Language*, 1799: *English Linguistics 1500–1800*, No. 72, Alston, R.C. (ed), Menston, 1968.

Aitken, A. J. 'Variation and Variety in Written Middle Scots', in *English Studies in English and Scots*, ed. Aitken, A. J., McIntosh, A. and Palsson, H., pp.177–209, Longman, London, 1971.

Aitken, A. J. 'Scottish Speech: a Historical View, with Special Reference to the Standard English of Scotland', in *Languages of Scotland*, ed. Aitken, A. J. and McArthur, T., pp.68–84, Chambers, Edinburgh, 1979.

Aitken, A. J. 'The Scottish vowel length rule', in Benskin, M. and Samuels, M. L. (eds) *So Meny People Longages and Tongues*, pp.131–57, Benskin and Samuels, Edinburgh, 1981.

Anderson, J. M. and Ewen, C. J. *Principles of Dependency Phonology*, Cambridge University Press, Cambridge, 1987.

Angus, W. *An Epitome of English Grammar*, Glasgow, 1800.

Angus, W. *A Pronouncing Vocabulary of the English Language: Exhibiting the Most Appropriate Mode of Pronunciation*, Glasgow, 1800: *English Linguistics 1500–1800*, No. 164, Alston, R. C. (ed), Menston, 1969.

Angus, W. *English Spelling and Pronouncing Dictionary*, Glasgow, 1814.

Arsleff, H. *The Study of Language in England, 1780–1860*, Princeton, 1967.

Bailey, R. W. 'Teaching in the Vernacular: Scotland, Schools, and Linguistic Diversity', in *The Nuttis Schell*, pp.131–142, ed. Macafee, C. and MacLeod, I. Aberdeen University Press, 1987.

Barrie, A. *A Spelling and Pronouncing Catechism*, ?Edinburgh, 1796.

Barrie, A. *A Spelling and Pronouncing Dictionary of the English Language*, Edinburgh, 1799.

Barrie, A. *The Tyro's Guide to Wisdom and Wealth with Exercises in Spelling*, George Caw, Edinburgh, 1800.

Barrie, A. *An Epitome of English Grammar*, The Author, Edinburgh, 1800.

Bickley, F. *The Diaries of Sylvester Douglas* (2 vols). Constable, London, 1928.

Bliss, A. J. 'Vowel quantity in Middle English borrowings from Anglo-Norman', *Archivum Linguisticum*, 4, 121–47; 5, 22–47, 1952–3.

Boggs, W. Arthur, 'William Kenrick's Pronunciation', *American Speech*, 39, pp.131–34, 1964.

Bronstein, A. J. 'The vowels and dipthongs of the nineteenth century', *Speech Monographs*, 16, pp.227–242, 1949.

Brown, T. *A Dictionary of the Scottish Language*, Simpkin and Marshall, London, 1845.

Buchanan, J. *Linguae Britannicae Vero Pronuntiatio*, London, 1757.

Buchanan, J. *The British Grammar*, London, 1762: *English Linguistics 1500–1800*, No. 97, Alston, R. C. (ed), Menston, 1968.

Buchanan, J. *An Essay Towards Establishing a Standard for an Elegant and Uniform Pronunciation of the English Language throughout the British Dominions*, London, 1766.

Bibliography

Buchmann, E. 'Der Einfluss des Schriftbildes auf die Aussprache im Neuenglischen', *Anglistische Reihe* 35, Breslau, 1940.

Burn, J. *A Practical Grammar of the English Language . . . for the Use of Schools*, Glasgow, 1766–99.

Cockburn, H. *Memorials of His Time*, Black, Edinburgh, 1856.

Cohen, M. *Sensible Words. Linguistic Practice in England, 1640–1785*. Baltimore, 1977.

Collin, A. Z. *An Essay on the Scoto-English Dialect*, Lund, 1862.

Colville, J. 'The Scottish Vernacular as a Philosophical Study', *Proceedings of the Philosophical Society of Glasgow*, pp.39 ff, 1899.

Complete Peerage of England, Scotland, Ireland, Great Britain and the United Kingdom, George Bell, London, 1892.

Crompton Rhodes, *Sheridan: Plays and Poems*, Oxford, 1928.

Danielsen, B. *John Hart's Works*, Part I, Almqvist and Wiksell, Stockholm, 1955–63.

Davies, C. *English Pronunciation from the Fifteenth to the Eighteenth Centuries*, London, 1934.

Dobson, E. J. *English Pronunciation, 1500–1700*, Oxford University Press, Oxford, 1968.

Donegan, P. *On the Natural Phonology of Vowels. Working Papers in Linguistics*, 23, Department of Linguistics, Columbus, Ohio, Ohio State University, 1978.

Dorow, K-G. *Die Beobachtungen des Sprachmeisters James Elphinston über die schottische Mundart*, Dissertation, Weimar, 1935.

Douglas, Sylvester (Lord Glenbervie), *The First Canto of Ricciardetto, translated from the Italian of Forteguerri, with an Introduction Concerning the Principal Romantic, Burlesque, and Mock Heroic Poets, with Notes, Critical and Philological*, London, 1822.

Douglas, Sylvester, 'An Account of the Tokay and other wines of Hungary', *Philosophical Transactions*, vol. lxiii, part 1, London, 1773.

Douglas, Sylvester, 'Experiments and Observations upon a blue substance, found in a Peat-moss in Scotland', *Philosophical Transactions*, vol. lviii, London, 1768.

Douglas, Sylvester, *Occasional Verses, Translations and Imitations, with Notes, critical and biographical*, Smith, Paris, 1820.

Dunlap, A. R. '"Vicious" Pronunciation in Eighteenth Century England', *American Speech*, 15, pp.364–7, 1940.

Ekwall, E. *A History of Modern English Sounds and Inflexions*, Oxford, Blackwell, 1975.

Elphinston, J. *The Principles of the English Language, Digested for the Use of Schools*, London, 1766.

Elphinston, J. *Propriety Ascertained in Her Picture: or, Inglish Speech and Spelling Rendered Mutual Guides, Secure Alike from Distant, and from Domestic, Error*, vol. 1, London, 1786; vol. 2, London, 1787.

Emsley, B. 'James Buchanan and the Eighteenth Century Regulation of English Usage', *PMLA*, xlviii, 3, pp.1154–66, 1933.

Flasdieck, H. 'Zum lautwert von ME ɛ im 18. Jahrhundert', *Anglia*, 60, 1936.

Fyfe, C. (ed) *The Sierra Leone Letters*, Edinburgh University Press, Edinburgh, 1991.

Gabrielson, A. 'The Development of Early Modern English ï/r (+ cons)', *Minnesskrift till Axel Erdmann*, Uppsala och Stockholm, 1913.

Georgian Era, The (Memoirs of the Most Eminent Persons, who have Flourished in Great Britain), 4 vols, Clarke (ed), 1832.

Gil, A. *Logonomia Anglica*, 1621: *English Linguistics 1500–1800*, No. 68, Alston, R. C. (ed), Menston, 1968.

Gray, J. *A Concise Spelling Book*, George Caw, Edinburgh, 1794.

Grierson, H. J. C. *The Letters of Sir Walter Scott: 1821–1823*, Constable, London, 1934.

Haggard, M. 'Abbreviation of consonants in English pre- and post-vocalic clusters', *Journal of Phonetics*, 1, pp.9–23, 1973.

Bibliography

Hart, J. 1569: see Danielsen, B.

Hill, A. A. 'Early loss of [r] before dentals', *Publications of the Modern Language Association*, 55, pp.308–21, 1940.

Hodgson, M. *A Practical English Grammar for the Use of Schools and Private Gentlemen and Ladies*, London, 1770.

Holmberg, B. *James Douglas on English Pronunciation c.1740*, Gleerup, Lund, 1956.

Hooper, J. B. 'The Syllable in Phonological Theory', *Language*, 48, pp.525–40, 1972.

Hooper, J. B. *An Introduction to Natural Generative Phonology*, Academic Press, London, 1976.

Horn, W. *Beiträge zur Geschichte der englischen Gutturallaute*, Berlin, 1901.

Horn, W. and Lehnert, M. *Laut und Leben*, 2 vols, Deutscher Verlag, Berlin, 1954.

Hornsey, John *A Short Grammar of the English Language in two Parts, Simplified to the Capacities of Children, with Notes and a Great Variety of Entertaining and Useful Exercises*, Newcastle, ND.

Innes Smith, R. W. *English Speaking Students of Medicine at the University of Leyden*, Oliver and Boyd, Edinburgh, 1932.

Johnston, P. *A Synchronic and Historical View of Border Area Bimoric Vowel Systems*, Ph.D. Dissertation, Edinburgh, 1980.

Jones, C. *A History of English Phonology*, Longman, London, 1989.

Kaffenberger, E. 'Englische lautlehre nach Thomas Sheridans Dictionary of the English Language (1780)', *Beiträge zur Erforschung der Sprache und Kultur Englands und Nordamerikas*, 3,1, Breslau, 1927.

Kenrick, W. *A Rhetorical Grammar of the English Language*, 1784: *English Linguistics 1500–1800*, No. 332, Alston, R. C. (ed), Menston, 1972.

Kiparsky, P. 'How Abstract is Phonology?', in O. Fujimura (ed), *Three Dimensions of Linguistic Theory*, pp.5–56, Tokyo, 1973.

Koeppel, E. *Spelling Pronunciations*, Quellen und Forschungen, Strassburg, 1901.

Kohler, K. J. 'Aspects of the history of English pronunciation in Scotland', Ph.D. Dissertation, Edinburgh, 1966.

Kohler, K. J. 'A late eighteenth century comparison of the "Provincial dialect of Scotland" and the "Pure Dialect"', *Linguistics*, 23, pp.30–69, 1966.

Kökeritz, H. 'The reduction of initial *kn* and *gn* in English', *Language*, 21, 1950.

Langley, H. 'Early nineteenth century speech: a contemporary critique', *American Speech*, 38, pp.289–92, 1963.

Lass, R. *Phonology: An Introduction to Basic Concepts*, Cambridge University Press, London, 1984.

Law, W. *Education in Edinburgh in the Eighteenth Century*, University of London Press, London, 1965.

Lloyd, R. J. 'Glides between consonants in English', *Die Neueren Sprachen, Zeitschrift für den neusprachlichen Unterricht*, 12, pp.14ff, Frankfurt, 1904.

Luick, K. *Historische Grammatik der englischen Sprache*, 2 vols, Chr. Herm. Tauchnitz, Leipzig, 1921.

Machyn, H. 1550: see Nichols, J. G. 1848.

Matthews, W. 'Some eighteenth century phonetic spellings', *English Studies*, 12, pp.47–60, 177–188, 1936a.

Matthews, W. 'William Tiffin, an eighteenth century phonetician', *English Studies*, 18, pp.97–114, 1936b.

Meyer, E. *Der englische Lautstand in der Zweiten Hälfte des 18. Jahrhunderts nach James Buchanan*, Ph.D. Dissertation, Berlin, 1940.

Milroy, L. *Language and Social Networks*, Blackwell, Oxford, 1980.

Mossé, F. *A Handbook of Middle English*, Johns Hopkins, Baltimore, 1952.

Müller, E. *Englische Lautlehre nach James Elphinston, 1765, 1787, 1790. Anglistische Forschungen*, 43, Heidelberg, 1914.

Bibliography

Nares, R. *Elements of Orthoepy, 1784: English Linguistics 1500–1800*. No. 56, Alston, R. C. (ed), Menston, 1968.

Nichols, J. G. *The Diary of Henry Machyn, Citizen and Merchant Taylor of London*, Camden Society 42, London, 1848.

Ohala, J. J. 'Experimental historical phonology', in Anderson, J. M. and Jones, C. (eds) *Historical Linguistics II*, pp.353–89, North Holland, Amsterdam, 1974.

Orton, H., Sanderson, S. and Widdowson, J. *The Linguistic Atlas of England*, Croom Helm, London, 1978.

Påhlsson, C. *The Northumbrian Burr: a Sociolinguistic Study*, Gleerup, Lund, 1972.

Parker, W. M. (ed) *The Heart of Midlothian*, Sir Walter Scott, Dent, London, 1971.

Perry, W. *The Only Sure Guide to the English Tongue or a New Pronouncing Spelling Book*, Edinburgh, 1776.

Perry, W. *The Royal Standard English Dictionary*, Edinburgh, 1775.

Pollner, C. *Robert Nares: 'Elements of Orthoepy'*, Europäische Hochschulschriften. Reihe xiv, Angelsächsische Sprache und Literatur, Bd. 41, Frankfurt, 1976.

Raphael, I. J. 'Preceding vowel duration as a cue to the perception of the voicing characteristic of word final consonants in American English', *Journal of the Acoustical Society of America*, 51, pp.1293–1303, 1972.

Rohlfing, H. *Die Werke James Elphinstons (1721–1809) als Quellen der englischen Lautgeschichte*, Heidelberg, 1984.

Savage, W. H. *The Vulgarities and Improprieties of the English Language*, London, 1833.

Scott, John, *The School-Boy's Sure Guide: or, Spelling and Reading Made Agreeable and Easy*, Edinburgh, 1774.

Scott, Sir Walter: see Grierson, H. J. C.; Parker, W. M.

Sheldon, E. K. *Standards of English Pronunciation According to the Grammarians and Orthoepists of the Sixteenth, Seventeenth and Eighteenth Centuries*, Dissertation, University of Wisconsin, 1938.

Sheldon, E. K. 'Pronouncing systems in eighteenth-century dictionaries', *Language*, 22, 1971.

Sheridan, T. *A General Dictionary of the English Language*, London, 1780.

Sheridan, T. *A Rhetorical Grammar of the English Language*, Dublin, 1781: *English Linguistics 1500–1800*, No. 146, Alston, R. C. (ed), Menston, 1969.

Sichel, Walter (ed) *The Glenbervie Journals*, Constable, London, 1910.

Smith, G. G. *The Scottish Language: The Cambridge History of English Literature*, vol. II, Cambridge, 1908.

Smith, J. *A Grammar of the English Language Containing Rules and Exercises*, Norwich, 1816.

Stampe, D. 'On the natural history of diphthongs', *Papers from the Eighth Regional Meeting of the Chicago Linguistic Society*, pp.578–90, Chicago, 1972.

Stephen, L. and Lee, S. *Dictionary of National Biography*, Smith, Elder and Co., London, 1908.

Sturzen-Becker, A. 'Some notes on English pronunciation about 1800', in *A Philological Miscellany Presented to Eilert Ekwall*, pp.310–30, Uppsala, 1942.

Telfair, C. *The Town and Country Spelling Book*, Elliot, Edinburgh, 1775.

Turner, J. R. *The Works of William Bullockar: Booke at Large 1580*, Leeds University Press, Leeds, 1970.

Valk, C. Z. *The Development of the Back Vowel before* [ɪ] *in early Modern English*, Ph.D. Dissertation, Muncie, Indiana, 1980.

Verney, Lady F. P. *Memoirs of the Verney Family*, 4 vols, London, 1892.

Vianna, M. E. 'A study in the dialect of the southern counties of Scotland', Ph.D. Dissertation, Edinburgh, 1972.

Walker, J. *A Critical Pronouncing Dictionary*, 1791: *English Linguistics 1500–1800*, No. 117, Alston, R. C. (ed), 1968.

Bibliography

Wallis, J. *Grammatica Linguae Anglicanae*, Oxford, 1653.

Wells, J. C. *Accents of English*, 3 vols, Cambridge University Press, London, 1982.

Whitehall, H. and Fein, T. 'The development of Middle English ŭ in early Modern English and American English', *JEGP*, 40, 1941.

Wyld, H. *A History of Modern Colloquial English*, Blackwell, Oxford, 1953.

Zettersten, A. *A Critical Facsimile Edition of Thomas Batchelor*, Part 1, Gleerup, Lund, 1974.

Index of words cited in the Introduction

Index to the Introduction

Index of words cited in the *Treatise*